ABDUCTION

Also by Jenny Randles

(From Robert Hale)

UFOs: A British Viewpoint (with Peter Warrington)
UFO Study: A Handbook for Enthusiasts
UFO Reality: A Critical Look at the Physical Evidence
Beyond Explanation?: Paranormal Experiences of Famous People
Sixth Sense: Psychic Powers and Your Five Senses

ABDUCTION

Over 200 Documented UFO Kidnappings Investigated

JENNY RANDLES

ROBERT HALE · LONDON

First published in Great Britain 1988

ISBN 0 7090 3276 5

Robert Hale Limited
Clerkenwell House
Clerkenwell Green
London EC1R 0HT

British Library Cataloguing in Publication Data

Randles, Jenny, *1951–*
Abduction : over 200 documented UFO kidnappings.
1. Unidentified flying objects
I. Title
001.9′42

Photoset in North Wales by
Derek Doyle & Associates, Mold, Clwyd.
Printed in Great Britain by
St Edmundsbury Press Ltd, Bury St Edmunds, Suffolk.
Bound by WBC Bookbinders Limited.

Contents

Author's Note

This book is about ordinary people who claim extraordinary things, so it is inevitable that some of them prefer anonymity. Wherever this has been expressly requested, I have, of course, not used the person's real name. On other occasions, witnesses have bravely come forward in their true identity. The difficult nature of that decision should not be overlooked.

If I have not used a real name, that fact is pointed out at the start of my discussion. However, in virtually all these cases I am satisfied that a proper and serious investigation has been conducted. Often I have spoken with the witnesses myself, although naturally (in particular with overseas reports) that has not always been possible.

I should acknowledge all the people who have assisted me in the preparation of this book. Indeed I was flattered by the tremendous support and encouragement given me, whatever correspondents' personal views on the abduction phenomenon. It would not be possible to list them all, but I have done my best to ensure that their work and their help have been credited in the text.

It seems rather unfair to select certain of these for special thanks, because it tends to suggest I undervalue other contributions. With the strict understanding that this is not the case, I feel mention must go to the following for their extra help and co-operation, beyond what was asked of them.

In Australia: Bill Chalker and Mark Moravec. In Britain: Dr John Dale and witnesses Shelley Dawn, Alan Godfrey and Elsie Oakensen. In the Far East: Ahmad Jamaludin. In Spain:

Vicente-Juan Ballester Olmos. In the USA: Dr Eddie Bullard and Dr Leo Sprinkle.

If I have offended anyone by not mentioning them here, or not giving due credit in the text itself, please accept my apologies.

Abbreviations

BUFORA	British UFO Research Association*
CUFOS	Center for UFO Studies, USA
FSR	*Flying Saucer Review* (independent magazine, Britain)
IUR	*International UFO Reporter* (CUFOS, USA)
JTAP	*Journal of Transient Aerial Phenomena* (BUFORA, UK)
MUFON	Mutual UFO Network, USA
MUFORA	Manchester UFO Research Association*
UFOIN	UFO Investigators Network*

* Explained when introduced at start of Chapter 5

Introduction

Something very strange is happening to the world. In Europe and the USA, across Asia and South America – in fact, almost everywhere – people are claiming an experience so bizarre that it is virtually unthinkable. It is said that aliens have appeared from another world and 'spacenapped' human beings, abducting them for often disturbing reasons.

Of course, one might say – with not inconsiderable reason – that is quite absurd. Aliens do not exist, so they cannot possibly abduct, cart off or spacenap anyone. Those sad folk who dwell under this delusion are feeble-minded, unbalanced or more than likely both. Yet this eminently sensible conclusion has to be set alongside some worrying discoveries. The total number of victims of this 'delusion' is growing annually at an escalating rate, such that it now borders on epidemic proportions. We already have detailed accounts from hundreds of witnesses who tell of their ordeal. We suspect thousands of others, hiding in the shadows for fear of ridicule or public reaction to such an admission. If it happened to you, would you talk?

But far more disturbing than this is the astounding belief held by some pretty hardnosed and experienced scientists that the majority of those who have undergone these very close encounters might harbour memories of that confrontation deep within themselves. Like a ghostly phobia, it lurks in their subconscious, changing the shape of their lives in countless subtle ways. That memory can be kindled from a flicker to a flame. Sometimes, when they least expect it, a mental time-bomb goes off unpredictably, destroying forever the humdrum existence of daily life.

If this sounds like a plot from some science-fiction B-movie, then ponder one other thing: there is no easy way to tell who these potential victims are. If it were dreamers or social misfits under this spell, an answer might be clear. The truth is that they are airline pilots and policemen, hamburger-stand waitresses and housewives – in fact, an average cross-section of any community. That these unsuspecting abductees are just like you and me raises a spectre that few can live with in comfort.

The more we discover about this strange new phenomenon, the less we really know about it, and the greater our uncertainty about who may be immune. This mysterious insanity has swept across our culture like an invisible plague during the last two decades. When it has been reported, it has been in the context of UFOs or flying saucers, but all stable-minded individuals know that UFOs are nonsense. That said, these reports of kidnap by aliens must be equally untrue. This simple logic may have blinded us to a weird and fast-expanding problem that cries out for exploration and understanding. These stories have been among us for more than twenty years but almost no one has noticed.

That changed in 1987. A best-selling novelist, Whitley Strieber, read one of my books. In passing I had referred to this problem, and suddenly his memory awakened. Something he had perceived as a dream, or perhaps as a sign that he was going mad, now looked quite unlike either of those things. Instead, he realized that it might really have happened – on whatever level an alien abduction can be said to happen.

Armed with this knowledge, Strieber set about investigating his memory. He worked with a psychiatrist and uncovered what appeared to be a shocking story. With the floodgates open, he produced *Communion*, one of the biggest-selling books of all time, now about to appear as a film. He became rich. He became famous. But most importantly the world woke up one morning to the realization that this phenomenon was not a joke but, in some sense at least, a real enigma. *Communion* changed everything. Television advertisements used witnesses to sell products. Even soap operas livened up their storylines with the new fad. The media had another toy to play with, inviting experts to explain it or, more often, to explain it away.

Meanwhile, in ordinary homes around the civilized world, people began to wonder. That dream I had a dozen years ago, when I thought I saw a strange alien face – was it really a dream?

That light in the sky during that late-night country drive – was it only the moon, as everyone suggested? A question that has vexed man since he first crawled out of his cave and viewed an indigo sky filling with stars raised itself once more into our consciousness. Are we alone in the universe, or do we share the cosmos with others? Perhaps 'out there' there are others who have answers to the horrors of the nuclear arms race, poverty, starvation and killer diseases.

Of course, if alien beings are visiting Earth to kidnap humans, it would be perhaps *the* most momentous occasion in history. No aspect of our lives would be left untouched by it. Science, medicine, philosophy, religion: all would face upheavals and challenges in the light of this news. How would we cope with the sort of revelation that suggested we were not the most intelligent or godly beings in the universe?

But what if the sceptics are right? Then this view is the nonsense it sounds. Then thousands, maybe millions, of otherwise intelligent people would be seriously mistaken or absurdly deluded. But we could not leave it at that, for if airline pilots and police officers believe they have been kidnapped by aliens who do not exist, the problem on our hands is hardly less disturbing. Can there be a new form of psychosis, capable of acting on a planet-wide scale? Are whole countries at risk from a psychological disease that would be the mental equivalent of a plague like AIDS? Or perhaps there is another form of answer, an intermediary solution. It may be that it is not contradictory to say that these people *are* sane and sincere but do *not* experience what they think they experience.

Because the question of alien abductions has been seen in the light of UFOs and spaceships, there has been a most unfortunate side-effect. This subject already generates two factions. There are those who say the witnesses speak the truth, so the Earth *is* being visited by aliens, and there are those who cannot accept this possibility, so come what may (irrespective of the evidence) these folk simply *must* be lying. Even worse, because UFOs are regarded as an 'occult' subject by bookshops, libraries and indeed the majority of people, they are considered alongside fortune-telling and witchcraft – which in most cases, and with most sensible folk, means not at all.

We have to overcome this predicament. There *are* other

options worth investigating. This is a new problem and we cannot prejudge it. To decide that it is nonsense is as much a prejudgement as to accept with open arms our 'friends from outer space'.

In the development of this book I have consulted scientists, sceptics, researchers, psychiatrists – indeed, anyone who has something to say about the abduction mystery, as well as the abductees themselves, those who say they have been victim of this strange epidemic. I have no obligation towards any solution. It is completely irrelevant to me personally whether our ultimate explanation for this puzzle lies in the frontiers of inner or outer space. It is too early to start taking sides, too dangerous to be overly prejudiced.

What I hope this book helps to elucidate is a recognition that all may not be as it seems. On the other hand, of course, it may be!

I have met many people who claim to have been 'spacenapped', in both Britain and the USA. I have sat in doctors' surgeries and psychologists' offices interrogating these frightened people under the influence of hypnosis, or completely conscious, as they relive the trauma which brought this crisis point in their lives. Such people sit at the sharp end of a situation which in their honest moments everyone who has been involved would admit has them baffled, confused, disturbed and frightened. All I ask is that you listen to what they have to say and try to decide for yourself what is going on.

Something very strange is happening to the world. We owe it to ourselves to find out what that is.

Jenny Randles,
Cheshire, October 1987

1 Alien Abductions: The Official Version

The story of the alien abduction officially begins in the early 1950s when such things as flying saucers were considered nonsense by most serious thinkers. When there were sightings, most people assumed they were the result of misperceptions or delusions. As the vast majority of such incidents were exactly that, such a view was eminently justified.

Amid all of this came a man called George Adamski, who looked after a refreshment stand on the slopes of Mount Palomar, California, near the famous astronomical observatory. He had written science fiction, with little success, and was deeply concerned about the state of the wicked world. From this background he came up with the claim that spaceships were visiting him and that aliens (from Venus and other such attractive places) were in contact. His saga of alien visitors was first told in *Flying Saucers Have Landed*, compiled by British author Desmond Leslie. It was such a success that it was followed by others, with titles like *Inside the Spaceships*. These told how Adamski had been abducted aboard the scoutships of these alien races and taken to see plants and rivers on the far side of the moon.

In this day and age such nonsense seems mildly amusing, if not quaint. In 1953 it was considered scientifically possible that there might be life on Venus and rivers on the moon, and space travel was the great dream of the era. Adamski seized on this quite cleverly to expound his philosophy, and there are few who nowadays do not regard his story as just a romantic fairy tale. Certainly his 'abduction' bears very little resemblance to modern cases. It involves Adamski's going aboard of his own volition, in complete control, and being treated as an equal by friendly chaps who might just as well have come from Clapham as from the far side of the moon, judging by their appearance.

Others followed in his wake. There was the sexy space alien Aura Rhanes, and the awful wailing noises said to be 'music' from the planet Saturn. There was even a religious cult, the Aetherius Society – it is still going strong today, proving that the desire for escapist fantasies did not die even in the face of the microchip and video age. This cult was founded by a London taxi-driver, George King, who in the more sophisticated contact tales of the late 1950s got one up on his American predecessors by suggesting that the aliens invited him to go with them, because the Earth had fallen prey to an intelligent meteor that was crunching through the solar system. All their fleets of UFOs had failed miserably, and King was needed to save the universe.

George (now an 'archbishop' and a 'sir' and with an amazingly durable appeal) has survived into a time when it seems odd that such stories should attract. But this shows that belief in aliens and 'little green men' is not dependant on fads or fashions: it is something we all seem to need.

One of the contactees (as these oddballs were called) was Cedric Allingham. He became the first true British rival to George Adamski, producing his book *Flying Saucer from Mars* in 1955. Recent revelations by intrepid UFO sleuths Chris Allan and Steuart Campbell have provided quite a shock, which I must admit my own investigations appear to have verified. The story of an extra-terrestrial visit to Scotland was brought to public notice by a then young space writer who went on to fame and fortune and one of the longest-running BBC television series of all time. He also became a very outspoken critic of all things ufological, possibly working on the assumption that if *he* could fool the world for thirty years, anyone could! This contactee was, according to researchers Allan and Campbell, described by none other than Patrick Moore MBE, the much-mimicked entertainer and one of the last of the great British eccentrics. The evidence *is* pretty damning, although he has neither confirmed nor denied these public disclosures.

I find it rather fitting that the origin of one of the finer tales from the 1950s should be laid on Patrick's shoulders. Others seem to consider it more sinister. When, in 1985, journalist and author of some of the more perceptive UFO books John Keel published his first thoughts for quite a number of years ('The Contactee Key', *Flying Saucer Review*, Vol. 31 No. 1), he claimed that one of the American contactees, Howard Menger, had later confessed that, 'His experiences with the UFO entities had somehow been engineered by the CIA' and that others, including people from Britain, had told of being kidnapped in rather terrestrial-looking cars, trucks and vans in which they were hypnotized by flashing lights and drugged into the delusion of a 'close encounter'. If I understand Keel's intriguing thesis correctly, this was all part of a plan to disinform the public and fool them into accepting that UFOs came from outer space, when instead they were psychic phenomena.

As we proceed with the traditional version of the abduction saga, it is widely held that the first true victim of an abduction was Brazilian cowhand Antonio Villas Boas. The twenty-three-year-old was ploughing his field near São Francisco de Sales at 1 a.m. on 16 October 1957 when his tractor was stalled by a UFO, which promptly landed and disgorged four men about five feet tall who dragged him aboard, gave him a rubdown and brought out a rather peculiar-looking woman. She had fair skin, high cheekbones, Oriental eyes and red hair. Seizing upon Antonio as a sort of inter-galactic toyboy, she proceeded to 'rape' him, then to rub her belly and point to the sky in a gesture not hard to interpret as, 'I am going to have your baby up there.'

The Villas Boas case was considered too wild even for ufologists. They saw in it a danger of ten years hard graft, trying to persuade a disbelieving world that something was up, being swept away by a tale so absurd that no one would buy it. Nevertheless, it was given a very good field investigation in Brazil by Dr Olavo Fontes, who examined the farmer in his Rio office in early 1958 and was favourably impressed by his trauma, his medical symptoms (which Fontes said 'suggest radiation poisoning or exposure to radiation') and particularly his willingness to be subjected to so many tests despite personal financial loss. (This was allegedly caused by his absence from work for long periods without any gain from his story.)

Later, in 1961, Dr Walter Buhler, a Brazilian UFO expert, came upon the case, interviewed the witness and submitted a detailed report to the then leading international journal *Flying Saucer Review* (*FSR*). They sat on it for quite a while, publishing in English, in 1964. It did not appear in Brazil until many years after that.

There was purpose in this seemingly odd decision. It was hoped, that other cases like it would surface – if it was not just in the mind of a sexually fantasizing young man. Critics would then have a hard time explaining such comparisons if it could legitimately be argued that nothing about the Villas Boas case had been put in print.

These researchers seem to have been vindicated in September 1961 – with the world still ignorant of what had happened in that South American field ...

Betty and Barney Hill were a mixed-racial couple. Betty was a social worker active in civil rights and Barney a postal officer. The Caucasian Betty is unquestionably the focus for this case. Her husband died tragically not long after it became public, but Betty went on to a sort of celebrity status and frequently reported seeing many other UFOs.

Returning from a holiday in Canada to their New Hampshire home, the Hills saw a white 'star' in the sky over the White Mountains, a 'star' which many have since come to argue must have been the planet Jupiter (on the grounds that their sketch shows the moon and the UFO in exactly the sort of relationship the moon and Jupiter shared in the heavens that night). A long 'chase' occurred, with the couple growing increasingly excited, before they saw the UFO (as a sort of pancake shape with windows) descend near Indian Head. It mesmerized Barney, and there was a memory jump after that – they found themselves at a spot further down the road than they thought they should be. On arrival home, a discrepancy appeared in their timing: the journey had taken a couple of hours longer than it should.

Betty's subsequent anxiety dreams involved faces and images of being medically examined, and Barney came to share in some of them. They sought medical help, and this ultimately lead them to Dr Benjamin Simon, a Boston psychiatrist who chose (in a fateful step) to adopt hypnosis as a tool to unlock Barney's, and later Betty's subconscious. Simon, it must be said, never believed that the UFO abduction was real. He saw the use of hypnosis, making them regress to the episode in 1961 and 'relive' it in their minds, as a means of catharsis. The fantasy which he thought lay inside could pour out and, the theory went, the anxiety would dissipate with it.

It worked something like that, but with unexpected consequences. The couple shared a very detailed 'memory' of being carried aboard the UFO by men with oriental, cat-like eyes and grey faces, for painful medical examinations (including one on Betty's navel with a long probe, described as a 'pregnancy test' by the alien captors). Such were the complexity of the story and the degree of similarity between the two separate versions that Dr Simon was temporarily thrown.

Simon's treatment began on 14 December 1963 and ran until 27 June 1964. By that time the story had been released from the minds of the witnesses but not made public, and the Villas Boas affair was *just* in print in a British UFO journal with a circulation of about 3,000. It is, of course, rather important that the two cases have substantial overlap, including the size and some of the features of the entities, the physical symptoms shared by the witnesses, and the gynaecological nature of the on-board experiences. None of the contactees had reported anything like this – or, doubtless, their books would have been even bigger sellers.

The Hill case set the stereotype in Western culture. Key features that it includes and which came to be seen as crucial include: a paralysis on first contact with the entities, a floating sensation prior to arriving on board, scene-jumps and memory lapses (which are features of dreams, of course), a long table or bed on which medical examinations are made, an eye-like instrument involved in the examining, the taking of skin and blood samples, interest by the aliens in novel features (for example, Barney's false teeth were studied with interest), reaction tests on the witnesses' bodies (Betty's knee was made to jump and jerk), and the sexual overtones (Barney reported these too, saying that a suction device was placed over his groin, causing considerable pain).

The story leaked to the press late in 1965 (it is not totally clear how and the Hills sought help from Dr Simon to avoid this). Ultimately they and the psychiatrist decided to co-operate with a famous local journalist, John Fuller, in the preparation of the 'true' story, a book entitled *The Interrupted Journey*. It was a major success, and syndicate reports on the case appeared all over the world in 1966 and 1967.

This is obviously important. It could no longer be argued that people were ignorant of the form of an abduction. In many respects it was perhaps very unfortunate that this first American case attracted so much interest, because it tainted everything that followed. However, it is difficult to imagine that many people took in the small details of the story, which, when reported, tended to concentrate on Betty's horrific pregnancy test, an attempt to take an alien book from the UFO as proof of the contact, and the supposed observation of a 'map' showing the aliens' origins as round a star called Zeta Reticulii.

Dr Simon felt that the most likely solution was a *folie à deux* – in other words, a shared delusion where Barney had reinforced Betty's dreams and they had both come to believe in them as a form of reality. He was supported in such an opinion by Barney, who under hypnosis fought against accepting the literal truth of the experience. In a 29 February 1964 session he said, 'I seem disassociated .... I am there – and I am not there', which appears to suggest that he is disputing the reality of his memory but which is actually now known to be a reaction remarkably similar to the response of many abductees. It is the sort of little detail that stands out on careful analysis of cases but which would not be considered relevant in a brief media account.

On 14 June 1966 Simon issued a serious warning to others who might think of using hypnosis in UFO cases: 'It can be the key to the locked room, the amnesic period .... Nevertheless, there is little produced under or by hypnosis that is not possible without. The charisma of hypnosis has tended to foster the belief that hypnosis is the magical and royal road to *truth* ... but it must be understood that hypnosis is a pathway to the truth as it is felt and understood by the patient. The truth is what he believes to be the truth, and this may or may not be consonant with the ultimate non-personal truth.'

Despite Simon's warning, the desire to find suspect cases and use hypnosis to reveal hidden memories was too great. From 1967 onward a new trend was in operation, and a slow trickle of similar stories began, at first in just the USA but spreading elsewhere. The encounter of a Nebraska state policeman, Herb Schirmer, in December 1967, was studied by a Government-funded team of scientists at the University of Colorado, and after his conscious memory had been logged, a short (fifteen-minute) time lapse was investigated under hypnosis by Dr Leo Sprinkle, a psychologist contracted in from the University of Wyoming. Another on-board memory appeared, and since the witness was a police officer, the case had unusual credibility. Sprinkle became so fascinated that he virtually devoted his life to the problem from that moment on.

Abductions did not reach the shores of conservative Britain until the mid 1970s – later we shall spend more time exploring international and historical trends and patterns.

There is no real doubt that, even in UFO circles, abduction (or close encounters of the 'fourth' kind, as it became labelled in specialist terminology) faced a rough road towards acceptance. Many investigators, and most of the public, ran from these weird and troublesome cases. It was easier to pretend that they did not exist than to wrestle with the hard problems and contradictions they often generated. Isolated cases continued, and teams of investigators looked into them, most notably artist Budd Hopkins in New York and lawyer Harry Harris in Manchester, UK. But the real extent of the problem (called an 'invisible epidemic' by Hopkins in his 1982 book *Missing Time*) remained unknown.

One of the things this new wave of research uncovered was the 'unofficial' version of the abduction. In this historical account the phenomenon seems to have begun well *before* the Villas Boas and Hill cases.

There are two ways in which this dramatic change in perception was brought about. Firstly, Hopkins discovered that witnesses to modern abductions claimed to have had childhood encounters too. Under hypnosis they relived events sometimes from nearly twenty years before the Hill abduction, which they had supposedly forgotten about in their conscious memory. British data (as will be seen later) offers more than a hint of support for this pattern, but when Hopkins first spotted it, he was justified in wondering whether the Hill case looked like a landmark only because of its extensive medical follow-up. This had released a hidden memory (or fantasy). Whilst recalling that some cases (for example, the Villas Boas encounter) had no reliance whatsoever on anything other than conscious memory, it was considered interesting to look at cases reported in the past that might look like the Hill report minus the hypnotic testimony.

They exist in some abundance.

One of the most crucial is that which allegedly occurred in the mountains of Italy near Villa Santina on 14 August 1947 (less than two months after the 'first' flying saucers were reported by a pilot flying over the Cascade Mountains of Washington State, USA).

The witness at Villa Santina was Professor Rapuzzi Luigi Johannis, a Milanese artist, writer of many things (including science fiction) and amateur geologist. It was this latter interest which had taken him, backpack and all, up into the lonely hills. His tale – of a UFO landing and of two strange 'boys' getting out and firing an invisible beam at him to induce paralysis – may seem like the product of a fertile mind, but it was well studied, considered credible and published for the first time in spring 1964, thus *provably* predating knowledge of either the Hill or the Villas Boas case.

The 'boys' were just three feet tall, smaller than either previous case, but they had other similarities, including large bald heads, slit noses and very large and prominent eyes. In this daylight encounter the geologist seems to have provoked attack by raising his pick and shouting, precipitating the beam that made him senseless. He noticed a dream-like state or aura surrounding the onset of the experience, which is a major clue spontaneously offered. It is frequently found in cases today (often referred to as a sense of timelessness or, as Barney Hill said, a feeling of disassociation). I use the term 'Oz Factor' to describe this state. The 'Oz Factor' is a set of symptoms very commonly reported by a witness to an abduction, which creates the impression of temporarily having left our material world and entered another dream-like place with magical rules. The onset happens rapidly, just as it did to Dorothy in the famous fantasy story *The Wizard of Oz*, hence the now commonly used name for this experience. It tells us several important things about what is occurring, most notably that the percipient has changed their state of consciousness. It is, in effect, an induced form of sensory deprivation that focuses attention on mental phenomena at the expense of otherwise overwhelming sensory input from the outside world. The result is a dreamy and weirdly silent state of mind that is recognized as peculiar by the baffled abductee, even though they do not appreciate what it implies.

It is possible that hypnosis on Professor Johannis would have provided an abduction scenario, but we do not know.

Nor do we know what hypnosis would have revealed of one of the earliest close encounters on record, a story that is exciting and fascinating whatever its status. It occurred one hot and thundery day in the summer of 1944. World War II raged around the village of Le Verger, near Toulon-sur-Arroux, France, when a thirteen-year-old girl, Madeleine Arnoux, decided to risk the many Germans and resistance fighters in the woods to cycle out and pick berries. In doing so, she confronted a strange object in the grass, like a small car but dull grey in colour. She then noticed that small men stood beside it, no more than three feet tall and dressed in brown one-piece suits. Feeling desperately afraid, she tried to run but was paralysed and lost all sense of time (the Oz Factor once more). Then, inexplicably, the object had gone and the hold on her was relaxed. She fled back to her village. If there was any time-lapse here, it is most unlikely that a girl picking berries would have noticed it, especially if it was not very extensive.

Fernand Lagarde published his report on the Le Verger case in the June 1972 issue of the evocatively titled French UFO journal *Lumières dans la nuit* (*Lights in the Night*) and he incidentally used it to mention that a major fault line in the earth ran straight under the woods at this spot. That might seem a very curious thing to bring into the discussion but, when we later move on to looking for explanations to these cases, this throw-away remark becomes significant.

In all respects these cases begin like modern abductions, and we have every reason to judge them along with the abductions revealed by hypnosis.

It is also worth looking at an early example of something often termed 'the bedroom visitor', although it has an obvious relationship with the abduction phenomenon. It was reported to me by a woman in her forties whom I shall just call Mary (anonymity occurs quite often in these early cases).

The 'visit' happened in 1950, when Mary was aged just five, sleeping with her younger brother in the nursery of a house in Dar-es-Salaam, in the African state now named Tanzania. Mary was woken by a strange vibrating noise outside the house, followed by a peculiar feeling of being watched, a sort of prickling/tingle, and other clues that hint of the Oz Factor taking hold. At the foot of her bed stood a figure only about 2½ feet tall, with the usual features already described: a pale greyish/white face, domed head, pointed chin, large staring eyes that dominated the face – in fact, an easily recognizable classic 'little man' of UFO lore. When the figure moved towards her, she screamed and woke the household. When her father rushed in, there was nothing to be seen. Even if it were not for Mary's subsequent experiences, she would now regard her father's inevitable dismissal of this 'childhood nightmare' as untenable. It has remained very vivid across the years and still terrifies her. She began to suffer bad migraine headaches afterwards, a common result of such episodes.

It is interesting that Mary did not report this figure in a UFO context but as a sort of ghost. This enhances its potential value, since it reduces the likelihood of contamination from other stories. Of course, if it truly happened in 1950, as stated, there *were* no other reported cases which could contaminate.

The event which catapulted the abduction into public prominence and led to the furore of global interest in 1987 and 1988 was the amazing story of best-selling novelist Whitley Strieber. For the first time a public personality had gone on record to say that he was an abductee and was willing to take the consequences. Those consequences, cynics point out, included fame and fortune, although Strieber can rightly say he had plenty of both already. He also adds that he suffered dreadfully because he dared to come clean.

The first hint the UFO community heard about this came from Budd Hopkins, writing one of his periodic updates on the now voluminous abduction cases pouring into him (*MUFON Journal*, USA, April 1986). He told how he had been contacted (in February 1986) by 'a rather distraught man who wished to tell me about a very disturbing experience he had had on 26 December 1985'. At the meeting this man (whom we learnt to be Strieber only in a later article) '… was unable to restrain his tears because the experience had been so terrifying'. Hopkins' technique is to ask about other 'odd, unresolved memories', and in this way he found that Strieber had several: 'Our interview turned into a kind of uncorking of masses of previously repressed memories', which it turned out included a childhood 'dream' of seeing aliens on an overnight train journey and a weird flying episode that is not unlike a scene from the film *Mary Poppins*, as the novelist floats over the rooftops of London.

I know Budd Hopkins to be one of the kindest, most affable men one could wish to meet. I am sure he devoted a great deal of time to Strieber out of pure concern and interest, just as he does to all those who come to his New York studio (where he is a superb professional artist when not chasing aliens). But where did Strieber's memory come from? Was it spontaneous? Did he remember everything?

We had to wait for the same *MUFON Journal*, ten issues later (December 1986), to discover the truth in Strieber's own words ('My experiences with the visitors' – Strieber refuses to call them aliens).

First Strieber gave his credentials: he gained a law degree from the University of Texas in 1967, spent the next year at the London film school and then worked as a newspaper and advertising man until he turned professional author in his thirties. He wrote a string of successful horror stories that were turned into films (for example, *The Wolfen* and *The Hunger*). From 1982 on, he changed tack to write what he calls 'serious fiction about important social and political issues'. These were big hits too and dealt with nuclear war (*Warday*) and the despoiling of the environment (*Nature's End*), both co-authored with Jim Kunetka.

It is interesting that the themes of his recent novels are precisely those which crop up in abduction stories when the aliens choose to pass on a message. They are remarkably concerned, it seems, with our apparent lack of action to stop ourselves destroying the planet. Strieber claims not to have known this prior to his encounters, and now wonders if there might not have been an element of 'dictation' in his earlier novels.

His 26 December 1985 experience actually took place in the early hours of 27 December, even though the earlier date is, for some reason, always cited.

At this point in time, as he puts it in *MUFON Journal*, 'I was pretty much of a skeptic. I really hadn't thought about the question [of UFOs] in years. I thought that the matter was extremely unimportant, and that the people who reported seeing objects were probably simply making mistakes. I was not aware of abduction accounts at all ...'

Early on 27 December 1985 he believes he saw a small figure in his bedroom. After this he floated out into a clearing where he next entered a room and was medically examined by beings of two types (the smaller ones robotic and others, around five feet tall, extremely similar to those described by Betty and Barney Hill and other abductees). Interest in his penis was also noted with some embarrassment, as they drifted skywards in a 'craft' and he lost consciousness.

Strieber had assumed this was a dream and says that his mind even substituted an image of an owl looking in through his window. It later appeared (from the lack of tracks in the snow) that no owl had been there. He says that only after several months did he learn from Budd Hopkins that such substitute animal images were common tricks played by the subconscious to replace a bizarre alien vision with something less disturbing. However, that is unlikely, because in *Science and the UFOs* (a book by astronomer Peter Warrington and myself, based on an article we published in *New Scientist* magazine) I referred to exactly this point, citing cases where rabbits and a dolphin had been used as a substitute image. Strieber had received this book as a Christmas present from his brother *the day before* his bedroom abduction.

Strieber says he did not read my book until early January 1986. He reports that, when he did, 'I was shocked .... I just stared and stared at the words .... They were talking about people who think they've been taken aboard spaceships by aliens. And I seemed to be such a person. My blood went cold: Nobody must ever, ever know about this ....' Now he realized that his dream (or sign of mental illness, which he had also considered) was something quite different. So he followed the clues in my book, tracked down Budd Hopkins in New York and had a couple of hypnosis sessions during March 1986 with Dr Donald Klein, a psychiatrist in the city.

The result of all this was a deeper memory, not just of his December 1985 experience but of several previous abductions that he had totally forgotten. After the first couple of hypnosis sessions he quit and '... preferred to struggle with the memories, to try to learn how to overcome the biological fear that seems to be impeding this experience' (*MUFON Journal*). He also went on to have recurrent abductions, *after* the spring of 1986, on a scale quite unprecedented: 'I have a relationship with [the visitors] ... and I have it on my own personal and human terms.'

In this respect he became far more like one of the contactees of the 1950s than any modern UFO abductee.

Despite his first remembered encounters occurring the day after he received a copy of my book (rather a coincidence), he struck a deal with a publisher remarkably fast. In May 1987 he told the *London Evening Standard* in an interview that nine publishers turned it down in disgust and he has frequently said that his own publishers reacted in horror at the thought of their star writer claiming to have met little grey men. They refused to have anything to do with it.

He chose to title his story *Communion* because of that 'special relationship' he felt he had developed with the 'visitors'. It was sold to William Morrow for a $1 million advance – easily the most any publisher has ever paid for a book about UFOs, by an enormous margin. Note also how long his desire had lasted not to tell anybody about his story! Strieber has never tried to hide the fact that he has no supporting evidence for his trips with the visitors. He does have corrobarative witnesses for one of the sightings to a limited degree, but not to the abduction itself. He went to some lengths to attempt to make people believe in his sincerity, taking lie-detector tests and brain scans. He even included friendly endorsements on the jacket of the book from some rather influential people, including a US Navy physicist and a NASA astronaut.

With hype like that, it should have surprised nobody (and UFO researchers were far from surprised) that the book was an instant success, retailing up to half a million hardbacked copies in the first few months and staying on the best-seller charts in the USA for most of 1987. Again this was unprecedented and allegedly astonished both Strieber and William Morrow. In *International UFO Reporter* for January/February 1987, Strieber related his adventures 'On the road [with visitors]', whilst promoting his book.

He appeared in eighteen cities and on forty live television and radio shows during this promotion. The 'gales of helpless laughter' he had feared did not materialize.

He was not treated so favourably when *Communion* was launched in Britain in May by Century-Hutchinson. It is interesting to speculate on why this might be so. Of course, he was less well known than in his native land, and the British are by tradition less willing to take stories at face value. He also suffered, in that the Aetherius Society used his forthcoming book to launch their own campaign. Being so attractive to the media with their wild tales, April and May 1987 saw countless silly stories published, and Strieber, coming in the wake of that, stood little chance of being taken seriously.

There were, in fact, some quite good reviews, for example by Val Hennessy in the *Daily Mail* (21 May 1987), who spoke of 'close encounters of the lucrative kind' and by Ann Shearer in the *Guardian* the day before, with the clever title 'A man who got carried away'. This was an excellent review and interview. Strieber himself said it was his best session with a British reporter, and it was one of the few where a crucial fact was stressed.

Strieber himself is not convinced that the visitors are from outer space. He merely wishes that '... more scientists [would] shed their prejudices about UFOs and start taking seriously the proliferating accounts of visitors in a new respect for people who for so long have been fearful of mentioning those experiences at all'.

In an interview with Mike Wootten, editor of *BUFORA Bulletin*, (No. 26, 1987), he added, 'One well-known UFO investigator has attacked my book because it is not "nuts and bolts" enough. It doesn't fit his preconceived ideas of these encounters. He wants it to be about little scientists coming down from a far-away place to teach our scientists how to get to the stars. They should be asking encounter witnesses how it feels. That's the important thing. I don't think the source of the experience is properly known at this time .... I cannot believe that the source of my experience is nothing more startling than visitors from another planet, quite frankly.'

When pressed, it seems that he favours an answer which suggests a new form of reality produced out of the collective mind of the entire planet. He also says, with remarkable perception, 'I suspect that the alien spacecraft imagery is a screen between the individual and the actual experience, which may at this time be impossible, or too awesome to comprehend.'

Unhappily, less intelligent interviewing dominated the British media. He *was* laughed at on the Terry Wogan television chat show, a somewhat predictable reaction. The *Star*, also predictably, chose to headline their interview 'Kidnapped by ET invaders – they operated on my brain', thus ensuring that no one would treat the story as more than comedy. The *London Evening Standard* (whilst admittedly later redressing the balance somewhat) even found it necessary to accuse Whitley Strieber of looking as if '... he has just stepped off the bridge of Fireball XL5 ... "Oh God, he's a looney," muttered the photographer as Strieber strode across the lounge of his hotel.'

Whatever else Strieber and other abductees may be, they are not loonies. They are in the main sincere and frightened.

The publication of *Communion* even provoked the doomed television soap opera *The Colbys* to try to rescue itself with a half-million-dollar final episode that saw Fallon Carrington Colby climb aboard a UFO in the ultimate abduction. It stimulated the Vatican into setting up training courses in extra-terrestrial studies for their priests, just in case they ever had to deal with the arrival of the aliens. And it made society on both sides of the Atlantic aware of these very close encounters.

This has two consequences. It means that no longer can anyone plead ignorance, as Strieber did. The theme of the abduction is now very public knowledge. It also means that the abduction phenomenon is now firmly under the microscope. People are wondering if there is any truth to these amazing claims, and if so, what sort of truth. Even Strieber seems to be pondering that. In *International UFO Reporter* he stressed, 'I have been saying that I'm 80 per cent convinced that the visitors are quite real .... But if they are not real, then the human mind is engaged in a really spectacular flight of collective fancy.'

These words convey the sort of beguiling honesty that I found about Strieber when I met him. If he is a conman, he is a disarming one, who speaks a good deal of sense about the phenomenon. It may not even matter if his story is *not* true, provided we realize that the abduction mystery does not stand or fall by this one case.

However, *was* Strieber ignorant of abduction cases before his encounter, as he claims? We have reason to wonder. In *Communion* he admits to being a supporter of a zealous anti-paranormal body (which produces the journal *Skeptical Inquirer*). This regularly debunks UFO and abduction stories. He also says that my book *Science and the UFOs* was bought for him for Christmas as a *joke*.

He told *BUFORA Bulletin*, 'This experience happens to a lot of people and they deserve to be treated with dignity. It's terribly important. My blood and my guts tell me it is so important that we have to take a clear headed and intelligent look at what is going on.'

Anyone who studies the abduction mystery will find it difficult to disagree with those words.

2 The Abduction Myth

In 1425 a French peasant girl named Jeanne saw a UFO. Of course, she did not report it as that. When a brilliant light continued to appear and several strange beings came with it, she assumed (quite naturally for that day and age) that it was a religious visitation.

The voices promised all manner of things, including that she had been chosen for a special task – basically to lead the French against the English invaders. They also gave her the dubious gift of psychic powers, enabling her to foresee successes and defeats on the road towards the ultimate defeat of her enemies, and let her know that she would not live to see this victory, as she was destined to burn at the stake (aged just nineteen). The reason for this tragic end was her frequent chats with other-worldly beings, clear proof of witchcraft.

Joan of Arc, as we know her, may in one sense have been what we might now equate with a medium but there are very distinct parallels between her story and those of modern abductions. Perhaps she was just one of the first to undergo a close encounter and to be manipulated by supposedly superior beings for some ill-defined purpose.

Possibly it is stretching things to draw comparisons between a saint and an abductee, but there are useful lessons to be learned by wondering whether the version of the abduction story viewed in the last chapter may not be just a modern interpretation of an ancient theme. It is, in fact, crucial to ask right at the outset whether the 'traditional' version has substance or is an illusion, for it may well be that we are deluding ourselves into thinking that the apparently recent epidemic of abductions has no historical precedent.

Some researchers have been extremely interested in this

possibility, even in days before the abduction case became recognized as a stereotype.

Dr Jacques Valleé is a prize-winning writer of French science fiction who moved to Silicon Valley in California and became a computer expert. He is, in fact, the man on whom the scientist in Steven Spielberg's movie *Close Encounters of the Third Kind* was modelled. Vallée wrote a trail-blazing book entitled *Passport to Magonia* in which he studied texts of myth and fairy lore from many countries (paying the price of including some weak and dubious stories, of course). Then he sought to compare or contrast the data found in these traditions with 'the space-age myth' of UFOs and aliens. Had these replaced gnomes and fairies in modern culture?

There were striking parallels. For instance, the UFO occupants are often small (although not usually as small as the tiny fairies). They also carry instruments like fairy wands, capable of doing things to mortals. When they cart folk off to fairyland, this usually involves a degree of time distortion, amnesia, kidnap to a wondrous place and ultimate return to disbelieving friends. There is even the apparent concern with gynaecology – for example, the 'changeling', a fairy child born of humans for some obscure purpose. Thinking about it, the Villas Boas case of cosmic rape is no more than a twentieth-century update on a theme, rather as the movie *West Side Story* placed Shakespeare's *Romeo and Juliet* in a modern American setting.

However intriguing these connections appear, there is a danger of going too far. Can one reinterpret the Bible, for instance, and say that Ezekiel's wheel was a primitive spaceship? Quite a few want to try! And a number of the comparisons are less than satisfying. For example, is it more than coincidence that the fairy abode of a toadstool happens to look something like a UFO with a beam of light from the underside?

Nonetheless, all but those most determined *not* to see any links must agree that there are grounds for suspicion. Perhaps there is a continuum between fairy lore from all over the world and modern UFO abductions. Of course, what this means is quite another matter. Have the aliens been around a long time, to be previously misinterpreted as fairies? Or is the whole thing a product of some strange desire in the human mind, made no more comprehensible by this historical antecedent but in a sense easier to accept if we do not have a phenomenon that has sprung out of nowhere since the early 1950s?

A classic case was found by folklore researchers Janet and Colin Bord, reported in the book *The Peat-Fire Flame* by Alasdair Alpin McGregor. This account of traditional stories in the Scottish islands was published (by Ettrick Press) in 1937, so there is no way in which it can have had any influence from UFO cases. It tells how two boys saw a strange 'boat' off the Isle of Muck one morning in 1912. Two small creatures approached; another stayed on the craft. The boys' fear was suspended by a trance (the classic Oz Factor), and the figures spoke to them, asking questions about their life and what they did at home. When the boys were invited on board, they refused to go, so the entities (fairies? ufonauts?) suggested they should watch the boat and when it reached a certain point they could go home. This sounds very like a post-hypnotic suggestion to bring them out of the trance state. By chance, their sister arrived and saw them staring out to sea (with no boat visible). Their eyes were vacant. As she spoke to them, the 'spell' broke and they began to tremble in terror.

Substitute a few words in this account (such as UFO for boat) and it becomes indistinguishable from a contemporary attempt to abduct two boys aboard an alien vessel. The pattern is so clear that one is caught unawares by it, since it must be independent.

To suggest that the first UFO abductees knew about this obscure Scottish text is improbable to say the least, and the author of the book (in the highly unlikely event that he made the story up) can have had no information whatsoever about UFOs, let alone UFO abduction cases. There were none recorded as far back as 1937.

It is not only fairy lore that shows such patterns. Of course, often 'fairy' is just a word, like 'alien', that helps a culture describe its bizarre experiences. We must never underestimate the parochial nature of our times. We tend to assume we know all there is to know.

Bill Chalker, an Australian researcher into close-encounter cases, is particularly interested in parallels with shamanism, the powers of the witch-doctor in tribal cultures. Here we find a large degree of belief in 'sky gods' of superior intelligence, and many methods of inducing altered states of consciousness (rhythmic dancing, eating plants containing hallucinogenic components etc), all geared towards a convening with spirits. The Aborigines have their 'dream time', where a sort of time-lapse effect occurs. In fact, almost everywhere you look there are hints of a possible connection. How vague these hints are is anyone's guess at this stage, but they are there and cannot be totally overlooked.

Another story of great interest shows how these revelations continue to occur. It was found by Masaru Mori and reported in the spring 1987 edition of *Fortean Times*, a wonderful storehouse of current folk tales.

This account, which certainly appears to be of a genuine incident, came from two sources, both long predating the UFO era. The oldest is the Japanese *Toen-Shosetsu*, written in 1825 by Kinrei-sha. It reports a strange 'ship' seen off the shore of Harayadori, near Tokyo, on 22 February 1803.

Japanese fishermen and villagers gathered to see the object, described and depicted in both accounts. The sketches are stylistically different but basically alike. They represent what we would now regard as a classic UFO.

The object was about fifteen to twenty feet in diameter, made up of two hemispheres, one atop the other and separated by a rim. The upper dome seemed to be made of glass or perspex and had transparent sliding doors. The lower one consisted of metal struts. Those who saw inside the dome said that there were strange letters written there. It also contained a bottle full of what looked like water.

The oddest feature of all was the figure of a very beautiful young woman seen inside the craft. She was about five feet tall and wore clothing of unusual material and design. Her face was white like snow, and she had long hair or a head-dress that fell to shoulder length behind her. She clambered out of the object, speaking in a language no one recognized, and clung jealously to a box about a foot long which she would not let anyone touch. Because no one knew who this stranger was, they bundled her back into the upper compartment and pushed it out to sea, where it drifted out of sight.

Again we see the obvious comparisons with modern UFO encounters. The strange woman turns up again, more than a century later, in another non-UFO story from a Leeds man, Iain

Johnston. He tells in his own words what happened when he was just six years old and living near Drumchapel in Scotland (letter to *Earth* magazine, midsummer 1987).

One sunny day in the summer of 1946 he walked into the local woods and then, 'All of a sudden, the sounds of woodland life were stilled, as if in expectancy of some new and fabulous event that was about to take place. I felt a very mystical sense of time, as if it had stopped or slowed down.' This is again the Oz Factor effect taking hold, perhaps indicating that he had entered an altered state of consciousness.

The figure then appeared to Iain. She was only about three to four feet tall and had a 'complexion [that] was an ivory white' and eyes that were 'large and slanted'. He later said of these that they were 'cat-like', a phrase used often by UFO abductees. The woman merely spoke with him, saying, 'Don't you recognize me?' and ending with the words 'You shall see me again.' Both these themes recur constantly in UFO encounter cases, as we shall see.

But perhaps the closest links of all come in cases of religious visions. Even the most famous of these, when a French girl, Bernadette Soubirous, saw the 'Virgin' at Lourdes and provoked the pilgrimages which continue to this day, had much of the abduction about it. Her story tells only of a 'girl in white, no taller than myself' (that is perhaps four feet tall). The Virgin Mary interpretation was placed on the vision by the Church, possibly just as now UFO researchers automatically put an alien interpretation on such cases.

In his book *Visions, Apparitions, Alien Visitors* Hilary Evans tries to show a common bond between countless apparitions, from ghosts to men in black. One of his cases particularly impressed me. It occurred on the night of 18/19 July 1830 and involved another French girl, Catherine Labouré.

Catherine awoke at 11.30 p.m. and saw a 'child of about five or six, dressed completely in white'. The child glowed with rays of light. In a sort of trance she was led to what she took to be a chapel, although it was radiating light from a source not seen and was brilliantly aglow. She felt no fear, as if controlled, as she watched the figure – which explained that it was the Virgin (in yet another disguise). However, rather perceptively, Catherine said, 'I can't explain why, but it still seemed to me that it was not her that I saw.'

The figure gave Catherine a message about how to be good and peaceful and then led her back to her room. A time lapse seems to have occurred (Catherine said, 'I don't know how much time passed') for when she arrived it was 2 a.m., even though she had no memory to fill up all this gap.

It is easy to see how today such a report would have a very different interpretation if it were featured in the local press.

These religious visions still go on. In Yugoslavia, for example, children in the village of Medju Gore have been seeing the 'Virgin', despite today's competition from UFOs. And an excellent case has been made out by Portuguese Ufologists that the famous Fatima visions may have to be seen as UFO encounters.

These occurred in 1917, again to village children. The difference was one of scale. The small figure in white that shone silver and carried a glowing ball in its hands promised to return on the same day each month and did so. It gave several messages, the first being a warning of the Communist revolution (then contemporary but probably unknown to these children), the second being World War II and the final one (allegedly) about a great 'tribulation' that is to come in the 1990s (presumably a third horrific war). In this last regard it is interesting that the current Yugoslavian visions have the Virgin warning that this will be her last appearance before that 'final cataclysm', but that a great sign in the sky will appear just before the doom is upon us. All the world will see that one!

The last appearance at Fatima was in October 1917, and thousands turned out to witness it. No one saw the Virgin (in keeping with all cases of abduction: outsiders do not see it happening), but there were many who claim to have observed a glowing light in the sky, said by most to be the sun spinning round.

Oddly, the solar effects of the 'Miracle of Fatima' were repeated on 4 October 1986, at Rhyl in North Wales!

Margaret Fry, a local sleuth who is most enthusiastic, was chasing many UFO sightings at the time. She kindly gave me a full report of the events which befell Mrs Cantrell, her daughter Sharon and their neighbours, Mr and Mrs Jones. They were also good enough to let me have a set of the colour photographs Sharon Cantrell took of the phenomenon.

In a curious about-face from the Fatima event, these witnesses were sure they had seen a UFO, but there is no doubt that the image on the pictures is that of the sun. Admittedly it seems to be creating an interesting illusion effect, and it is puzzling why more people in this popular holiday resort did not witness the spectacle. Yet many questions arise. Is it pure coincidence that there were genuine UFO sightings at the time? What do we make of the fact that a house in Prestatyn, very near by and at the same period, was invaded by a poltergeist? The family claim that an energy force drove them out and even threw their pet dog down the stairs – luckily with no ill effect.

One of the first indications I had of the way in which myth and modern UFO encounters interface with religion came in August 1978 when I went on holiday to the Mediterranean island of Ibiza. I spent some time with a delightful expatriate Scottish couple who owned a villa in the mountains above San Antonio Abad. They had many strange tales to tell, including the orange ball that hovered over their bedroom, created an air-pressure disturbance and left illness in its wake.

But the oddest was the story of some local peasant children. They had seen two figures and a glowing light in the woods. One figure was an archetypal robot (even complete with antennae). The other was seen in a religious context – not the Virgin, on this occasion, but, I think, a sort of Jesus entity, although my lack of Spanish made it hard to be certain. This weird placing of such divergent beings next to one another always stuck in my mind. Nowadays we see it often in UFO abductions, where witnesses talk of robot 'captors' and more human-like 'experimenters' in charge of the robots. So the connection seems important.

Surprisingly few novelists have seen the importance of these links. One who did was British science-fiction author Ian Watson. His 1978 novel *Miracle Visitors* poses more questions than it answers, but at least it poses them! By setting the UFO abduction into a miraculous framework, it challenges the basis of reality. Watson is not saying that this is all a myth. If it were that simple, we would need to go no further. It is a lot more complicated than that.

Others have recognized this. Indeed, everyone who has really analysed the clues offered by the connections we have touched on in this chapter seems to have come away certain that they deepen the mystery rather than help resolve it. This was true of Vallée. It was true of the famous Swiss psychiatrist Dr Carl Jung, whose 1959 book *A Modern Myth of Things Seen in the Skies* is often mistaken for a sceptical dismissal. In fact, he was more puzzled after he wrote it than before.

Another person this is true of is Bertrand Méheust, a French researcher whose work was the catalyst for Watson's novel. Sadly he is little known outside France. He has tried to unravel the threads that merge UFO cases into folklore. In recent years he has been more and more intrigued by '*enlèvements*' (as the French call abductions), yet he still cannot quite believe that the parallels mean the answer must be just psychological.

In his latest book, *Soucoupes volantes et folklore* (*Flying Saucers and Folklore*, Mercure, 1985) he says: 'If every person who found himself in a state of extreme emotional crisis observed UFOs, the sky above the English Channel would have been full of them on 6 June 1944.'

The links we have discovered are certainly worth filing away to be thought about later. They are not to be treated lightly and dismissed if they do not fit what you *want* to believe about abduction stories. But in themselves they solve nothing. There *is* more to it than that.

3 Abductions and Science Fiction

In a perceptive analysis of the 1961 Hill abduction (*BUFORA Bulletin*, December 1984), John Spencer makes an important point. He quotes from the hypnotic regression carried out on Betty Hill by Dr Benjamin Simon and notes that she said to her husband, Barney, 'I laughed and asked him if he had watched the *Twilight Zone* recently on television.' The doctor asked why she brought this up and she added, 'Because the idea [of a UFO abduction] was fantastic.'

Spencer uses this as part of his argument that the case, and CE4s ('Close encounters of the fourth kind') are psychological in origin. He suggests that '... the stimuli exist for a fantasy' and that these stimuli come in the form of science fiction.

In a British abduction, that of nine-year-old Gaynor Sunderland from Flint, North Wales, in July 1976, one hypnosis session, three years later, was conducted by an experienced (though not medically qualified) researcher, under the direction of the *Liverpool Daily Post*. The hypnotist, Joe Keeton, is best known for his experiments into alleged reincarnation. However, whilst Gaynor added nothing new to her conscious recall (just a few more details), Keeton did think he had caught her out.

Having met the now adult Gaynor on several occasions, it is quite fascinating to compare her calm, self-assured nature as a busy nurse with the recording of her voice as a young child made during that session in early 1979. (The three-year gap occurred because Gaynor had undergone a mental block after her sighting, requiring that she tell no one of her experience until triggered to do so in the spring of 1978). The July 1976 encounter does not seem to have been an abduction, although a memory gap exists and there are other clues to imply that it might be. When I investigated the case in 1978, abductions were uncommon enough for us not to look too hard.

The crucial part of the session (after seeing a UFO in a field is as follows:

Gaynor:	The man is walking round the spaceship .... I feel funny.
Joe:	How do you know it's a spaceship?
Gaynor:	Because it's funny .... I feel funny.
Joe:	Did you see it come out of space?
Gaynor:	No.
Joe:	Then what makes you think it's a spaceship?
Gaynor:	I've seen ... picture.
Joe:	You've seen a picture of it .... Well, where did you see a picture of it?
Gaynor:	On telly [television].
Joe:	You saw it on telly .... And when did you see the picture on telly?
Gaynor:	It was on *Nationwide*.
Joe:	It was on *Nationwide*, was it? [This was a BBC early evening magazine programme of the time] ... When was it on *Nationwide* – the day before?
Gaynor:	No – before I broke up [i.e. left school for the summer holidays, presumably before the sighting].
Joe:	Before you broke up from school you saw this programme on *Nationwide* .... And does this thing in the field look exactly the same as what you saw on *Nationwide*?
Gaynor:	Er ... exactly the same ....

It was not totally clear here whether she was saying that the object *was* the same. Witnesses under regression tend to mumble (and in this February 1979 interview Gaynor was still aged only eleven). She was not asked to repeat her answer, but careful listening seems to suggest that she *had* allegedly observed a UFO on television just like the silver cigar she saw in the North Wales field. And this had been only a few weeks before her close encounter.

That would be vital information, and Keeton was quick to see that it might imply a sort of mental trigger for a fantasy. A few weeks after the hypnosis, when he, Gaynor and I had a three-way debate-cum-interview on BBC Radio Wales, he put forward the idea (which the now twenty-one-year-old Gaynor still utterly rejects) that she fell off her bicycle and in a period of sleep or unconsciousness 'dreamed' the experience based on this prior television programme.

Later in the session Joe Keeton tried twice to get more out of Gaynor about these television images. First she insisted that no entities were associated with the *Nationwide* UFO. Then she was regressed to the time when she was watching the show and asked to describe what she saw. She said: 'Like a cigar ... silver with a rim ... no windows ... there's nothing on top.' The only comparisons with her encounter are the use of the word 'cigar' and the silver colour. But her sketch clearly shows that she observed a typical disc with a flat base and windows round the curved edge. On top was a red light. Indeed, when questioned under hypnosis about this discrepancy, she called the UFO 'round'. In retrospect it appears that the two objects (the one she saw on television and the one 'really' witnessed) were quite different, and the term 'cigar' was applied to her UFO sighting only because she had heard this word linked with a UFO on television. There is scant evidence to suggest that the mind of a child in a suggestible state of hypnosis tried to make her UFO identical with the one on TV.

In addition Gaynor saw two aliens, very close up for a protracted period – coming within a few feet of one. In later abductions she discovered that the phonetic names of these were 'Ana' and 'Parz'. The female entity (seen more closely) was about five feet tall, with a silver one-piece suit, white, elongated face, very thin features and large round (pink) eyes – very much a stereotype, although it is hard to imagine that a nine-year-old would be familiar with that.

When asked whether aliens had got out of the UFO in the *Nationwide* programme, she matter-of-factly announced, 'I went away.' It was later confirmed that she was so uninterested (or frightened) by the UFO that she walked out before the item finished. No aliens such as she saw *were* involved in that case.

Keeton also tried to ascertain whether she had seen a television film about aliens, *The UFO Incident* (a dramatization of the Betty and Barney Hill case). This was not screened in

Britain before July 1976 and under hypnosis Gaynor denied seeing it later. When asked about favourite television programmes, she mentioned *Blue Peter*, a children's magazine show. Had she watched *Dr Who*, a popular time-travel and space monster serial? She admitted that she had (along with ninety-five per cent of the children in Britain, no doubt). What did she think of its silver-suited 'Cybermen'? She was insistent – they were 'Silly!'

I have dwelt on this because it is the best experimental data we have on the influence of science fiction in a real case. Whilst at the time we all assumed that the *Nationwide* programme had been *before* her 1976 encounter, there is room for doubt. No such feature has turned up in June or July 1976, and the most likely case is the one a year later, describing some children who saw a 'silver object' in a field near their school in Dyfed, South Wales. This was the subject of television features in the spring and summer of 1977, after her sighting but two years before the hypnosis. If so, it would explain the choice of such words as 'cigar' but could obviously have had no direct influence on her sighting in the first place – only, perhaps, her *memory* of it.

Incidentally, those who doubt that witnesses in these situations are sincere need only hear the adult Gaynor or hear her relive the experience on my tape of that 1979 hypnosis session. I spoke to her some hours before it took place, and there is no question that she firmly believed that one cannot lie whilst hypnotized. This is nonsense, but for an eleven-year-old to be told that and still agree to go ahead speaks volumes for her integrity. Hearing the very real tears and the natural terror that pour out from Gaynor during certain phases of the memory (always the most appropriate phases), makes it difficult to believe that this is a genius actress. Whatever the explanation for her experience, Gaynor Sunderland relived it as if she were there, enduring a waking nightmare.

However, the suspicion that witness stories might rely in some way on science fiction will not go away. Hilary Evans writes on the theme in an article entitled 'Abducted by an Archetype' (*Fortean Times*, autumn 1980). He is particularly intrigued by the fact that people who go on board a UFO almost always refer in their stories to the fact that the doors opened like magic and the lighting oozed out all over the room without visible sign of where it came from. These exact features, he claims, appear in science fiction. He talks of one 1920s story from obscure French science fiction which shows the hero aboard a spaceship that pours out a diffuse green light from nowhere and has doors that appear unexpectedly when needed. But that is just one minor detail, culled from a work which had only the most limited readership. Today's science-fiction best-sellers (stories that sell by the million) conjure up the most fantastic of alien monsters, who *never* appear in abductees' reports. Nor are threatened invasions of Earth, staple matter of modern science fiction, ever replicated among the warnings issued by aliens to abductees. These are far more striking images than the mere appearance of a UFO and might be expected to register more strongly on the subconscious, to be reproduced in abduction reports – but they are never featured.

Visual images are more potent than words, so it might be argued that science fiction in films and television drama has coloured 'popular imagination' – that is, accounts of abductions reported by the easily impressed. Since abductions are a post-1947 phenomenon, the link is feasible.

There is no film before 1951 of any relevance, but the film *The Day The Earth Stood Still*, of 1951, *is* highly significant. The story was based on the first UFO reports then coming to popular notice. It took the theme and developed it, with a giant disc landing in Washington DC and a silver-suited (otherwise quite normal) man getting out. With him was a huge, lumbering robot. That is not too auspicious a start, and the man/robot theme continued in several later films (e.g. *Forbidden Planet* in 1956). It is not auspicious because the normal man and giant robot are not at all common in UFO encounters (save one or two of the early to mid fifties contactee cases, which it is fairly safe to assume were often unconscious, if not outrageously conscious, hoaxes reliant on these movies).

Where *The Day The Earth Stood Still* scores is in its plot concept of the aliens coming with a message of peace. In order to demonstrate superiority, all electrical power (except emergency services) is brought to a standstill right round the world. It is worth wondering whether the now very familiar theme of electrical impedence in car engines, house lights, television sets, radios etc (not uncommonly alleged in UFO close encounters) might not have *begun* with that movie. In fact, it occurs in standard UFO cases that are *not* abductions (and far more often), and so is actually one of the few features of the UFO evidence which is strong, extremely well-documented, highly consistent and open to scientific research. There are excellent grounds for the belief that a real energy of some sort (and it may be from an entirely natural phenomenon – after all, lightning has a lot of electromagnetic energy) may lie behind these cases.

Yet Geoff Falla produced a major study for BUFORA of over 400 such 'vehicle interference' reports in the literature, and only a tiny handful (about eight) pre-date the 1951 film. None is of the precise sort we are talking about, and it was not until the October 1954 wave in Europe (the first time aliens were reported as appearing in any abundance) that they occurred in present form. Why is this? Is it due to the growing use of vehicles, television sets and other electrical equipment from the mid fifties onward? If the theme in the film *was* the catalyst, why was there a three-year gestation period?

Other hints can be found in films such as *Invaders From Mars* (1953), where humans were taken aboard and operated on, and *This Island Earth* (1955), with its scene of 'beaming up' an aircraft into a UFO, just as today witnesses sometimes claim their cars are abducted.

However, again the overwhelming tone of these films has been of 'bug-eyed monsters' intent on taking over the world by force. If any motifs from the films were to filter out into the human subconscious, why were they not the most dominant? Why do we not have abduction cases involving horrible creatures who strike terror into the witness and say they intend to invade Earth?

Absolutely none of these films (which in the main were not all that popular or successful) features the scenario so ever-present in modern abduction lore: the smallish entity with large eyes pointed chin, grey skin and a peaceful (if somewhat stand-offish) scientific interest in humanity.

Television fares no better. As the 'official' or 'traditional' version of abduction history showed in Chapter 1, it was 1967 onwards when the abductions really came onto the scene. This was *contemporary* with the heyday of *Star Trek*, one of the most popular television series of all time, still being repeated all over the world and currently spawning the fifth in a sequence of films starring the same characters. An amazing variety of monsters appear as aliens here including, 'Mr Spock' with his red skin cast, slanted eyebrows and wickedly pointed ears. If science fiction was creating an archetype in the human mind, what happened to all the Spock-like aliens in post-*Star Trek* abductions? They just do not exist. Nor do any Klingons.

There have been some far-seeing ideas in films from the 1960s to date. Nigel Kneale's *Quatermass and the Pit* (screened on BBC TV as a six-part black-and-white serial in late 1958) absolutely terrified me as a child. The aliens here were small and insect-like, and his linking of their rediscovery to a sort of human genetic engineering project is remarkable in its relevance to our current problem. Yet that serial was never screened outside Britain, and when it was made into a film in 1968, it had very limited success. It cannot realistically be seen as the cause of anything, especially as it then post-dated some abductions.

Similarly, John Wyndham wrote a good deal of amazingly apt science fiction, some of which has been made into low-budget films. *The Village of the Damned* (1960), based on his book *The Midwich Cuckoos*, tells of a village put into a sort of Oz Factor trance which wakes to discover twelve of its women pregnant. They bear children who are all alike, with deep, staring eyes, blond hair and telepathic powers, engineered as alien half-breeds.

His novel *Chocky* is even more relevant, since it discusses children who are contacted by an alien, Chocky, who uses their ability to manipulate images. The children's innate psychic powers help Chocky change the world. This is a recurrent abduction storyline and has more than a passing resemblance to the real-life Gaynor Sunderland saga already referred to. *Chocky* has been turned into three children's television serials, shown in Britain during the 1980s. I had documented all the Gaynor Sunderland data *years* before these television programmes, so, if anything, one could argue that they were based on Gaynor's story. It cannot be the other way around, since Anthony Read's purpose-written sequels *Chocky's Children* and *Chocky's Challenge* are actually more interesting in terms of UFO abduction cases.

It almost tempts one to see these Kneale and Wyndham writings as examples of 'back-door contacts' – that is, that their fiction comes from their subconscious which, without knowing it, is directed by aliens!

Perhaps it is not quite so daft as it sounds. When, in 1976, Ian Watson put together his 'serious UFO novel' *Miracle Visitors*, he did not know that he was in the midst of 'Britain's year of the abductee'. Cases like that of Gaynor Sunderland, and others we shall look at later, suddenly gave Britain abductions when it had not had any before. 1976 remains the single biggest year on record for British CE4s, although most of them came to light afterwards and, as Watson was conceiving his book, he could not have known about them.

In *Miracle Visitors* (1978) he finally published the only sincere fictional attempt to understand the abduction. When interviewed several years later, he commented that it was his most forceful work, because whilst he wrote it (living in Oxfordshire) UFOs seemed to 'home in' on him. Considering that his plot was that UFOs are a quasi-reality forced into existence through the medium of people with the ability to enter a state of 'UFO Consciousness', this may not have been irrelevant. But what he was really noting was the spring 1977 wave, when more sightings occurred in Britain than ever before.

Watson set his plot in the North Yorkshire Dales, apparently not far from the satellite monitoring base at Menwith Hill. His hero, Michael Peacocke, sees a UFO land, loses memory of it and later, at a university hypnosis experiment, comes out with a typical abduction story, including details that Watson based on the Villas Boas case of sexual liaison. He throws in many other true-to-life ideas from real UFO cases and weaves them cleverly with theoretical discussions about what is going on, through the mouth of characters such as Dr John Deacon, the psychologist who sets out to prove that Michael is fantasizing but soon realizes it is not that simple. One debate between two UFO investigators shows this well and mirrors real discussions I have often been involved in: 'Mightn't there be hallucinations that are also at the same time, in a sense, real? Hallucinations that have a temporary conditional reality?' one researcher asks. When he is told that something is either real or unreal, he challenges, 'But need it be? UFOs seem to act as though they both *are* and *aren't*, at one and the same time. As though they occupy some middle ground.'

This paradoxical truth does not aid the credibility of UFO abductions but remains present however much we might prefer that it did not. It may indeed be our perception of reality that is at fault, in which case questions such as 'Are abductions real or are they imaginary?' would be meaningless.

As Watson's story develops, we find that Michael has been rescued from death earlier in life when a runaway tanker should have flattened him and that bizarre coincidences take a hand (although, of course, coincidences are a part of the fabric of reality, and thus of UFO consciousness). Meanwhile Dr Deacon starts to theorize about what he calls 'solidograms', holograms that are produced out of pre-existent matter and based on the mythic idea in the mind of the witness. To test his thesis he hypnotizes Michael, who conjures up a pterodactyl (flying dinosaur) over the Yorkshire moors, which swoops around before dissolving back into the ether.

There is a great deal more to the book than this, but the flavour of the yarn is illustrated, and what really matters are the staggering consequences that emerge from its writing which are mind-boggling yet unhappily quite true.

The Yorkshire moors around which he set the story became a hotbed of UFO sightings, particularly in 1978 (the very year it was published) and especially around the Menwith Hill base and the microwave tower that features in his plot, but *before* publication (though after preparation) of the novel.

One of the witnesses to these events was Paul Bennett, a youth whose history makes Michael Peacocke's seem tame. He too claimed to have had his life saved when he was thrown from his bicycle into a tree and nearly died, recovering from coma as a UFO hovered over the Bradford hospital where he lay. Between 1973 and 1977 he also conjured up all manner of entities and had very close encounters of the abduction type. Many of these things were recorded by Nigel Watson (!) and myself in 1977-8, in an obscure magazine (circulation under 100) *before* Ian Watson (no relation) published his novel in late 1978. A fuller account of some of them appears in my books *Alien Contact* (1981) and *The Pennine UFO Mystery* (1983), which depend in no way upon Ian Watson's novel. Paul Bennett went on to edit a journal of mysterious goings-on in the Yorkshire area. One of the first cases he received (apparently without knowing of the coincidence and from a sincere witness) was the sighting of a pterodactyl over the moors!

As if this was not enough, Ian Watson had moved on to other (equally fascinating) novels, not about UFOs, and was living in Northamptonshire. He is right in the centre of the one place in Britain where – for some reason – abduction cases seem to be happening like crazy. Four of the British cases recounted on later pages occurred near his home. When I wrote to tell him, Ian Watson was clearly surprised. He certainly did not know about these cases, only one of which received any media publicity – just as his book was published in hardback!

Did the success of *Miracle Visitors* generate these events? The hardback science-fiction novel sold only modestly, and the paperback appeared in 1980, after many had happened. One of his editors told me that Watson is known as 'the ideas man of science fiction' because he comes up with often brilliant and revolutionary suggestions; he has a limited but devoted following.

Again we find that the most theoretically accurate in a theoretical sense are the least commercial. They tend to influence fewer people than the horrific space-invasion tales that are so popular.

The only mass-market true-to-life UFO story on film has been Steven Spielberg's *Close Encounters of the Third Kind*. This was released in the USA in late 1977 and in the UK in spring 1978 and was a huge success. Its aliens are small and have large eyes and more resemblance to those in abduction cases than any other film. But that is hardly surprising, since Spielberg based his fantasy on abduction cases. It can hardly be said that his film provoked reports, because hundreds were on record by 1978. It is also worth nothing that there was no wave of either UFO sightings or abductions generated by the film – not in the USA, nor in Britain. There was, in fact, a mini-wave of British alien contact cases in January 1978, but they happened *before* the publicity campaign began.

The only film actually about an abduction is *The UFO Incident*, a dramatization of John Fuller's book on the Hill case. This was a low-budget US television film, and its screening in the States in October 1975 was prior to a small glut of abduction cases. But it was by no means the most important one of the decade) and the next wave (in Britain during November 1980) was totally without reference to any catalyst.

All of this shows how difficult it is to claim that science fiction or SF films are the trigger for UFO abduction stories. The evidence simply is not there, just as Méheust pointed out that it is not there for a direct correlation with periods of tension. The Cuban missile crisis in 1962 was at a record low in UFO events. There were no recorded abductions. The Suez crisis in 1956 brought no cases. And the Falklands War of April and May 1982 was in no sense correlated with activity.

What seems to happen is that science fiction sometimes *uses* UFO interest after the fact but does not stimulate it.

Perhaps the oddest discovery is that Ian *Watson* was writing as fiction what Nigel *Watson* was then investigating as fact. No simple theory of spaceships or imagination can account for that. And at this exact same time, with full independence, someone else was putting the same ingredients into a pot and coming up with an identical brew. His idea for a quasi-real UFO hallucination was a book called the *Lifetide* (1979). His name was Lyall *Watson*.

4 Rogue Cases

There is one more link we must examine before moving on to a detailed discussion of world-wide alien abductions. This is what might be termed 'rogue cases'.

These stories appear inherently implausible, bizarre extremities of the evidence. However, a brief look at such reports assists greatly in the task that is to come, for the cases that *are* real, in the sense that they involve sincere witnesses without psychological hang-ups or any obvious reasons for trickery, can then be viewed in comparison: whilst the rogues are a mixed bag of weird anecdotes, the essence of the alien abduction is consistency and credibility.

For reasons which I trust are apparent, I will not use real names for cases discussed in this chapter, but they are not fabrications. The first in particular, I have little reason to doubt – at least to doubt that the witness believes it took place.

Summer 1942 – Britain

Bernard lives in a British town, is in his fifties, has been married quite happily for many years and, after spells in the RAF and working on the railways in a skilled job, became a nurse in the 1950s and has worked in that field ever since, rising to a position of some influence. There is no doubting his sincerity or his intelligence.

However, Bernard's life masks a very odd secret, which has led him through a gamut of doctors and psychiatrists. He sought my help to try to persuade them that his memories were real. Of course, all I could do was endorse the fact that, astonishing as his tale may be, it has to be seen in the light of others.

During World War II, as a child, Bernard made friends with a girl who was evacuated from Surrey. Whilst I have renamed him and not located his home to protect his privacy, I think it important to give the real name of this girl (who is married and of course now has a different surname). This is because both Bernard and I would like her to come forward – she may write, in confidence, to me. She possibly holds the key to this mystery.

Angela Shine, as she was then, has a fascinating name, rich in symbolism.

There was an immediate rapport of friendship between Bernard and Angela, aged eleven or twelve at the time. One summer day, at the height of the fighting (probably 1942), they went to a local hill where it was possible to find spent bullets from a practice range. Bernard says: 'For the first and only time in my life I felt a sense of complete peace come over me'. Although they lay on the grass he is certain they did not fall asleep. Suddenly a man's voice interrupted their reverie. 'Here they are,' it was saying. Another man was with him, and both the children sat up. One man came and knelt by them, the other stayed behind. He seemed to hold something in his hands, and every so often the kneeling man would turn and look at him. They spoke to each other, quoting numbers and talking about time in a strange way. They also made peculiar remarks like, 'They are beautiful children, aren't they?' Bernard can remember little about them, except that they were very handsome and '... gave off an aura of pure peace and tranquillity'. Oddly, later he and Angela disagreed as to whether they wore bright-coloured clothes or a shiny suit.

The men appeared to know everything that would happen in the children's future but warned them not to tell anyone they had seen them no matter what happened. They also issued a promise that they would see them again. When Bernard asked where they came from, the man who did the talking gazed into the sky and said, 'I come from a long way away.' A lot more was supposedly said, but even forty-five years later Bernard has not recalled most of it. Then the children were told to go to sleep. A brilliant light above them (taken to be the sun at the time) radiated heat onto the ground. There was then a memory gap (during which, he thinks, they may have slept), and then they set off to walk down the hill.

Coming to a farm, they were greeted by someone who asked

their names and told them to get off home quickly. It was here that Bernard noticed a strange bluish mark, as if he had been bitten or punctured. It was on the elbow, on what he now knows was the brachial arteries. When he mentioned it to Angela, she showed that her arm had an identical mark.

When they got home, they were met with relief and horror – nobody believed they had just been up on the hill looking for bullets. They had not been on the hill for a couple of hours, as they had thought: they had been missing for one whole day and night. Angela had to return to London soon afterwards.

The effect of this strange experience never really left Bernard. There are aspects to this case which do fit the abduction pattern, but it is very peculiar. It may for that reason be unusually important. I have respected Bernard's desire not to go public with his story, but it is naturally important that, if Angela is there and does remember these events, she should come forward. Who knows what she might remember.

1965/6 – Birmingham

Another truly unusual case came my way from a British woman married into a strict religion (hence her desire for anonymity). Her story is amazing.

Margary, as I shall call her, and her first husband lived in Birmingham at the time (December 1965) and she had just obtained her degree and begun a professional career.

One night her husband told her to prepare for a shock and some kind of test. It was obvious that he was being quite serious. They got into his car and drove off, although her memory of the trip became hazy and confused and she does not know where they went. Then she was in a room that was dimly lit and there were people standing around a long table or flat bed. She was put onto it and seemed 'drugged' and unable to resist. The most memorable of the men in the group was tall and thin with a long nose and white beard. He had thick eyebrows and supposedly said to Margary, 'Remember the eyebrows, honey.' A strange medical examination, using odd equipment, was performed on her.

Her husband then took her on a trip to all the houses she would occupy in the future. This was accomplished by a click of the fingers, followed by a barrage of images. Her mind was filled with information but she was told that she would remember it only bit by bit as the future unfolded. The memory of the experience did return only from 1978 onwards.

At one point one of the 'examiners' in the room said to Margary, in a tone that made it seem as if he were amused, 'They will think it's flying saucers.' Her husband also revealed who he really was – but she declined to tell me this.

The day after the abduction to 'a house somewhere in Birmingham', her husband left, said he was 'going abroad', and Margary never saw or heard from him again.

It is not only in Britain that rogue cases happen. Irene Granchi reports (in *FSR*, 1985, Volume 31, No. 2) on a story from Brazil.

4 January 1975 – São Luis, Brazil

For teenager Antonio Ferreira, the adventure began at 9 a.m. on 4 January 1975, when a UFO supposedly hit the wall of his home. Later the same object came back and hit him with a beam of light. Three-foot-tall, dark-haired and dark-skinned aliens emerged and dragged Antonio aboard. During a three-hour trip to their planet he was interrogated about cars and Earth food by one being who called himself Croris. Evidently not satisfied with the boy's answers to their questions, Croris gave him a hefty punch in the chest.

Antonio now devised a plan to deal with these hooligan abductors. In exchange for eleven more rides to other planets, he agreed to find them subjects for vivisection and experiment. Luckily Croris was quite happy with a dog, a cat and a parrot! As a reward they gave the youth all manner of things (which he has not kept), from statues and medals to a gun which emits a puff of smoke and destroys anything in its path.

Presumably the experiments on the parrot did not succeed, because on the final trip Antonio was put in a glass case alongside an alien who was then magically transformed into his double. The kidnapped boy could only watch as the alien impersonator was sent to Earth 'as a test' and successfully fooled Antonio's father.

There are dangers in South American cases. Abductions are reported there more often than anywhere in the world, and there are grounds to question the veracity of many. One man fishing at Navegantes in 1974 said that three beings got out of a UFO and carted his wife Francisca on board, and he had not seen her since – which rather sounds like a wish-fulfilment fantasy. And it is difficult to believe that farm-labourer José Nobre Uchoa from Balem, Brazil, would have been daft enough to agree with the suggestion of two aliens who invited him to go for a ride. He was told to walk down the middle of the main highway at a certain time the following night and await the arrival of the next scheduled UFO. He did so, but before the big light in the sky had the opportunity to land, a car came steaming down the road and flattened José.

The British can probably outdo the Brazilians in the stakes for the least credible UFO abduction.

1983 – Wirral, Merseyside

One day in 1983, when I was working for the Liverpool ILR station Radio City, I found in my mail a letter from a man whom I shall just call Rupert, from the Wirral peninsula. Superficially, it sounded promising, and during my next feature I appealed over the air for him to contact me. That was my first mistake. The second came a few days later, when Rupert arrived on the doorstep of my home (then in Wallasey). I decided to let him in to tape an interview, and it proved very difficult to stop him talking after that.

Rupert's experiences are long and varied. He had had an elf on the wardrobe in his bedroom as a child. This 'proved' its powers by pointing out a bottle of whiskey that was out of sight. Then he met an alien called Algar, who became such a chum that eventually Rupert's wife was allowed to see him. Apparently another man on the Mersey waterfront also saw the silver-suited creature and was so excited that he lost his hat in the river. Later a UFO appeared over Rupert's house and provided an extra-terrestrial dry-cleaning service by projecting a beam of light through the roof, causing an expanding fully cleansed patch on the carpet. Then Rupert began to go for trips with Algar, becoming his sidekick in an interplanetary war.

With total sincerity, Rupert related his many adventures through the 'gateway' on top of Bidston Hill, a local beauty spot.

These included battles with what he called the 'hairy pillar-boxes', a particularly nasty bunch of extra-terrestrials. He was later rescued from certain death by some tiny furry creatures with beaks that carried him down the hill to safety. Sadly Algar was not so fortunate. He forfeited his life to an alien ray gun.

I was now favoured with frequent visits from Rupert – I was wanted as his apprentice. He could arrange for me to go on a trip any time I wanted. There was a UFO base under a reservoir in Wigan, I was informed. All we had to do was find the way in. Explaining that I could not swim had no effect.

This was the summer of 1983, and Rupert was keeping tabs on the Tesco supermarket in Birkenhead, where aliens regularly appeared. He knew that because he had met them, cunningly disguised as humans but a dead give-away thanks to their telepathic conversations. Nobody else was able to hear these, of course. The fact that they were piling dozens of tins of dog food into a shopping trolley as part of an experimental programme was another hint.

Rupert's mistake (and my salvation) came the day he chose to visit when my boyfriend was present. Not being in the least tolerant of any sort of UFO story, he was certainly none too keen on Rupert's suggestion that I accompany him to Spain, where we could board a UFO and fly off to join the war of the worlds. Although Rupert undoubtedly believed what he was telling me, I was not unhappy when my boyfriend advised of a way our intrepid traveller could get to see stars without the presence of a UFO.

We might find stories like this amusing, but they are really little different from the one which has allowed George King to found the Aetherius Society. That has appeal. All these rogue abduction cases do. But they do not follow the pattern set by the Hill and Villas Boas abductions – or many more examples that follow. The very eccentricity and deviance of these odd cases helps to establish what is normal in a field that barely qualifies for that description. They also answer those critics who say abductions are just imaginative fantasies. If they are, why does the standard case pale in the face of such rogues?

If we can see even the glimmer of a standard type of

abduction (and most of the cases in this chapter are definitely not standard) we shall be better able to judge individual stories against the mould. In whatever terms we eventually try to explain them, this advantage is one well worth bearing in mind.

5 Alien Abductions – The British Catalogue

The British Abduction Catalogue is an attempt to record one nation's entire experience. One of the things which the British Catalogue will allow is the ordering of abduction cases into groups, to compare with patterns around the world (Chapter 7).

The groups that suggest themselves begin with simple time lapses – instances in which time disappears during a UFO encounter. This is a major clue that suggests an abduction may have happened and that something has caused a period of time to have vanished from the witness's mind.

The next step up the ladder from these basic cases is what might be called a Type I or entity case. This involves the observation of entities but adds something to suggest deeper things. Two key additions here are serious physical effects, where inexplicable damage is done to a witness by the encounter, and the presence of the mysterious 'Oz Factor', an induced form of sensory deprivation which seems to alter the state of consciousness of the percipient. It can become visible as a sensation of time standing still or interfered with, or it manifests as all sound vanishing, a very odd feeling of being isolated from our world into a magical world. It is less easy to describe than it is to recognize, since witnesses often refer to it without having any idea of its significance. This underlines its importance.

There are a number of possibly relevant medical conditions, such as temporal-lobe epilepsy, where the person can enter an 'aura' before the onset of an attack and suffer a 'time lapse' in the form of a black-out. After recovery, the epileptic may even continue doing what they were previously doing without realizing they had not been conscious all the time. Narcolepsy is another disease where the patient 'falls asleep' briefly and repeatedly, sometimes without knowing that this has happened. Virtually no work has been conducted by specialists in such matters, examining abductees. But a number of suspicious circumstances point out the potential. For instance, many abductees are known to suffer tightening sensations around the head, flashing lights and severe migraine attacks (Elsie Oakensen reported this on a regular basis around the time she had her encounter). Others (for example police officer abductee, Alan Godfrey) suffered frequent blackouts or mini time-lapses on occasions other than their abduction, leading (in Alan's case at least) to one doctor suggesting that he might be either epileptic or narcoleptic without realizing it. (Both these abduction reports will be discussed later.)

Type II cases, contacts, go even further beyond. Not only are entities seen but there is communication with them. Quite often this comes by way of odd dreams or nightmares that follow an encounter. (That was how the Betty and Barney Hill abduction came to be uncovered.) It is a common way to access these deeper memories, which are buried in the subconscious mind but which are often very hard to coax into the open.

Finally, there are the ultimate cases, Type IIIs, full-blown abductions, with the witnesses remembering being taken aboard a UFO.

Those who are inclined to do so may use these details to carry out further research, which might add valuable new insights. But, on the other hand, the summaries of these cases may be read simply as narratives.

The cases we shall look at in this catalogue are those which have been reported to serious UFO organizations in Britain. Principally, this means BUFORA (the British UFO Research Association, formed in 1962 and with a team of accredited investigators), UFOIN (UFO Investigators Network, an informal system of several independent field investigators in the 1970s, now mostly incorporated into the BUFORA team) and several small local groups. The one which features most is MUFORA (Manchester UFO Research Association, founded in 1963), largely because it once included lawyer Harry Harris and his team of abduction researchers; they are now independent of the group.

There are doubtless other abduction stories, even in British

UFO circles. But I have included only those with which I had some personal involvement (as an investigator or co-ordinator of the investigations team) and those for which I have seen the case file and am reasonably satisfied that a competent analysis was carried out.

I am grateful to all those investigators whose reports I summarized, often put together over many months and with great expenditure of their time, money and effort.

Naturally, these reports are not to be taken as in any sense representative of the full total. Many witnesses to such an experience would be far too frightened or embarrassed to report it. Even if they wanted to, few would know of the existence of a UFO group and, even if they did, might feel natural reluctance to get mixed up in the sort of thing UFO groups are perceived to be.

Sometimes a case might be reported to the media, or police stations, or air bases, others probably only to close family or friends. In some of these instances the story might have reached the attention of serious researchers. Most often it would have gone no further than the nearest bin. This is a tragedy, but understandable given the bizarre nature of these claims. However, it seems certain that abduction stories fail to be reported far more often than they do filter out. So the cases in this catalogue should be regarded as nothing more than the visible part of a much greater problem. Not until proper reporting channels are set up will we learn just how large the invisible part may be.

Time Lapses

Late 1972 – Medmenham, Buckinghamshire
Investigated by John Makin of UFOIN, reported in *FSR*, Volume 24, No. 3.
Ten years earlier, aged nineteen, this witness had undergone a terrifying experience. Late one night he had been parked in his MG sports car with his girlfriend (an RAF nurse) when a rotating mass of whirling lights had landed nearby and all the car electrics had failed. He had to push the car away from the location (near Holton airfield in Berkshire). He later obtained his pilot's licence and became manager of a pub. Now, aged

thirty, he was driving on the A4155 from Henley to High Wycombe – a regular route, with which he was familiar – when, rounding a bend, he saw a vertical cone shape with what looked like fluorescent striplighting down the sides. There was a whistling noise and he felt a strong urge to get out of the car. The next memory he has is of driving through Marlowe and having no idea how he got there. One and a half hours had vanished. He did not wish to be hypnotized.

September 1973 – Little Houghton, Northamptonshire

Paul, a twenty-one-year-old Italian living in Bedford, had been to a dance in Northampton and had a strange experience whilst driving home alone. At first he thought he had been in a car accident, but one night he got drunk at a family wedding and memory of the truth came back. He told his sister. It was from her that the story reached *FSR* in a short letter published in 1976.

Because this case was so remarkably similar to another ten years later (p. 63), I tried to follow it up. I could not speak to Paul, because he did not wish the story to be taken further, but I did talk to his sister. She remembered it very well.

He had been approaching the village of Little Houghton, noticed the time on the village clock, 2 a.m., and then inexplicably found himself wandering on foot at Bromham Bridge just outside Bedford – at 7 a.m. He was wet through, although it was not raining. He found a friend and told him he must have had an accident, and they drove back along the A428 to find Paul's car. It turned up in a field near the Olney B-road. It was locked up, and Paul still had the keys in his pocket, but despite the rain that *had* fallen overnight, there was no clue as to how it had got into the middle of the field without leaving tracks and with the gate shut. The farmer had to tow the car out with his tractor.

Paul's final conscious memory at Little Houghton is of a brilliant white light in the sky heading straight for his windscreen. His sister told me that he has seen ghosts and has frequent vivid dreams but unfortunately she would not elaborate.

January 1974 – Werrington, Staffordshire
Jeff (aged twenty and a student teacher) was driving his Austin 1100 with his fiancée, Jane (same age). It was 9.30 p.m. A green light in the sky appeared and followed them towards Leek. Though it seemed to 'give up' and head off towards Cheddleton, the couple had a peculiar feeling that they were being observed. They stopped the car and inexplicably got out, standing in the middle of nowhere. Above them was a black oval shape which shone two beams downwards. A green one lit the road and a blue one the 1100. Then they drew together and encircled the car. In panic the couple jumped into the car and drove off, but Jeff had an urge to follow the light. Suddenly there was a bump, which turned out to be them travelling over a cattle grid. They were at Ilam in Derbyshire, with no memory of how they had got there. It was 1.30 a.m., and several hours had vanished. A few minutes later there was a second bump and they found themselves surrounded by street lamps after having been way out in the country. They found a police station and were astonished to learn that this was Macclesfield in Cheshire, twenty miles from the previous location. It was now 3.30 a.m. They were so concerned about what their families might think (Jeff had promised to get Jane home by midnight) that they asked the police to send a car from the Staffordshire force to explain to her parents that they were lost and would not be home for another hour.

Derek James investigated the case for BUFORA in 1976, and confirmed the story with the police. Sadly the couple did not want any publicity and would not consider hypnosis. This was certainly no attention-grabbing exercise.

August 1975 – Wessenden Head, West Yorkshire
Alan Fallows was aged twenty and a service engineer. After spending a day with friends in Yorkshire, he was driving home to the Pennine village of Mossley at about 8 p.m. The road over the moors was desolate, and thick hill mist closed in. His mini-van headlights cut through the half-light, and he had his head out of the window. Then he saw a bright light off to the side. After dismissing the idea that it was a farmhouse light, then a huge truck bearing down on the narrow road, he saw that it was a monstrous oval shape, glowing eerie white, gliding across

his field of view just feet above the surface. He stopped, having no idea what else to do. Then he switched off his engine and headlights, thinking they might be attracting it. There was no sound, and it seemed to take a long time for the 'egg' (about twenty-five feet across) to drift only yards in front of him. He was seemingly paralysed, and there is evidence of a time lapse, since his next memory is of being shaken into awareness by two dark shapes wandering in front of him. They turned out to be sheep, he says, that must have seen the UFO, been mesmerized by it and were following it to the valley bottom where it had headed. In his hand Alan was clutching a screwdriver like a weapon, although he does not know how he had got hold of it. Peter Warrington and I, from MUFORA, investigated this case and we were very much impressed, but again the witness would not be hypnotized. This might have been because Dr Richard Gregory, a famous specialist in perception at Bristol University, told the local press it was probably just an illusion caused by the mist. Had Dr Gregory spoken with Alan, it is unlikely he would have reached such a glib conclusion. Witnesses do not like being taken for fools and are constantly in fear for their reputations.

October 1977 – Low Moor, Bradford, West Yorkshire

Thirty-three-year-old Angela Brooke and her husband Stan were returning from Keighley through Bradford towards their cottage. It was about 5.30 p.m. They observed a white light above the road which 'followed' them home and then hovered above. It remained there all night. This description makes it appear probable that the object must have been a planet (such as Venus) or a bright star.

Something very odd occurred to Angela a week later. It was after midnight, Stan had gone to the bathroom, and she said she would make sure the front door was locked, then go up to bed. She remembers turning the door handle to check, and then her next memory is of waking up in bed 'as if from a very deep sleep'. She was confused but gradually pieced together what had happened when Stan said, 'I hope you are not going to go on a walkabout again like last night.'

He had been in the bathroom about half an hour and was surprised not to find her in bed. So he went downstairs and saw the front door open. As this was during the time of the

Yorkshire Ripper scare, Angela knew better than to stand outside after dark in the lonely spot where they lived, but Stan had to drag her back inside, since she was staring at the sky with a vacant expression 'as if in a trance' and did not respond when he called her name. She feels that something happened during that time but does not know what. Angela described this in several letters to me.

February 1983 – Little Houghton, Northamptonshire

This case ties in remarkably with the previous one in this same tiny village (p. 60), but there appears no other connection between them. The witness, forty-four-year-old Peter Rainbow, wrote to me six months after the experience and has since been interviewed in detail by Ken Phillips of BUFORA.

On 21 August 1982 Peter had a close encounter with a brilliant dome outside his Northampton home. His teenaged autistic son also witnessed the event, and files show that it was recorded by others in the area at the time, proving the basic integrity of Peter's testimony.

Six months later he decided to drive to visit his elderly, sick mother at Little Houghton. He left at 6.45 p.m., expecting a fifteen-minute ride on his motorcycle-sidecar along the A428. At Great Houghton, rounding a bend, he lost all power (engine, lights, horn etc). Deciding that a fuse must have gone, he dismounted and took out a piece of silver foil to wrap around the fuse (an old bikers' trick). But this did not work, so he took out a new fuse. He was just about to put it into the machine when he saw a strange 'football' of white light in the field beside him. He also noticed for the first time, how quiet it was. All night noises had gone silent. The object was swaying from side to side and rotating, and he watched as if hypnotized. Then it shot vertically upwards. Suddenly he realized that the fuse was gone from his hands (he had *not* put it in), and he was holding the ignition key (although it was previously in the lock). When he put it back into the motorcycle, it fired immediately, and off he went. On arrival at Little Houghton, the church clock (the same church clock involved in the previous case) showed 8.30 p.m. An hour and a half had vanished.

1 September 1983 – Weaverham, Cheshire
Billy Lowry, a young man from Belfast, was touring on his motorcycle, riding from Brighton all the way to Blackpool to stay with friends. Passing through Whitchurch in Shropshire, he stopped to telephone his friends to tell them his estimated time of arrival. He noticed that it was then about 11.45 p.m. Continuing, he came upon a hotel with a coloured fountain out in front, he also noticed a bright light in the sky. He proceeded north on the A49 until he passed a sign indicating that Warrington was just six or seven miles away (thus placing him on an open country road near the River Weaver). The light in the sky seemed to be coming towards him, and he stopped his motorcycle in the road, with an acute sense of being watched. Deciding he wanted to photograph it, he went to get his camera but had a definite impression not to do this. Instead he turned his lights out, plunging the deserted road into blackness. The dark wedge-shaped object was silhouetted against the sky, with lights around it, hovering directly above him. Suddenly car headlights appeared around the bend ahead, and the object moved away. Billy came to his senses and realized the folly of being in the middle of the road without lights on this dark bend. He could easily have been killed. He carried on towards his destination but then found a signpost indicating he was just outside Chester! This was on the wrong road, well out of his way, and he had no idea how he got there. He checked the time on a travel alarm he carried with him. It said 2.15 a.m., indicating a loss of almost two hours.

Billy Lowry was interviewed in Belfast by Jennifer Campbell of BUFORA, and Peter Hough and I also met him when he visited England in September 1986.

There are many interesting parallels between these cases. For now, simply note that they tend to happen late at night (or in the early hours) on very quiet, country roads. Often these are roads that have few distractions, suggesting perhaps that a form of 'highway hypnosis' might occur (when a driver goes miles on 'automatic pilot' without realizing that he has done so). But here there are other features too; the urge to get out or stop, the UFO itself, the almost hypnotized state that the witnesses appear to enter.

It would certainly have been interesting had some of these stories been subjected to hypnotic regression experiments. But, as will soon become apparent, they share features with cases that did involve regression and became abductions. It is also very useful to have a stock of cases where only conscious memory is involved, for then it cannot be argued that the hypnotic state caused them. Whatever their solution, they are truly remembered as real events.

Type I: Entity Cases

4 February 1951 – Withdean, Sussex
Investigated by Andy Collins of UFOIN.
At 6.30 a.m. a young girl, Sheila, was enjoying the sunny morning at her mother's home in the week prior to her wedding. In the garden was a flattened dome, coloured greyish green but glowing silver. 'It seemed to be throbbing inside,' she said. Three strange men got out, wearing khaki-coloured clothes and carrying a weird object. They floated towards her and then mysteriously returned to their craft, which took off and spun away. They had bald, domed heads, and their method of retreat was 'like a film going in reverse'.

In 1970 Sheila moved to Perth, Western Australia, and worked as a catering officer on the night shift at the airport. Driving home at 2 a.m., she saw a brilliant fluorescent light swoop at her Ford Falcon from over the Darling Hills. She had to swerve into a ditch to avoid it and got out to watch the object spinning away into space.

January 1977 – Huyton, Merseyside
Investigated by Brian Fishwick, UFOIN.
This complex and unusual case involved a thirty-two-year-old woman called Barbara and her twelve-year-old son, Robert. It began as Robert went into the garden to empty the waste paper basket into the dustbin. He came rushing into the house to say that he had seen a light. Dismissing this as imagination, Barbara went out to pick up the contents of the bin (scattered over the garden) and saw a very tall figure in a silver suit standing or floating in the bushes. After shouting at what she assumed was someone playing a trick, she ran back inside and locked the

door. Over the next couple of hours several neighbours arrived and went out to confront the stranger. One woman attacked it with a broom, then fled back when it failed to react. A man went at it with a knife and ran in saying that it was not human! This man, Barbara's cousin Don, went upstairs with her and watched the silver man through a window. It was examining the knife. Suddenly a strange sensation overcame them. ('It was like we were on tranquillizers,' Barbara told Brian Fishwick.) Their next memory was of walking down the stairs in a trance.

There also appears to have been a time lapse, as this all went on for an extraordinary long time in a house on a busy suburban road. In the end the police arrived. Two officers went out to arrest the alien, but as they approached, it vanished in front of their eyes and they came back shocked, explaining that they had no intention of reporting this because, 'Who would believe a word of it?'

Late September 1977 – Parkstone, Poole, Dorset
Investigated by Leslie Harris of UFOIN
Sixty-two-year-old Ethel May Field was taking in washing when she heard a humming sound and saw a grey disc hovering in the dark night sky over the garden. Two figures stood in a dome at the front. They were of normal dimensions but wore silver suits. One looked down and pointed to the ground, appearing to suggest they were planning to land. A bluish beam issued from the underside, and Ethel put both hands up to her face to protect her eyes. Then she fled indoors, and the UFO flew away. Later her hands began to turn red, and they were sore for several days.

27 January 1978 – Frodsham, Cheshire
Investigation of this case was very difficult as it involved four men, aged between seventeen and nineteen, who were out poaching in a farmer's field beside the River Weaver. Since one was the son of a respected local official, they were naturally reluctant to do more than give me written statements via a local intermediary. This is a shame as the case is quite extraordinary.

They claimed to have seen a silver balloon float along the river and land. A fuzzy purplish glow came out which could not be stared at directly (it sounds very much like an ultra-violet radiation). Two figures of normal height dressed in silver suits got out. They had lamps on their heads, like miners. These also glowed purple. Cows nearby were standing immobile, as if paralysed, and with a sort of metal cage of thin frames they seemed to pen in one beast and measure it. Not surprisingly, the men decided not to be next on the list and fled from the bush where they had hidden. One, who was willing to describe his experience in more detail, reported that as he ran there was a pulling sensation on his genitals. Others were less specific but referred to 'tingling sensations'. All felt very sore when they reached home.

Unhappily, due to the inadequacy of investigation, we do not know if there was a time lapse here.

March 1979 – Sheffield, South Yorkshire
Investigated by David Clarke, BUFORA
Another peculiar case, because it happened in a built-up area. The witness, a thirty-two-year-old assistant in a local hospital had gone to make a phone call from a box near the Co-Op and was chatting to a man who lived locally. He was called Ken but we were not able to trace him as she had moved before reporting the story. A grey disc with a dome on top appeared over the fish-and-chip shop. Inside, through a transparent window, they could see two figures who were staring down. One of them was watching the two witnesses on the ground, the other had his arms behind his back as if bored. The entire area was unusually quiet, and both witnesses had a fine view (for an unknown length of time). The two aliens wore ice-blue 'ski-suits' and had long blond hair. Not a single car passed by during the encounter – which was considered very odd but which is a classic feature of the 'Oz Factor'.

Following the UFO sighting the woman began to experience psychic phenomena, including noises and objects moving about in her house on their own, and saw an apparition of her dead husband. This is another common sequel to a close encounter, possibly suggesting that it is something about the observer which is special, rather than something about what they observe.

One of the interesting patterns to spot here is that all bar one of these cases took place in an urban area. It seems puzzling that

UFOs and bizarre aliens could be seen over a chip shop without being noticed by the entire neighbourhood, yet this often occurs, and the peculiar silence or magic tricks of the Oz Factor (making all the traffic disappear, for instance) seems somehow tied in with it.

Also, most of these cases do not rely on the word of a single witness. In both the Huyton and Frodsham cases there were a minimum of four witnesses.

Finally, it is worth pointing out that the Poole and Sheffield cases are remarkably similar. The UFO was almost identical in appearance, and both involved two entities looking down as if they were on a guided tour and gazing at the wildlife down below. (One can almost envisage the aliens with cameras ready to capture the scene – and this has even been claimed in some overseas cases.) These events were independent and could not have been based on each other. They are also extremely like the next story. Without too much stretch of the imagination, it is possible to see all three of these cases as involving the same UFO and occupants doing almost identical things each time. Can this really be coincidence?

Type II: Contact Cases

21 October 1954 – Ranton, Staffordshire

This case is legendary in UFO circles, having featured in several books during the 1950s, but no one seemed to have looked at it recently, so on 6 August 1987 I interviewed the chief witness, Mrs Jessie Rœstenberg.

She was in her late twenties in 1954 and had two children, Anthony (aged eight) and Ronald (six). They do remember the events, but only vaguely. Jessie had felt 'tingles' all day, prior to 4.45 p.m., when the incident occurred. She heard a hiss and went outside expecting to see a jet aircraft (then quite a novelty). What she saw was even more of a novelty. It was a disc with a flat base, shiny like aluminium and with a large transparent window on top. Through this two figures were staring down as if observing. They seemed distant, almost wistful and yet oddly compassionate. They wore blue 'ski-suits' and had long blond hair. Their skins were very white, and their chins were pointed, but they seemed otherwise human and normal in height.

This is a description identical to that offered in the Sheffield chip-shop sighting a quarter of a century later. Indeed, the two cases are so similar that there are really only two viable options: either both witnesses saw the same phenomenon or the woman in the Sheffield case based her story on having read about what Mrs Rœstenberg experienced. We could find no evidence that she did.

Whilst nothing Jessie said indicated to me that she was familiar with UFO cases, she spontaneously reported that, when the object hovered over the roof of her isolated farmhouse, 'It felt like hours passed, but it must have been seconds. Time was suspended. I was also paralysed. It was like I was in a vice. But my mind was working overtime. I wanted to say "hello" but I was worried about my children, so I turned to look at them, and when I looked back up, it was gone.'

Jessie ran indoors and hid under a table with the children. One of them spotted the object through trees, apparently circling. It gave off a purple flash of light and disappeared. Since then she has often thought about it: 'This was something absolutely marvellous. The saddest part to me is that I have never been able to fully understand the greatness of this thing.'

However, she says that she has since had a 'great, almost extreme, development of ESP. I *know* things about people. I *understand* situations. All this probably sounds crazy, but it is true.' Some of the things that have happened include seeing the aliens again *in* her house '… out of the corner of my eye …. But I think it could be a "thought thing". It could be my imagination'.

These contacts have implanted feelings into her mind about the aliens: 'I think they'll be here when I need them …. They are surveying us. They're afraid that we might panic. But some of them are living amongst us.'

Jessie Rœstenberg impressed me because she had not become a 'UFO nut' and had seemingly read no books on the subject since 1954. She had seen the Spielberg film *Close Encounters of the Third Kind* but in typical fashion said about it, 'I remember thinking whoever did this film has a good understanding of the subject. But when those little funny aliens came on I almost stood up and shouted, "They're not like that!" I don't believe in little green men. Not after what I've seen."

8 November 1954 – Croydon, Surrey
Investigated by Janet and Colin Bord, BUFORA.
Late October and early November 1954 saw a massive wave of entity sightings in Europe. Jessie Rœstenberg (whose sighting was one of the first) could not have known that. Nor could a thirteen-year-old orphan, Philip Molava.

At 1 a.m. on the night before his contact Philip was out looking after his rabbits when a plate-sized disc flew over. He jumped up to try to catch it, but it flew off. Next day he became sick and ended up in the infirmary with suspected food poisoning. At 2 a.m. (twenty-four hours after the previous experience) he was in bed paralysed and numb when three figures in cloaks materialized out of a glowing mist at the foot of his bed. He lost all sense of time, and his next memory was of being up the following morning, suddenly fit and well again.

Philip told the Bords that the experience triggered ESP, and he went on to have numerous strange out-of-body projections, premonitions and telepathic messages. He believes the aliens are trying to warn the Earth against disasters looming. 'I wasn't awake until they came,' he said.

18 November 1957 – Aston, Birmingham, West Midlands
Another classic contact story from the past. I had the kind assistance of psychologist Dr John Dale, who met and interviewed the witness, twenty-seven-year-old Cynthia Appleton, on many occasions during 1958 and 1959. He has access to a lot of previously unpublished information.

Cynthia, the wife of a sheet metal worker, had no esoteric interests and was concerned only with running their large terraced house and looking after their young baby. Two days before her first contact, she had suffered a black-out or time lapse. She never regained memory of what happened but was supposedly told later that this was a failed attempt at communication.

At 3 p.m. on the afternoon of the 18th a rose colour appeared in the sky outside and there was 'an atmosphere, like a storm'. There was a whistling sound and from nowhere a figure materialized in the living-room. Then the light outside returned to normal. The figure was more than six feet tall and had very blond long hair. His complexion was extremely pale, and his features were elongated. (This is very reminiscent of what Jessie Rœstenberg reported.)

The man communicated directly into Cynthia's mind, saying, 'Do not be afraid.' This calmed her and she said, 'He seemed to have some control over me. I should say it was like hypnosis.' He told her many things, including that he came from another world and that his people wanted to live in harmony with us but dare not try overt contact until we stopped having wars. Scientists were trying to 'get to them' but would fail. They were '... pulling against the great force of gravity by going straight up ... we should travel with a sideways attitude.'

The being then opened his arms wide and 'a TV set switched on' in the gap, in which moving three-dimensional images of UFOs appeared. Reading the account Dr Dale recorded in 1958, it is hard to avoid the impression that Cynthia is describing a hologram. The only problem is that we do not have three-dimensional holograms now, and in 1958 not even the concept of a hologram had been invented.

The extensive records of this case are frequently impressive, for Mrs Appleton was told that she had a brain tuned to the correct frequency and so could be contacted. A total of four visits by this man and a colleague were alleged (the last being on 18 August 1958). Once she touched his silver suit and found it horribly slimy. Her daughter saw the man too, on the visit when he left in a big black car and wore a dark suit and old-fashioned hat! On that occasion the alien had burned his finger and she was asked to bathe it in hot water. He injected himself from a tube and then put a spray of jelly on the wound and it healed miraculously.

Of the masses of detailed information conveyed by this man from Gharnasvarn (the name he gave for his planet), there was philosophy about how man 'invents' time, a lecture on the structure of the atom and another on how all life is joined at some inner level. She was told about the development of a laser, (Dr Dale's records show that this was before news of this discovery was released), then she was given a report on the nature of cancer and tips on how to cure it. These involved shocks to the body organ most in use at the time, creating a sort of frequency change in the vibrational rate of the particles inside the atom.

Much of this is way over my head and apparently Dr Dale's. It certainly meant nothing to a twenty-seven-year-old Birmingham housewife three decades ago.

The fact that so little was done with this case and because Cynthia Appleton never went on television to reveal these alien secrets makes it all the more fascinating. If it was a hoax, what on earth was its purpose?

There was some astonishing physical evidence. On the first visit (November 1957) the alien is said to have stood on a sheet of newspaper discarded on the floor. This was reported at the time. Photographs of the 'scorch' mark left do exist. Dr Dale claims that during their February 1958 visit, when the alien burn was healed, Cynthia later found a piece of skin in the bowl of water! The psychologist took it away with him and had it analysed under an electron microscope at Manchester University. It was not human skin but was said to be rather similar in composition to animal skin. There did not appear to have been anything obviously extra-terrestrial about it, but its precise nature was never identified. For some reason the doctor chose never to publish a report on these findings, although he has all his records and showed them to me.

December 1971 – Rowsham, Buckinghamshire

Investigated by Andy Collins and Barry King, UFOIN

The witness was a twenty-year-old supermarket manager given the name Sydney to protect his identity. He was walking home at 1.30 a.m. after a visit to his fiancée (now his wife) when, on the A418 Wing to Aylesbury road, he spotted a light that flashed onto the ground and turned into a greenish bullet-shaped object. A beam projected out and hit the ground, and from this came a single, very tall being in a silvery one-piece suit. It seemed to glide towards Sydney, who was standing paralysed and yet surprisingly calm. The being moved its hand up and down over Sydney's face, and he felt a warm tingle come over him. He also had the sensation of information being drawn out of his mind. During this contact, time seemed to stretch out. Eventually the figure returned to the beam and was pulled up into the bullet, which vanished with a brilliant flash of light. Sydney ran the mile or so into Rowsham village and met a police car. The police saw his distressed state and gave him a lift home.

He arrived at 3 a.m., which strongly implies a time lapse of an hour or so, but Sydney had not kept accurate note of the time, so we cannot be certain.

Years later he still got the regular urge to visit the spot and stare at the sky. He became very artistic afterwards and told UFOIN investigators, 'I am sure that some of this experience is still missing.'

4 January 1979 – Rowley Regis, West Midlands

This became known as 'The Mince Pie Martians Case', although the media headline I enjoyed most read, 'Take Me To Your Larder'. It concerns forty-five-year-old housewife Jean Hingley, a car-factory employee. She had waved her husband off to work at 7 a.m. when she saw a light in the garden. Thinking he had left the carport lit, she went to investigate, but it was dark, so she returned to the kitchen. She put down some food for Hobo, the family Alsatian, and called him from the garden, but he flopped down as if drugged and gazed at the ceiling, glassy-eyed. Then, with a 'zee … zee … zee' noise, three weird creatures flew past into the lounge.

They were only 3½ feet tall and had waxy white faces and coal-black eyes with no eyebrows and very thin mouths. They wore silvery clothes. This is remarkably like the aliens Whitley Strieber claims he saw some years later, with the difference that Jean Hingley says they had wings and were floating.

She was clinging to the sink paralysed but then, she says, 'Suddenly I floated towards the lounge. I had my hand on the door but my feet didn't touch the floor.' Such was the glow that she had to cover her eyes to shield herself, but Jean did notice that they were inspecting the ornaments on the Christmas tree with interest. They also probed into her mind with telepathy – 'It was like a light or an X-ray penetrating.'

They told her she would not be harmed and, when she asked where they were from, they said (or rather she could not tell which one said), 'We come from the sky.' Then she explained why the house was all dressed up to celebrate Jesus's birthday. 'We know all about Jesus,' they claimed. She offered them water and some mince pies but they did not eat. They said they would return and, 'We come down here to talk to people but they don't seem to be interested.' Finally, when she showed them how to light a cigarette, they fled as if in terror, taking a mince pie each with them!

Outside, on her garden, was an egg-shaped object with windows. They floated into it, and it took off with a flash. The dog returned to life, and Jean called the West Bromwich police, who did little but put our investigation team onto it. The electric clock in the house had stopped, and all her cassette tapes were magnetized and unplayable. She also had very sore eyes for about a week and felt sick. The doctor told her to take a rest. In the snow, where the object had sat, was an oval outline which, thanks to being called in immediately, the local UFO team were able to photograph before the snow melted soon after.

June 1980 – Sproston Green, Cheshire

A twenty-five-year-old insurance broker approached UFO investigator Harry Harris to say that she had had a dream of UFOs. Jenny, as she was called, could only remember that these recurred and had something to do with aliens. Harry decided to get a doctor to perform hypnosis, but Dr Joe Jaffe could get nowhere. Then researcher Mike Sacks, who was present in the doctor's surgery in St John Street, Manchester, suggested that Jenny try to recall a real event that she might be remembering as a dream. Immediately she succeeded.

She found herself in a car with her boyfriend (now husband) Jim and being forced to drive, because Jim was almost asleep through drink. It was late at night, so she took back roads through Cheshire on her way back to south Lancashire where they lived. Suddenly an object with red and yellow lights appeared in the distance. Under hypnosis she said: 'It can't be an aeroplane.' Then brilliant lights appeared on the road ahead and she was forced to stop. Out of the glare two figures walked towards the car, and she desperately tried to wake her now sleeping boyfriend. He would not budge. One figure went to the window by Jim and seemed to tap on it. The other was right by her and tried to get in. She had turned the car engine off, although she did not know why, and kept repeating under hypnosis that the doors were locked so he could not get in. The figure was seven feet tall and wore a silvery suit. He seemed to walk in slow motion, almost gliding, whilst Jenny was paralysed. There was a battle of wills as the entity's eyes stared at her.

Eventually Jenny called out in triumph, 'I'm not getting out. They are not going to come again. They didn't make me do it.'

It is hard to remember that this is based on nothing more than a dream. Watching the video tape of Jenny under hypnosis easily demonstrates the real fear which oozes out of her.

A number of cases have been held over for more detailed discussion in the next chapter. Also quite a few other stories might have been included in the catalogue, but I chose not to use them. Some were less than fully researched, although fascinating. A few others have features which require me to keep them confidential at this stage to protect the witnesses.

You will possibly have noticed that contact cases have interesting new features. Young women are involved in a proportion that is noteworthy, particularly in view of the fact that every day UFOs are reported by men more than women in a ratio of about two to one. Also the complexity of the story increases. The contact is almost always said to involve telepathic communication and floating sensations. There are patterns in the event that stand out. Then there is the way in which promises of return are made and the manner in which the encounter seems to be just part of a continuum that often includes ESP and other alleged psychic phenomena.

I should stress that I am making no claims as to the reality of any of these things, merely reporting stories, but the fact that these stories are so alike must be significant.

Type III: Abductions

September 1942 – Cresswell, Northumbria

Albert Lancashire was aged twenty-seven when he claims he became Britain's first true abductee. This occurred when he was on guard in a sentry box of a then secret radar base just north of Newbiggin on the craggy North Sea coast.

Out to the east a light appeared over the sea, then a black 'cloud' rolled in. Albert thought he was witnessing some new sort of secret weapon. An impulse made him go outside and look into the sky, whereupon he was struck by a beam of yellow light and felt a floating sensation. His next conscious memory was of waking on the ground outside his box, dazed and confused. For years this experience languished dream-like in his subconscious. He knew that something had happened, but not what. In 1963 he spoke to friends about his belief that he had 'been inside a UFO'.

Then he became a British Rail signalman in his home town of Ashton-under-Lyne, Lancashire. In October 1967 there was a huge wave of sightings in Britain, and several odd lights manifested in his house and around the signal box. These were partially of a psychic nature but also involved seemingly objective phenomena, because other railwaymen saw them. Their main function was to trigger his memory of the 1942 abduction.

Seeing a report on the Hill abduction case during this 1967 wave, Albert wrote to Lionel Beer of BUFORA, and his story was later followed up by Eric Richards and Norman Oliver. It was documented in one of Oliver's publications in 1970. I met Albert briefly in 1975, and he was still working in his signal box and having repeated strange experiences. He felt that Oliver's report was a little inaccurate.

The local group MUFORA, under the auspices of Georgina Mills, have been compiling a full account of this case. Mr Lancashire appears to have incorporated his encounters into a semi-religious framework and quotes freely from the Bible. He says that his abduction memory returned in a series of dreams during one month of 1967. They involved his waking in a room, seeing an Oriental woman lying on a bed, and being given 'goggles' to put over his eyes. A man in white was also present.

Naturally this case suffers by its long-delayed report, but its features are so similar to recent events that it could be significant. Even when it was first told, there was really only the Hill abduction to base a fantasy upon. It does share aspects of that but also incorporates others that might endorse its validity, because they were not in that report. The Albert Lancashire case is almost unknown even in UFO circles and cannot conceivably have been a template for post-1967 abductions. It was never publicized.

16 October 1973 – Langford Budville, Somerset
Investigated by Barry King and Andy Collins, UFOIN
The importance of the last case can be seen by the fact that the

next true abduction in British records dates from *after* it was reported and more than thirty years later than it supposedly happened. However, there is no possibility that the Albert Lancashire story influenced this current case. It is well to remember that, as there are obvious similarities.

Mrs Verona (a pseudonym) was then aged thirty-three and, like her older husband, an Italian from Turin who came to Britain in 1963. At tea-time on the date in question, the daughter of a friend came to Mrs Verona and asked if she would drive with her to Wellington, since her mother was ill. Mrs Verona had work to do but promised to drive to Wellington later in the evening. She was delayed much longer than expected, and it was about 10.45 p.m. before she could set off. The daughter had gone on ahead, but Mrs Verona still felt she must keep the promise to visit her friend's mother.

Taking a back road, the B3187, she found herself at around 11.15 p.m. in the dark, on a lonely stretch past the Langford Budville turn-off, just a couple of miles outside Wellington. Suddenly a light appeared in the field to her right (south-west), but she was more concerned that her 1967 mini saloon was failing and the headlights were going out. Coasting to a halt, she struggled to restart, but there was no power.

Although Mrs Verona's knowledge of car mechanics was negligible, having a look to see was preferable to sitting in the dark. So she got out and had the bonnet open in seconds. It was then that she became aware of a faint humming sound. Looking into the field, she saw the glow was still there and she became sufficiently scared to want to get back into the safety of her car. Slamming the bonnet down, she was about to do just that when a force struck her on the shoulder and pushed her downwards. Turning, she saw a tall, metallic 'man' and a flashing light and then lost consciousness.

There is a brief recall of being outside the light in the field and seeing that it came from a metal disc with a flat base and dome on top. The yellowish glow she had seen from the road issued from windows. But then she passed into unconsciousness again, awaking only inside a room.

In the room she was strapped at the arms and ankles to a long table or bed. The metal man, which she was later informed to be a 'robot' or 'trained retrieval device' for sampling-gathering, stood immobile in one corner. Three normal-height men were in the room – they wore skull caps, face masks and light-blue apron-like clothes and looked like surgeons. Whilst two stood back, one performed a medical examination all over her body by moving cubes along a rail guide that surrounded the bed. These glowed different colours as they moved.

The fair-skinned, round-eyed man who did the examination also used an instrument held in his hand which he moved over her body. It was small. She was totally naked and felt as if the room were icy cold. A pencil-like device was also used to prod her, and nail pairings and a blood sample were taken. None of these was painful, but when a suction device was placed on her reproductive organs she felt a pulling sensation. (The youth in the Frodsham Entity case described the same thing.) This caused discomfort. Mrs Verona felt that the examiners were treating her like a laboratory animal and had little emotion.

She was left alone for a few minutes after this but could not get free. She also felt sick and had a sore throat. Then one man returned, stared at her lower regions for a few moments and placed a small pin in her thigh. This seemed to make her go numb. She could not move. With her eyes closed and feeling terrified, Mrs Verona says that she was raped. Immediately the pin was removed and she was helped off the table by the men. She passed out again.

She recovered her senses, fully clothed, standing by the car. Although totally disorientated, she climbed back in. It functioned normally and she drove home in a state of turmoil.

Mrs Verona had a full memory of the details just recorded, although there are obvious time or memory gaps.

Upon arrival home at 2.30 a.m. she was shaken and crying but told her husband the entire story. They resolved to tell no one.

Four years later, in October 1977, they came across Barry King's name as a UFO investigator. After much reluctance Mrs Verona rang to 'put it on record'. He and colleague Andy Collins of UFOIN made a full investigation, but the unwillingness of the witnesses to have any public mention of the case remained strong and counts much in favour of their sincerity. Mrs Verona has not been hypnotized.

I have recounted the details of this medical examination at some length because it has remarkable parallels with cases recently reported by Budd Hopkins in the USA. I first saw the Collins and King report when they submitted it to me early in 1978, and Hopkins published no data at all until his 1981 book. His sexual abduction cases were not revealed until the build-up to his 1987 book.

Even in 1977, when this case was reported, the only precedent for such a story was the sexual abduction of Antonio Villas Boas in Brazil. It is clear that Mrs Verona's story differs markedly from this, but it does not deviate greatly from Hopkins' recent American cases. Since neither Hopkins nor his witnesses could have had any idea of the depth of this British abduction, and it was totally impossible for Mrs Verona to have known about the American cases (which had yet to be found, let alone investigated, in 1977), this important story bears consideration when we attempt to understand what is going on.

I am sure science-fiction buffs may have noticed the symbology of the tall robot with the flashing light on its head, and the way the case borrows images from the movie *The Day the Earth Stood Still.*

27 October 1974 – Aveley, Essex

At the same time as the above case was discovered, Andy Collins and Barry King were investigating another abduction. This had also not been discussed by the witnesses for three years, and when it was reported (to a small Essex UFO group) they failed to see any significance in the time lapse. Collins and King saw it and immediately ensured that the Aveley encounter became the first British abduction to be explored under hypnosis.

John and Sue Day were returning from a trip to relatives by car. It was 10.20 p.m. In the back seat, dozing, were their three children (two boys and a girl aged between four and eight). John was twenty-eight, Sue twenty-five, and they were a typical East London family. Later I met them at their home and sat in on one of the hypnosis sessions, and I was very impressed by their no-nonsense approach. There was no evidence that they were familiar with American abduction stories. They could not have been familiar with British ones, because in the autumn of 1977 none had been made public.

The family saw a blue light in the sky, discussed it briefly and then forgot about it. Rounding a bend, they came upon a patch of green mist straddling the road just outside their home village. They could not stop themselves driving into it but, as they did so, the radio sparked. Fearing a fire, John instinctively yanked out the wires. Meanwhile they were out of the mist and after a slight 'bump' were on their way home.

John wanted to watch a play on television, and they had been hurrying back for that, but he took a few moments to fix the wires whilst Sue took the children in for bed. She put the television on but it was giving the 'off-air' signal. Amazed, she checked the time, found it was now 1 a.m. and had to confirm this with the speaking clock, so unbelievable was the time lapse. They had lost 2½ hours without any memory.

In the period 1974 to 1977 many things happened to the family. There was a kind of spiritual transformation. They stopped eating meat and began to care about the environment. When I met them, John was just about to begin work in an artistic profession, such was the dramatic increase in his skills in that direction. They were also having numerous psychic experiences, such as objects moving about the house on their own and apparitions being seen, and they had observed several previous lights in the sky.

None of these changes was really connected with the UFO by the family, but their recurrent dreams were nightmares of being in a room with horrible-looking small creatures. It drove them to UFO research to seek an answer to the blue light and the missing time.

Hypnosis was carried out by Dr Leonard Wilder, a London dentist who has specialized in regression but who was a novice in UFO terms (everyone was in Britain!). A very long account emerged, wherein the family were 'drawn out' of their car. Sue described it to me in detail, and it struck me that she was relating an out-of-body experience. The floating sensation and hazy memory of entry into the UFO again featured, but there was a puzzling period where they 'saw' themselves and the car, even though they were floating about the UFO. You will see this odd detail in other cases.

It soon developed into a conventional abduction story. There were tall human-like figures in silver suits with 'balaclava helmets' and fair skins. The eyes were large and almond-shaped. The small creatures were trained 'examiners' and rather resembled the bat-like 'Tetraps' in the 1987 *Dr Who* television serial (although much smaller in stature). These creatures have not appeared in *Dr Who* before, and it seems more than likely that they were based on the Aveley case, as it is probably Britain's best-known abduction.

There was a medical examination. John was shown the engine room of the UFO. They all viewed videos in hologram form of the alien world, a rather sad place. The aliens told them that humans were a sort of genetic experiment of theirs, hence the great interest in us. Information and tasks were planted into the family's subconscious, particularly the children's, and then the memory was wiped clean.

The hypnosis opened up a minefield of information and controversy.

23 January 1976 – Bolton, Lancashire

Shelley was a seventeen-year-old receptionist. At 5.15 one evening she got off the bus returning from work, intending to walk the few hundred yards to her home on a then new housing estate in a quiet area on the edge of town. Suddenly she saw two lights in the sky. One was amber, the other red. They were 'bumping into each other'. Then an object seemed to swoop down and was virtually on top of her. It had a curved base and flat top, and the lights were inset into its metallic side. It was the size of a small house, at rooftop height, and she was terrified. A pressure was on her shoulders, pushing her into the ground, and her teeth were vibrating, hurting her mouth. As it turned on edge, she ran home and tried to scream but could not. She dragged her mother into the street, pointing vaguely at the sky, but nothing was there. Thinking she had been attacked or raped, her mother called the police, and a female officer came, interviewed her, concluded she had become hysterical after seeing an aircraft and left.

That might have been the end of the matter, but for some reason the police chose to tell the local press. This was utterly irresponsible, especially if they really did not believe the poor girl. (Sadly this is by no means the only incidence of such treatment of a witness.) Other girls had seen lights the same week. These were followed up by UFO investigators and explained as stars, but the police obviously decided that

Shelley's story might fit in and informed the Bolton paper when they enquired about the other girls' encounter.

To her credit Shelley refused to have anything to do with the press and even declined financial inducement from Granada TV (which would have been very useful to a young girl on a small income). However, she did agree to give one interview to Arthur Tomlinson, a local UFO investigator. Arthur's report was forwarded to me. In fact, Peter Warrington and I referred briefly to the case in our 1979 book *UFOs: A British Viewpoint* because the teeth-vibrating effect was interesting.

Then in January 1984 Shelley telephoned me at home. She had picked up another of my books and, now a mature woman about to be married, felt it was time she added the details she had left out in 1976. She had done this because, in her words, 'I was not able to cope with public pressure at that time, and had I given anyone the full story they would not have left me alone.'

Shelley gave the date as January/February 1977 and later (even under hypnosis) said the two lights were red and green. It is, of course, provable that her memory of the date was a year out, and her written account on the BUFORA report form describing the lights as red and amber exists. It was completed only days after the sighting, which is crucial information, because it immediately shows that her hypnosis memory was wrong in at least one respect. Hypnosis clearly does not reveal the full truth.

There are many aspects to Shelley's case that emerged during the new investigation by MUFORA, which involved myself, Harry Harris (video-filming all interviews), Linda Taylor and Mike Sacks. These 1984 interviews broadened out into a hypnotic regression experiment with Dr Albert Kellar, a Manchester MD. In April 1986 a second and more productive session occurred with clinical psychologist Dr John Dale of Cheshire.

Briefly, the subsequent 'new' data involved serious physical illness effects which included burns on her arm and side (noticed the day after the encounter when she had a bath). She also suffered from sore eyes and felt sick and dizzy. Her GP was called but assumed she was merely ill with a cold or flu. Her fillings also allegedly crumbled into powder over the days following the sighting, and she required emergency dental treatment to correct this. (Medical verification of neither of these things has proven possible, despite extensive efforts to do so, but there is no reason to question Shelley's version of the story. There were several psychic experiences in Shelley's past, the most interesting of which were 'floatings' where she regularly drifted into the air. On one occasion she was seen to do this levitation act by her mother and sister, who have confirmed this fact.

In addition there was a weird series of phone calls followed by the visit of two men in dark suits who spent hours interrogating the girl in her own home. They had a box-like implement and appear to have used telepathy to condition her. One called himself 'the commander'. He had only one arm. This strange incident is recounted in great detail by Shelley and her parents, who were present at the time. Her father cannot explain why he let the interview (which would have done the SS proud) continue as long as it did. He was just unable to stop it. Shelley was regressed to this visit by Dr Kellar and responded in such an emotional way (her pulse and heart beat being monitored throughout) that it was considered medically unsafe to take it further.

However, the most important new factor revealed in 1984 was that, despite positively seeing the UFO at 5.20 p.m. and being just a few seconds from home at running pace, she got in at 6.05 p.m. Three-quarters of an hour had lapsed.

The first hypnosis revealed little except that when the pressure hit her Shelley tried to run away but felt as if she were doing so in slow motion. There was then a switch to being inside a room, and a female alien in a long gown was present. Shelley felt that her feet were being studied and the word 'Babinski' came into her head. This is, in fact, a medical test that is used to check muscle operation, particularly on the feet and often in young babies. Shelley claimed not to know this.

Dr Dale's technique seems to have worked better at controlling her emotions. She spoke of the object 'throwing me around' and under hypnosis said, 'It came in front of me .... It zoomed in front, spinning.' Then, on arrival home she kept saying, 'I don't think I should have seen it.'

Her re-creation of the experience was graphic. She described using her umbrella to push into the ground to try to resist the pressure that was forcing her down. There were other, minor forgotten things, such as that added impact. She even knew that her mother had cooked roast beef but she had been too sick to eat.

Of the 'on board' memory quite a lot poured out. She was on a table or bed, her head was flat, and she could only just see the woman standing over her. She was tall, had blonde – almost white – hair and was putting information into her head 'like hundreds and thousands'. The continual refrain, 'Do not be afraid. We will not harm you' was coming into her mind as if it was being played by a tape-recorder. She also felt that the time was not yet right to remember all the details. 'I haven't been told yet *when* to remember,' she said under hypnosis. But she was told that they will return to see her again, when '... man rises against man and nation against nation .... During and after the sequence of events.' She does not comprehend the full meaning of this phrase, but the night after this second hypnosis session she had a terrible nightmare of countless bodies lined up along the hard shoulder of a motorway and she now has a morbid dread of atomic energy.

There is more to this case and at some point it may be told, but I have promised Shelley some peace and quiet. I respect her too much to disagree. However, the story as it stands is too significant not to be reported. In her no-nonsense Lancashire fashion she told me, 'I saw an *Unidentified*, which means I don't know what it is, *Flying*, which it certainly was, *Object*, which it also was. Beyond that I cannot say.'

February 1976 – Keighley, West Yorkshire

Described in *UFOs: A British Viewpoint* and investigated at the time by Trevor Whitaker of BUFORA.

Reg, an ambulance driver, was supposedly visited in his bedroom by two beings who were tall, had grey faces and large, cat-like eyes and treated him as a sort of specimen, despite apparently needing his help. He was shown an image of a piece of tubing, and the idea seemed to be that he should go with them to see if his mechanical talents could help fix their stricken UFO.

Before you smile, this *seems* to have been a ruse to lure poor Reg, because he was then told to lie prone on his bed, whereupon he was paralysed and felt himself float up through the ceiling into the sky where a UFO (like a bath tub) was hovering.

His next memory is of being on board the by now very familiar table or bed, undergoing (familiar) medical examinations. A large purple eye-like device was moved across his body as if scanning him. Quite a number of Biblical references, were uttered by these strange creatures (into his mind), including comments about the Alpha and Omega. But when Reg tried to find out who they were, he was firmly advised that, 'An insignificant being such as a worm should not ask such questions' and was helpfully informed that, 'A thousand of your years are but a day to us.'

Once they had done with him, the ambulance driver found himself back in his bedroom, totally unable to move for some minutes, and with large gaps in his memory. However, the details recorded above were consciously recalled immediately and followed up by BUFORA within weeks, thanks to a contact known to both Reg and the investigator.

14 July 1976 – Oakenholt, Flint, Wales

This is the Gaynor Sunderland case discussed in Chapter 3. The only points to note are that Gaynor's later 'abductions' (to an alien zoo and a sunny planet) occurred in a way rather similar to that described by Reg: she was pulled up, as if going out of her body. The Sunderland case involves no medical examination, but there is an element of fear of apocalypse and implanted messages. (See my book *Alien Contact.*)

14 November 1976 – Winchester, Hampshire

This story became public in late 1976 but its follow-up was never recorded. It was investigated by an army of BUFORA people, including Dr Geoffrey Doel MD. The witnesses were forty-two-year-old British Rail powder-room attendant Joyce Bowles and an ex-farm manager, fifty-eight-year-old Ted Pratt.

During the first (of three) encounters, an orange glow appeared in the sky, and the car in which they were travelling was pulled across the road by a strange force. Joyce and Ted ended up on a grass verge with no lights or power but with an egg-shaped object beside them. From this came a tall figure in a silver suit with a beard, long blond hair and pink eyes (although that might have been accounted for by the orange illumination from the object). He leant on the car and then, as Joyce and Ted looked away, simply vanished. The object had gone too, but the car headlights suddenly glowed unusually bright, power came back on its own and they drove off. No time lapse was noted.

On 30 December Joyce and Ted were on another nocturnal drive near Winchester when Ted saw a glow in the sky. He pointed it out to Joyce, who saw it after a few seconds. Then a terrible whistling noise began and the car started to vibrate. Joyce Bowles said: 'When I had my previous sighting I can remember everything that happened, but with this incident my mind on some of the things is blank.'

The next recollection of both witnesses is of being inside a room with three of the tall beings. They spoke in a strange language, and not everything that was said was understood – one word, 'Mil-ee-ga', was uttered. Ted was asked to walk up and down and report on whether it was hot or cold. There were other memory gaps, but the couple recall seeing transparent images on the wall and being told: 'This is our field.' Ted misunderstood and, being in the farming world, assumed they meant fields of grass. They looked upset at this and said, 'No. No. *Our* field.'

Joyce seems to have felt a little left out and when they explained that they had not come to invade, she replied, 'That's what Hitler said!' At this one of the men said, 'You have a very strong tongue' and Joyce thought she was in for it. Happily the aliens did not react. A great deal more was said but the information seems to have largely gone over their heads. Then there was a flash of light and they were back in their car, lost on an unfamiliar road. About an hour seems to have disappeared.

Quite a number of interesting other details are known. Joyce reported being sick and to have had a red burn or rash on her face for a few days after the first encounter. She also had to remove her wedding ring because the skin underneath it was red and sore. And her watch began to gain time and became too magnetized to be usable.

But perhaps the most interesting news is that Joyce Bowles had a track record of psychic experience and was noted as a healer of animals. She had also suffered a poltergeist attack of noises and moving objects in her home. This sort of thing often crops up. Abductees tend to be psychic.

After the second encounter Joyce was certain that the aliens would return, and they allegedly did in March 1977. This time Ted Pratt was not with her, and she has never revealed what occurred in any detail. A message (of a religious nature) was given, but she can release it only when the time is right. So far it does not appear to have been. Recalling the cases of religious visions discussed in Chapter 2, this curious feature is important.

19 June 1978 – Faringdon, Oxfordshire

Full details can be read in Frank Johnson's book *The Janos People*, but all bar the scene-setting opening chapters should be treated with some caution.

This five-person abduction is fascinatingly similar to that of the Day family in the Aveley case, which was then unpublished. It is also important because it is the last reported before the Aveley case went on public record in Britain, thus setting some sort of standard for the abduction case. The family concerned telephoned their story in on a hotline operated by UFOIN, and I was responsible for putting university lecturer Frank Johnson onto it. I assumed that Johnson's academic background and lack of contamination by previous abduction stories would make his work of value; it did not turn out quite that way.

Briefly, John, his wife Gloria, their children (girls aged five and three) and John's adult sister Frances were travelling by car back to the Gloucester area after a funeral in Reading. A light was seen (it seems rather likely that it was just a bright planet), and all manner of confusion set in: they passed a brightly lit house that does not exist; the car 'drove itself'; time stretched out in Oz Factor fashion. They ended up passing the same scenery again and again. Budd Hopkins notes this feature from his American cases and calls it 'the cover story'. It seems to be a substitute image to blot out troublesome ones. Then a spinning disc-shaped UFO appeared. The witnesses drove home and arrived an hour later than expected.

So much for what was known when I put Dr Johnson onto the case. He arranged for Gloucester hypnotist Geoff McCartney to take the family under his wing. Such was the extraordinary story that came out that they spent month after month of endless sessions on it. No consideration of the problems of hypnosis seems to have entered Frank Johnson's mind, and he became totally convinced of the literal reality of the saga. Yet when, six months into his investigation, we met at the Welsh home of writers Janet and Colin Bord, it was our opinion that the hypnotic technique had played a key part in inducing some of the material.

Later I discovered that the witnesses were not happy about how the story had swollen from its simple beginnings, and there were quite a few problems because Johnson now had a book deal. They did not back out, because the case *was* factual, but they refused to let their names be publicized and were disturbed at the consequences unleashed upon them. I could only sympathize and regret what I had unwittingly set in motion. UFOIN had to opt out of the case, and Johnson went it alone.

For what it is worth, the family's hypnotic testimony involved being taken on board by tall, fair-skinned beings with no facial hair. There was the usual medical examination and taking of blood samples. ('We wish to examine you to see if we can adapt,' John was told). There was also a tour of the UFO, holographic picture-shows – a good many features that make the case astonishingly similar to the Aveley case. Whilst the witnesses could not have known about this when they first reported seeing a UFO, the abduction memories seem to have been generated by the over-zealous barrage of hypnosis at a time when the Aveley case *had* just been published in the UFO literature. It must be faintly possible that these witnesses had seen it or heard Frank Johnson talk about it.

This is a great shame, because it is possible that some of these memories might be important. For instance, they were given a salty drink that would help them forget and told that it was for their own protection – if they remembered immediately, it would bring more trouble. Remembering later was all right, since it was easier to cope. This is a little-known feature of a few foreign abduction cases.

The thing which really destroyed the case in most people's eyes was the way in which Johnson wrote it up, insisting it was true word for word, although the witnesses could only vouch for their out-of-hypnosis memories. He even ended his book by featuring a bizarre open letter to the Earth asking that we accept these aliens from Janos! This was the visitors' alleged planet of origin, but also a mythological god of two faces. It had been destroyed by their moon, Saton.

It hardly needs a scholar to see the symbolism in that, but nonetheless Johnson was convinced that the Janos people were really 'up there' and left the country in despair when UFO researchers refused to endorse him and the media laughed his book into oblivion. He certainly did not help himself by proposing that the inhabitants of New Zealand move off one island and turn the other over to these kindly aliens who, even now, must be getting very frustrated after a decade as interstellar refugees!

28 November 1980 – Todmorden, West Yorkshire

This is another quite well-known British abduction, largely because it involves a police officer (thirty-three-year-old Alan Godfrey) who was on duty at the time.

It was 5.15 a.m., and he was coming to the end of his nightshift. Looking for a herd of straying cows, he instead found an oval-shaped object hovering over the road ahead. He sketched it onto his accident report pad and then, mysteriously, it had vanished and he was further down the road than he should have been. He drove back to the site and found the previously wet road surface dry in a swirled pattern. His police boot was split, as if he had been dragged, and a message kept reverberating in his mind that he should not have seen this thing, another common tale.

PC Godfrey was silent until the next night, when he learned that three officers out on the moors chasing stolen motorcycles had seen a brilliant light head towards Todmorden. They had radioed it in to their base (Halifax). This gave Alan all the confidence he needed.

MUFORA, a local UFO team, picked up on the story immediately. Norman Collinson, a high-ranking CID officer with the Greater Manchester force, was a member, and he involved Harry Harris to video-film the interviews. Upon reconstruction, an apparent fifteen-minute loss of time was discovered, and Harris set up regression-hypnosis sessions with Dr Robert Blair and Dr Joe Jaffe in Manchester. Some of these were also filmed.

A full account of what Alan Godfrey recalled under hypnosis is reported in *The Pennine UFO Mystery*, which I wrote on Alan's behalf. Briefly: he was floated into a room (without recalling entry) and given a medical examination on a table or bed. There was a tall human-like being in a white cloak which said its name was Yoseph, but the examining was done by smaller beings, about 3½ feet tall 'with heads shaped like lamps'. Godfrey was promised that the aliens would return (frequently said). The aliens also told Alan (by telepathy) that they knew him.

Perhaps the most interesting feature of Alan Godfrey's case is that he recalls several previous time lapses in his past. These have not been explored under hypnosis, but it is interesting to speculate what might emerge if they were. In all the times I have met him and discussed his case, Alan Godfrey has struck me as a very sincere man who is merely puzzled by what has happened. He paid dearly: he lost his job as a consequence, thanks to a West Yorkshire force who took it upon themselves to try to prove that he was mentally unfit for duty. They failed miserably. When he gave up the fight and retired (with honour), they even raided his retirement party. Such actions were, in my view, disreputable.

The most crucial thing he has continually said is, 'I know what I saw on the road that night. It was real. As for what I said under hypnosis, I just don't know. It *seemed* real but it might have been a dream.' Of course, if it *was* a dream, the question is why it was so similar to everyone else's dreams of abduction.

January 1981 – Worsley, Manchester

After the Godfrey case Harry Harris and colleague Mike Sacks decided to investigate as many time lapse cases as they could find. Initially this was under the auspices of MUFORA, but later alone. I attended quite a few of these sessions, which mostly involved Dr Albert Kellar of St John Street, Manchester, the northern equivalent of London's Harley Street.

Little information on these cases has been published, since Harry Harris preferred simply to video-record them. He gathered them in an unsystematic fashion by listening out for stories among friends.

One case involved Linda Taylor, then in her late twenties, who went on to join Harry's team and offer first-hand abductee advice to others.

Her encounter took place when returning by car with her mother from Southport to Chorlton, a district of Manchester. The normally busy East Lancs Road became oddly quiet (very strange at 7.30 p.m.). To the south a huge light appeared and seemed to pace the car. Linda tried to accelerate, but could not, and the car then 'jerked about' and slowed right down. Suddenly a very peculiar 'old-fashioned' car appeared ahead, dangerously close. Linda was distracted from the UFO by this, and when she looked back, the light had changed to a metal disc hovering over this main road on a stretch between Leigh and Worsley. The old car in front then vanished instantly.

Immediately Linda swerved into a petrol station. The UFO was still visible and she pointed it out to a man filling his car. She was anxious to get away when the UFO tilted and accelerated skyward. She failed to note his reaction, and he has never been traced or come forward. If he reads this, his testimony might prove vital.

Linda reached home feeling nauseous, and her coat was missing. She had certainly had it in the car, but it was never found. Two hours had also vanished somewhere, since it was now after 9.30 p.m. This led Linda to Harry Harris and a long series of hypnosis sessions. But these have never got past a 'cover story' first met as a dream. In these 'memories' she is in a big, clean room with a tall man in a white suit. He has blond hair and blue eyes and leads her to a dolphin in a swimming pool. The dolphin is supposedly ill, and Linda is asked to touch it. She feels its slick skin.

Since then Linda Taylor has had several odd psychic experiences or visions, and a time lapse, and she fears for a future war involving immense destruction and death.

12 August 1983 – Aldershot, Hampshire

The witness was a seventy-seven-year-old man, Alfred Burtoo, who was fishing on the canal bank near an army barracks. His dog was with him. It was 1.15 a.m. and he had just poured a cup of tea when a bright light landed on the towpath some distance away. It then dimmed.

Alfred watched as two figures came towards him from the light. His dog growled. The figures were only four feet tall and had pale green costumes and visors. He told the dog to shut up and followed the beings, who had beckoned to him. They led him up the steps into what he could now see was a spinning-top-shaped object spanning the path. Once inside, a voice told him to stand under an amber light. He did so. Then he was asked his age, which he faithfully reported. After a few minutes he was told, 'You may go. You are too old and too infirm for our purposes.'

He went down the steps and looked back to see the object start to glow and hum like a generator. Then it climbed into the sky. He returned to his dog and went back to his tea and fishing.

This man's attitude is perhaps puzzling, but Omar Fowler, an investigator who interviewed Alfred a few weeks later, considered him sincere. 'At my age what have I got to worry about? I can only die once .... I don't care a damn who believes it or who doesn't, but I definitely went into that machine .... If they had taken off with me, then it was just my lot. It would have been just the same as me going out in the street and being knocked down .... [But] Whoever built that thing certainly did a good job of it.'

I am grateful to Omar, who sent me a full transcript and copies of Alfred's signed statement and his sketches of the outside and inside of the UFO. Mr Burtoo had complete conscious recall. Did this have anything to do with his age? And what exactly was he too old and infirm for?

I do not intend to discuss patterns in these Type III cases just yet, but many will be obvious. There is a clear theme to these stories, which are far more alike than they are individually different – too alike for there not to be some underlying answer.

For me the most important factor is the credibility of the witnesses. These are positively *not* people out to gain fame and fortune. That is the last thing these witnesses usually want, and I do not know of any money being made by any of them. If anything, they feel embarrassed about what has happened and as puzzled about what it means as any objective thinker would be.

It cost one man his job to speak the truth. Others, such as Mrs Verona and Shelley, have suffered different sorts of pressure because of their revelations. Talking about an abduction generally leads to social stigma, disbelief, loss of status and endless emotional problems. It is like being raped and then

then having no one to talk to who can possibly understand. The last thing it provides is higher esteem or rewards.

Shelley summed it up with something she revealed under hypnosis. She said that she kept saying to the aliens when with them, 'You've got the wrong person. I'm just ordinary. Look, if you let me go, then I promise I won't report this.'

That sort of bargaining smacks of honesty and would, I suspect, be understood by all victims of these encounters. In almost every case they have said, 'If I had the choice, I wish this had never happened, but it did!'

6 Those Who Were Abducted: Some Case Histories

In 1979 a young scientist, Allan Hendry, was employed by the J. Allen Hynek Center for UFO Studies (CUFOS). This was a period immediately in the wake of the Spielberg movie, which had relied heavily on both Dr Hynek and the Center. For this reason it was seen as a sensible and valuable step to allow one scientist (a graduate astronomer) to 'man the office' and investigate UFOs full time.

Sadly this was an experiment which did not last very long. UFO research has very limited money invested in it and, despite the large sums Spielberg and Columbia Pictures made from *Close Encounters of the Third Kind*, a paltry amount found its way back to ufology. But at least they used what they had well, and Hendry published a superb book about his two years at the helm of American field investigations. Under the misleading title *The UFO Handbook*, this is really a major review of more than 1,000 cases studied as they happened by a man who could devote all his time to them.

Not many of these cases were close encounters, and fewer still possible abductions, but on 27 August 1979 something took place that illustrated the importance of the CUFOS experiment and justified all the money spent on it. It produced an investigation around which Hendry could easily have built a second book and which is a model of what *should* be done. Unhappily there is rarely any possibility that these things can be carried out, because the UFO groups have neither the resources nor the expertise to cope, and science in the main considers such material unworthy of consideration.

Time Lapse: The UFO Collision

At 1.40 a.m. on 27 August 1979 Sheriff Dennis Brekke of Marshall County, Minnesota, called CUFOS on a special 'hot line' subsidized by the Center, which allowed people to make calls toll-free, thus encouraging many hoaxers but also providing some promising cases that might otherwise never have been forthcoming.

Allan Hendry took the call, referring to a sighting only hours before. He immediately saw the potential significance of the case. After making several enquiries to airports, radar sites and military bases close to the location of the encounter, he was able to show fairly quickly that no aircraft was known to be in the area at the time in question. Whilst, as Hendry correctly said in his case report, 'None of this disproves the role of, say, a low-flying aircraft', it did suggest that a proper on-site investigation was imperative. At the Center's expense he flew from Chicago to Warren, Minnesota, the next day.

By interviewing all the key people in the story not much more than twenty-four hours after the events, this was the account which emerged.

Deputy Val Johnson, aged thirty-five, was driving his 1977 Ford LTD patrol car on County Road 5, about ten miles west of Stephen. This is a very flat piece of agricultural land with an unobstructed view on either side. It was also a very clear night. (Hendry later got weather data from Grand Forks, North Dakota, forty miles away. Taken ten minutes after the encounter, this showed a temperature of 57°F, high scattered cloud, twenty miles visibility and a light 7-knot wind.)

Johnson saw a bright white light above trees about two miles south of him. It was low and appeared stationary but was too intense to be a car or truck headlight beam. As he drove towards it, he seriously considered the possibility of an aircraft that had set down in this remote area, because there had been reports of drug-smuggling across the nearby Canadian border. He turned south onto Highway 220 and did not call in because as yet he had nothing positive to report.

After he had been driving along the highway at a speed of about 65 mph for about one minute, the light suddenly shot towards his windscreen, covering the estimated one-mile gap in the blink of an eye. To say the least, Deputy Johnson was startled.

He was virtually blinded as the light rushed at him. He recalls the sound of breaking glass, and then he plunged into unconsciousness.

Johnson recovered his senses an unknown time later. The warning light was lit on the dashboard, and the car had stalled. As he became more aware, he realized that the vehicle was slewed across the road sideways and straddled the carriageway opposite that on which he had been travelling. With no street lighting at all, it was very fortunate that this road was so quiet at that late hour.

Johnson was more concerned about his physical condition. His head was resting against the steering wheel, and his eyes were so sore that he could barely see. He immediately called headquarters for assistance.

Happily this conversation was recorded back at Stephen by Pete Bauer, the radio officer. The recording shows Johnson giving the standard 'officer in distress' code with a very shaky voice and through an unusually bad transmission quality. When asked what had happened, the deputy said, 'I don't know. Something just hit my car. I don't know how to explain it .... Something attacked my car. I heard glass breaking, and my brakes lock up, and I don't know what the hell happened.'

Deputy Greg Winskowski was immediately sent to assist. The time was 2.21 a.m., showing a lapse (presumably caused by Johnson's being unconscious) of almost exactly thirty minutes.

Winskowski helped his colleague out of the car a few moments before the ambulance arrived. He said that Johnson was not wearing a seat belt and had a bump on his forehead evidently caused by hitting his head on the steering wheel. The ambulance driver found the patrolman shivering and in clear shock and drove him straight to the hospital at Warren, about twenty miles away.

In the confusion nobody told the night shift at the hospital that Johnson had apparently been unconscious. When he was examined at 4 a.m. by Dr W. Pinsonneault, it was only the eye trouble that was a cause for concern. X-rays had already ruled out any broken bones.

Dr Pinsonneault told Hendry the next day that there was a mild reddening irritation on the surface of both eyes but he could not examine the pupils because the light probe hurt the policeman too much. He considered the injury consistent with 'welding burns' and, after putting ointment on, sent the deputy home. After giving a statement to his superior officer, Johnson was allowed off duty at about 5 a.m.

Before calling CUFOS, Sheriff Brekke checked the car at the site and found several interesting things. One headlight was smashed, there were dents in the car, the windscreen was cracked, and the radio aerial was severely bent (presumably the reason for the transmission difficulties). Yet the car was in a position where it could not have sustained this damage by hitting any roadside object.

By far the strangest feature of all, however, was the fact that the car radio and Johnson's watch agreed perfectly with each other, but they were fourteen minutes slow! It was possible for Hendry to demonstrate, from a study of Johnson's other radio calls before the encounter, that his timekeeping had previously been perfect. So the curious effects *were* a factor emerging from the collision.

Meanwhile the deputy was driven by Brekke to Grand Forks, North Dakota, to see an eye specialist. Dr Leonard Prochaska removed the bandages placed by the hospital and found at 11.45 a.m., ten hours after the encounter, that the eyes were healed. He suggested that this rapid return to normal was consistent with flash burns caused by strong ultra-violet light sources. (In previous cases identical eye problems have been reported.)

Naturally a full 'accident' inquiry took place on the road, where broken glass and skid marks showed that the Ford had travelled 954 feet from apparent point of impact with the UFO to its final resting place. Ninety-nine feet of this was in full skid. Sheriff Brekke went over the highway with a geiger-counter, and Hendry similarly checked out the patrol car. Nothing above background levels was recorded. The two men also scoured the place where Johnson said the light had appeared, looking for evidence that a light plane might have landed. There was no such evidence. Nor, of course, were there any ground lights that might have been mistaken.

Obviously, there are those who will argue that Johnson's car was simply hit by the wind blast from a light aircraft fleeing the scene when it saw a police car approach. The main problems with this are the very rapid movement alleged by the officer and the effects on his eyes, the clock and the watch, none of which can be accounted for that easily.

CUFOS really went to town on this case and spent quite a lot of money following it up (something which unfunded groups cannot do, thus losing the chance to investigate fully many interesting cases). It cost $130 to obtain a radar print-out, for example. This covered the entire county from 1.30 to 2.30 a.m. but showed beyond doubt that no air traffic flew through the area. It is possible that a very low-flying aircraft would be below coverage, but it would have had to remain that low for forty minutes after the encounter or until it flew out of the county.

Meridan French of the Ford Motor glass division inspected the windscreen (which was cracked in several places). There was no evidence of heating above 120°C (the minimum figure detectable). He was very puzzled because the only way the damage could be explained involved the simultaneous raising of pressure inside the patrol car and lowering of it *outside*. As French said, 'I can only reassert my conclusion that all cracks were from mechanical forces of unknown source.'

The other car damage (for example, the aerial) was investigated by Honeywell Inc at Minneapolis. Their engineer, Roland Wardell, found that roadside grit had imbedded in the car, causing a lot of the damage. But this was not what had bent the antenna. After much discussion, their best guess was that 'a highly charged electrical "thing" ' had flown over the Ford and that the windblast had produced the mechanical damage.

Dr Warren Lamb, Johnson's optician, was also interviewed. He noted that the police officer's spectacles had light-reacting lenses that darkened automatically and would protect against ultra-violet emission. This led to a study of the windscreen, showing that it also would block off ultra-violet light. After much discussion with all the medical people involved, one conclusion was unanimous: the damage to Johnson's eyes could not have been caused by ordinary light but probably required something like mild infra-red radiation.

The effects on the watch and clock were even more puzzling. The car clock was electric but the wristwatch worn by Johnson was a cheap three-month-old Timex wind-up that was not anti-magnetic. Both worked perfectly when reset to the correct time, and neither the watch nor the car showed any evidence of having been subjected to an intense electro-magnetic field. The only plausible cause appears to have been a strong electrical charge that temporarily ionized the air.

Much else was attempted by CUFOS without adding to the data – for instance, an infra-red aerial photographic survey of the accident location. But the cumulative results leave this a baffling case.

We might wonder if all time lapse cases start like this. Certainly Deputy Johnson suffered some later suggestive abduction effects (for example, head pains), but he did not wish to 'become a sideshow', and regression hypnosis was never conducted. So the lost half an hour remains lost, and we have nothing but a strange encounter with 'something'.

Contact: The Very Strange Cloud

In December 1985 I was invited to help teach a seminar organized by Manchester University, entitled 'Science and ESP'. Dr John Shaw, the psychologist who ran the weekend of lectures and experiments, set up several things for me to do, including a group session on the question of psychic after-effects to UFO encounters.

After this seminar I was approached by one of the women in my group who thought I might be interested in the experience of a friend of hers. This lady, whom I will just call Dawn, lived in Cheshire and had no interest in, or knowledge of, the UFO subject, but she had undergone two quite remarkable encounters. Roy Sandbach, a retired print engineer who investigates with our group, conducted the first interview with Dawn. I recorded an interview with her later.

Dawn's sincerity was obvious. She is a deeply committed Christian who is utterly perplexed by the things which have happened to her and, although unafraid to tell her story, is totally uninterested in gaining publicity. Now the widow of a colonel in the REME, she spent many years in India and has since organized charity relief work for India, though she has an illness that causes her to become progressively blind as the day wears on. A less likely person to hoax a close encounter I could not imagine.

In autumn 1947 Dawn made a trip to Tibet. This was a great adventure for anyone in those days, let alone a young

Englishwoman. With a Gurkha guard and in a convoy of trucks, she and her husband were led across the desert plateau from Nepal. They journeyed for about a week, making very slow progress along the dreadful roads when they stopped near a 'village' (a collection of two or three huts), with a magnificent backdrop of mountains, she asked the Gurkha sergeant as they ate a light supper if these huge peaks contained Everest. He smiled, saying, 'My lady, those are just hills.'

Sitting on the truck's tailboard Dawn first became aware of a strange feeling: 'I was icy cold and it was a hot day. We all felt the same. Then I felt that something was touching me. The Gurkha said he felt it too.' The Colonel was in charge of other travellers in the convoy (including two Plymouth Brethren) and ran to the front of the truck. As he did so, he crashed to the ground as if felled.

This pressure in the air was now causing the vehicles to vibrate. Dawn jumped to the rescue of her husband, who was dazed and winded. It was then that she realized that the Gurkhas and villagers were staring at something sweeping towards them. 'It was a strange blurred object .... It looked like a grey, floating mass slightly above the surface but definitely moving.'

By now the villagers had fled but Dawn was mesmerized by the object, which went around the back of the truck as if inspecting it. In size it was 'as big as a large house', and then it changed shape: 'It wasn't a hard object. It was sort of woolly edged. It seemed to be solid in the middle but the outside seemed like vapour.' It was basically round but unlike anything she had seen before. She remembers in a sort of frozen tableau the faces of the soldiers struck dumb by fear. The thing just hovered beside them and was now so solid '... that I expected a door to open and the driver to get out'. This did not happen. Instead there was a manifestation of the Oz Factor. Everything went extremely quiet. Time stood still.

The next thing Dawn remembers is picking her husband up off the ground, with the object no longer in sight. The villagers refused to talk about it. The soldiers were silent for hours. Eventually, in a state of shock and by mutual consent, the entire group decided to return to Nepal. This was very disappointing after such a long, hard trek (although later Dawn did become one of the first Englishwomen to be entertained by the Dali Lama). However, as she says, 'I was quite glad to be getting out of there.' This certainly shows the effect of the encounter.

MUFORA explored the possibility that there might have been a 'dust devil' or whirlwind. The meteorological office confirmed that on hot days they can occur in Tibet. However, there are a number of factors that rule against this otherwise attractive idea. One of these is Dawn's second encounter, described below; others are more directly pertinent to this 1947 experience.

During the close proximity of the object Dawn had felt 'strange'. She elaborated on this to me, saying, 'It was a prickly feeling … as though my hair was standing on end. All my exposed parts were touched by it. I came out in goose pimples, and it was almost like an electric shock, but not quite as severe.' I suggested a tingle and she agreed, 'Yes, but it went on for quite a long time.'

This description sounds very much like an electrostatic charge. You can feel a similar mild version if you hold your arm against a TV screen when it has been turned off following several hours continual use. The charged particles on the screen create a field which attracts the fine hairs on your skin. It is quite possible that this field was attracting tiny dust or sand particles around whatever lay at its centre, giving the 'fuzzy' state of the object. One of the more impressive sets of UFO photographs, taken by the crew of a survey ship in January 1958 off a remote Atlantic island, depicts the same effect. They say that they observed a fuzzy haze around the Saturn-shaped object, and the pictures (since verified by computer enhancement) clearly illustrate this.

More significant than this interesting physical description is the fact that after the encounter in the Tibetan desert Dawn, her husband and the Gurkha sergeant (the three witnesses who came closest to the object) all became ill. This persisted for several hours, and no one could eat until the following day. The next morning they had all developed an '… itchy rash, bright red and frightening. It covered all the places I had felt I was being touched – my face, neck, arms and legs.' It lasted for about two days and then cleared up. Medically, this is suggestive of exposure to mild radiation.

As if this experience was not enough, Dawn had an even more terrifying encounter in October 1981 (reconstruction appears to have suggested the 8th as the precise date).

She had gone on holiday to Scotland as part of a Christian group and decided to visit the Isle of Mull. Two Americans, named Dwight and Geraldine, went with her. They hired a car, and Dwight drove. After taking the ferry, they toured around a bit and then decided to explore Tobermory, the main town. They were on a remote mountain road in the midst of the island, surrounded by the Salen Forest and with heather-clad hills inland and the sea to the north. It was a fine sunny day, and Dwight wanted to take some photographs, so they slowed to a stop. As they did so, a mist began to congregate around the car, thickening and solidifying. With it came a heavy pressure. Dwight, who was no scared rabbit (having faced armed bandits in Turkey during his travels), yelled and jumped back. Both he and his wife ducked below the windscreen, burying their heads in their hands. Then the car began to vibrate.

Dawn was more composed. She had the advantage of having been through this before and was determined to see more of it this time. As the object became black and now totally enveloped the front of the car, she would see something vague moving inside it. 'This was different from Tibet. There was this blurred silver shape, like a thing or a person, I don't know. But it was moving. I shouted to the others to look up, but they didn't. Then it – ah – disappeared.'

This sudden vanishing act intrigued us, so we probed it deeper. That was very important. At first Dawn had simply said that they got out of the car and were astonished to find the boot open and its contents all strewn about. They bundled them back in and set off, all thoughts of staying on the island now gone. Within hours the two Americans were refusing to discuss it, and when Dawn asked them about the boot, they just said, 'An animal must have done it.' Despite requests, the couple have not been willing to talk to anyone else. Indeed, in recent phone conversations with Dawn they have denied any memory of the incident.

When Dawn was carefully asked about how long the close encounter lasted, key anomalies emerged. 'It seemed like twenty minutes … probably. But I was not conscious of time. My wind-up watch was going but I never thought to look at it. Dwight and Geraldine both had quartz digital watches and – now that's a funny thing – they both stopped. They had to take them to a jeweller to get them going again. Oh, and there was a clock in the car too. That had stopped and did not start again. We just did not mention it when we took it back, because how would you explain it?'

This is the exact effect Val Johnson suffered in his patrol car, with the exception of Dawn's wind-up watch. Also the car engine had apparently failed on the first couple of tries, despite its being a virtually brand new hire car. Again, there appears to have been some sort of energy field surrounding the car on Mull that day.

But was there a time lapse? Dawn now made an interesting remark, after our discussion about the timings: 'You know, that is very, very strange. I've never thought about it before. We left on the ferry very early, and it was just after noon when we saw the thing. But when it had gone, the sun had moved well across the sky. Is that important?' I assured her it could be, and we looked deeper. 'You know, when we got back into town the shops were shutting. The afternoon just disappeared. Where did it go to? There was no traffic either. I mean, it is a deserted spot but there should have been some cars. Next day Dwight said, "That's the one good thing about it. Nobody else saw it." He took himself off then, saying that he wanted to be alone for a bit. That wasn't like Dwight at all.'

I include this case because it shows very well a number of things. This is a story that has been languishing in the mind of the witness for years. It is like many of these abduction scenarios that no one dares to report or no one knows where to report them. Superficially they may seem just like a strange tale, but when you probe further, clues tumble out. As here, witnesses frequently have no idea of the significance of what they are saying.

Another fascinating clue comes from Dawn's background. She is certainly what many people might call a medium. She has many anecdotes to tell about childhood premonitions. For instance, she once reclaimed her room after it had been taken over by an uncle, aware, although no one else was, that he was 'on a big thing looking at dirty water' – not a bad description of the boat he was sailing on. He had run away that morning to the USA, but nobody knew. The three-year-old Dawn had never seen a boat.

She has also undergone a classic out-of-body experience during surgery, watching the whole process. When she told the surgeon everything he had said during the operation, his jaw fell open and he warned, 'Never tell a surgeon that again. No one will ever want to operate on you!'

Are these things important? If you find 'psychic stories' hard to believe, you will doubtless think not. But remember, I am not claiming to explain what they mean, only to point out that this correlation between abduction witnesses and their previous strange encounters does exist.

Dawn has not been regressed to either encounter. She is too unwell to undergo that sort of strain. But she has 'feelings' about her experiences. 'I know that whatever lies behind these UFOs picked me out because I am sensitive. It tuned in. But I am positive they are *not* from space. You will think I am daft, but I am sure they come from right here.'

Contact: The Men from the Ministry

Perhaps the importance of those so-called 'psychic' experiences in the background of witnesses seems unconvincing. We found them in Dawn's story because Roy Sandbach and I knew by experience to enquire; often we are left wondering if they would be there had they been requested during other researchers' interviews.

However awkward they might appear to be, we are not in a position to pick and choose our data. We have to base our theories on what the facts advise, not select facts that fit a theory we may like. On that basis the extent of these claims about psychic phenomena in the history of a witness simply cannot be evaded. This will become increasingly obvious as the discussion develops.

Here is another case where they figure strongly – although there was no suggestion of that in the original report which I came upon, a tiny press cutting in the *Stockport Advertiser* dated 24 August 1972. It had been reprinted in *FSR*, a UFO magazine, and there were things about the story which cried out for a deeper investigation. It was one of the cases I set aside, as I was researching this book, with the intention of looking more closely into it, partly because the witnesses lived in my home town of Stockport. It is perhaps like hundreds of other reports from all over the world, which do not look particularly exciting on the surface but which upon investigation turn out to be real goldmines.

Roy Sandbach and I interviewed Peter Taylor and his wife Sandra almost exactly fifteen years after their close encounter, which had been at 2 a.m. on 17 August 1972.

This is the case as the media had it. Peter Taylor (then aged thirty) was a successful contractor. Sandra (then aged twenty-nine) was a professional dancer. She had been working at a club in the north-east and, as was his normal practice when he could, Peter had been to collect her. The long ride home took them through the Yorkshire Dales, then across the Pennines, entering Cheshire near Macclesfield. On this occasion they had bypassed York and were on the way towards Harrogate when they came upon a strange object by the road. It was melon-shaped and seemed to have just landed. On its side was a fluorescent door that appeared to be opening. Then the story just petered out.

Cases of this calibre are few and far between, so it was fortunate that in 1985 the couple still lived in the same home near Manchester Airport, so a reinvestigation could begin.

The first surprise was that there had been a third witness, not mentioned in the press report. She was a fellow dancer who was dozing in the back seat of their car. As it turned out, her eyesight was very poor, and the combination of these things, plus other factors, meant that she did not observe the object.

Our suspicions were aroused when the Taylors said that they had initially seen some red lights. 'It looked like hundreds of them. I asked if we were near an airport. I thought they were maybe poles with lights on,' said Sandra. The police later suggested that these were 'the lights on the base'. At first we thought this might mean Menwith Hill, a top-secret establishment in the Dales near Harrogate, used for satellite communications by America's National Security Agency, an intelligence unit. In the past many strange UFO encounters have occurred around here. However, it appears that the base referred to was Topcliffe, an RAF airfield (above which, incidentally, a crucial UFO case involving RAF jets took place many years ago and changed the attitude of the British Government on the subject). These red lights, therefore, appear to be quite explicable, but they did mark the start of the experience, because shortly after they had appeared the car radio began to falter. 'We had the radio on to keep Peter awake. It had been a long day. But it just filled with static and we had to turn it off. Then about one minute later we saw the UFO,' said Sandra.

She described it: 'It was huge ... definitely melon-shaped. I've never heard of a UFO shaped like that before. It was way above the trees.' Peter confirmed this but added, 'I think it was landing in a copse when we first saw it. As we drove towards it, I slowed down. Then it was just sat there behind the hedges.'

They had come to within about fifty feet of the very strange thing. It glowed green, 'like those glowing socks you used to be able to buy,' said Peter. We reconstructed the height and distance with the witnesses, and we were certainly dealing with an object about thirty feet high and sixty feet long.

Two cars were ahead of them on the road and one behind. They had formed a sort of convoy, as traffic on dark Pennine roads often does when it is quiet. The company can be very reassuring, especially as the lead vehicle in this instance was a police car. All the occupants obviously saw the object and stopped, but no one got out. It is here where the encounter begins to get very strange indeed.

On the side of the 'melon' a brilliant blue/white 'door' was appearing. Sandra described it as looking like a sunbed light (suggesting it was ultra-violet). Peter related it more to 'a very slow flashbulb'. It began as a dot and then spread outwards into a T-shape several feet high. The way this happened, just growing from the wall of the object, fascinated them. Peter likened it to '... the dot that you used to get on an old-fashioned TV set when you switched it off ... you know, the picture fading to a dot. This was in reverse. It grew from a dot and spread out into a door.'

This happened for a long time – Sandra felt it was several minutes, Peter rather less, and this dispute provided a major new clue, for Sandra said, 'You know what was strange. There was no noise. Even the trees. Not even normal night noises.'

Peter agreed, adding, 'Yes. That was the weirdest part. It was only when Sandra opened the door to try to get out and we were talking about it that we noticed just how quiet it was. There's always some twittering. But nothing was doing nothing .... I don't know if that helps.'

Yet again, as you will see, the witnesses to a close encounter quite spontaneously relate the Oz Factor without knowing its significance. As soon as they did so, our suspicions about there being more to this story were confirmed.

Sandra actually got half out of the door on her way over the hedge. 'Something made me want to get out,' she said. Peter meanwhile was dragging her back in. He said to his wife, 'You were fascinated by the object. I was fascinated with getting out of the way.' 'Yes,' she smiled. 'I still remember your exact words. You said, "Sod this for a game of soldiers." '

When they left the scene, the door on the thing was still opening. But their memories of what happened next are very dim, compared with the clarity of the rest. Whilst at no time did Roy Sandbach or I hint at missing memories or the possibility of abduction, Peter suddenly looked puzzled and spoke as an aside to his wife. 'You know what's odd: I don't remember us overtaking that police car. Where did it go to?' Does this imply that a good deal more took place after the opening of the door on the UFO and Sandra's compulsion to get out of the car? Were they there longer than they consciously remember?

When they got home (they cannot recall the time but think it was after 3 a.m.), they were met by a police car patrolling the road near their house. 'Have you anything to report?' was the odd question that Peter says the patrol car officers asked. Then they made all kinds of enquiries as the couple tried to enter their front door, which might be regarded as reasonable given the late hour of their arrival. 'They wanted to know where we had been and also must have noticed our state of shock, because they tried to intimate we had been drinking,' said Peter.

Whilst Sandra was more willing to ascribe this confrontation to coincidence, Peter felt that the police were fishing for information and knew about their UFO sighting. 'That other police car must have radioed in with our number,' he had long since concluded. However, it was learnt that such police activities were common in the area at that time, as there are many quite expensive properties nearby. So it might have been natural suspicion on the part of the police.

Although Sandra says that the light from the 'door' hurt the eyes to look at, there do not seem to have been any after-effects. She did say that on the following day, 'All day, for some reason, I felt like I was high on drugs or something.' Needless to say, she has never taken drugs. By 7.30 a.m. she was wide awake and up, and with a compulsion to report the matter. Peter would have preferred to forget all about it.

Two local officers came to take their story. They appeared to know it already. They explained that York police were investigating, suggested that the Taylors had seen a large tent and asked them if they wanted to change their story. 'There were other cars there, weren't there?' the police insisted. Sandra Taylor simply responded, 'Officer ... I am not blind. I have very good eyesight, and I know what I saw.'

A week later the Taylors were surprised to see a story in the Stockport paper: 'Heald Green couple flees in terror,' Peter said. 'We wondered "Who's this?" and were amazed when we saw it was us! The police must have given them the story.' Calls followed from all over the world.

Sandra went to Gibraltar to perform in cabaret the day after the press story. She missed the arrival of national newspaper reporters, who came in droves, obviously having picked up on the local story. The police had arranged it all, and a policeman was in the kitchen making tea for everyone while the journalists lined up in the hall to use the phone. This was cut very short when two official-looking men arrived in a black car and showed a card bearing the title 'Ministry of Defence'. They interviewed Peter at length, but he says, 'They were only really interested in the door. They kept asking me to describe that part over and over.' Then they advised, 'It is best that you say nothing of this.'

Pointing to the horde of pressmen in the hall (none had been allowed into the MoD interview), Peter wrily asked what he was supposed to do about them. The men from the Ministry agreed to handle it and promptly got rid of them all. Later, 'A man in a real old banger turned up and tried to get us to say we arrived home later than we did, for some reason. We just told him, "Look, mate ... when you see something like this you don't spend time looking at clocks!" He went all over us and the car with a geiger-counter, then left very disgruntled.'

All of this is fascinating and hints at deeper memories, but what turns this case into a real contact are Sandra's subsequent experiences.

She did not surprise us one bit when sheepishly admitting, 'I see things. I always have done. I seem to see things that others can't see.' She related a very vivid apparition experience where she helped an old lady back to her cottage in Cheadle village late one night, only to discover the woman vanishing in front of her and the house now appear to be boarded up and empty. Peter also confirmed that when they went on holiday to Sweden for the first time she astonished them both by directing them around Gothenburg, a city neither knew. She even addressed shopkeepers in Swedish, although she has not learned a word and has no idea how she did it.

Fascinating as these anecdotes might be, they are less intriguing than her claims about very vivid dreams post-dating the UFO encounter: 'I kept having the same dream over and over. It was this funny chap. He had yellow boots, like waders. His mouth was just like a little slit. And his eyes were terribly piercing and very blue. It was really odd, because he used to talk to me but he never opened his mouth. Yet I knew all that he said. We used to have long conversations but I have forgotten all of them. He was no Don Juan. He was like this little, really quite small man, with funny, rather leathery features. He looked like he'd been out in the sun for a long, long time. When he touched my head, he made me feel so calm. It was like a feeling of peace and contentment ... being put at ease. The last time I had the dream, I woke up sobbing because he had gone away.'

Treated as either a dream or a manifestation of a hidden memory, this remains of note. There are a number of comparisons between Sandra's description and Whitley Strieber's 'visitors', but the dreams predated the publication of Strieber's book by several years and, consciously at least, the Taylors appeared not to know about the American writer's story.

As a postscript it is worth adding that Peter Taylor also features in another anecdote, offered with reluctance and only after careful questioning. I fear that most investigators would not find such details because witnesses generally fail to realize the significance. They believe they are reporting their UFO encounter, and that is all that matters. It may well not be.

Peter's other experience was in the winter of 1973, just a year after the UFO sighting. He was returning from a job past Daresbury, a Cheshire village near Warrington. The car had shuddered and stopped at a certain point twice before. On this night it did so again. It was an almost brand-new Ford and had no defects (it was checked over and worked well afterwards). The time was 7.30 p.m. and Peter was looking forward to getting home, the drive from here being no more than thirty minutes at the outside. But suddenly he was driving forty miles north of Daresbury, in Preston! He found the first callbox and phoned home. His wife remembers this well. 'I don't know how I have got to Preston,' he told her. 'It's weird.'

It was 9.30 p.m. and, even allowing for an hour to drive to the town, that means an hour of his life had disappeared somewhere. But where?

Contact: The Armageddon Man

So far we have seen that alien contact and abduction themes may underpin many innocuous sightings, but we have not really learnt a great deal about the purpose of the contacts. However, the visions and fears of a holocaust in the Bolton contact and Linda Taylor stories have been echoed by others; abductee Gaynor Sunderland even offers a precise date for the disaster, 1992. At a time when arms treaty talks seem to be going well (autumn 1987), such a dread of Armageddon appears vaguely outmoded, but it is consistent in these cases. To review the situation, let us look at another example in more detail.

Keith Daniel of Bristol wrote to me initially to report a light in the sky. It was early July 1981 and he was with a friend, Davey. Together they were in charge of a group of children from one-parent families. Keith and Davey had set up a camp site on Thurstaston Common, a beauty spot on the Wirral peninsula which looks out across the Dee Estuary towards the North Wales coast. In fact, they were looking precisely at Flint, where Gaynor Sunderland had her close encounters.

As Keith put it, 'After bedding the mob of kids down for the night, neither of us could sleep, so we set off to walk across the common towards the sea. Here we sat, chatting, at about 2 a.m. on a fine, clear night.'

Opposite them was a factory with a red aircraft hazard light on top. But, 'Directly above that was another light. This was yellow/white and seemed to be giving off the power of a large bulb close by.' They were a long way from a phone, so all they could do was watch. After a while it drifted up and moved away to the south-east. They were contemplating possible explanations – for example, a helicopter, despite the silence (the wind was blowing towards them across the estuary) – when it changed to blue/white, climbed vertically, hovered and then streaked away 'like a God-knows-what', so they had to conclude otherwise.

The sighting was reported to the parkland rangers the next day, but they were totally uninterested.

This would hardly be very exciting were it not for a piece of information that Keith could not possibly know that I had. Some months before, I had been told by one of the Dan-Air ground staff at Liverpool Airport that the company did not like to discuss UFO sightings involving its aircraft. Nevertheless, they knew of one concerning a cargo flight from Belfast. Crossing the Point of Ayr, the crew had seen a brilliant light and had reported it to ground control, who had recorded it on radar. The light flew off over the Dee Estuary, and the plane landed. This had been at 2 a.m. on 12 July 1981.

Whilst Keith had no way of knowing about this unpublished story and did not even know the exact date of his encounter, he had already told me that it had been a weekend in early July when there was a moon. Checks of astronomical data showed that Sunday July 12 fitted, whereas the previous weekend had had very little moon at all. The same sources showed that there were no bright planets that might be responsible, such as Venus or Jupiter.

So the independent corroboration of the sighting makes it all the more impressive.

This gave me cause to look back into the past of Keith Daniel. He had already mentioned that it was so full of strange things that he was attempting to produce his autobiography.

Briefly, these incidents began soon after his birth in 1952. He lived in an old, rambling house at Tranmere, Merseyside. Many odd happenings took place here, including what we might call a poltergeist making noises and moving objects. The noises included crying sounds, lights turning on and off on their own, and his father being flung across the landing by an unseen force. Mr Daniel senior described one interesting event from Keith's childhood:

'It was 3.30 a.m. I got up to go to the toilet. Whilst standing there in the bathroom I began to black out and as I reached the landing I had blacked out completely. When I came to, my wife said I was fighting something during [that time] .... I have also seen a person or whatever standing beside my chair with some form of habit on .... This appeared to be holding a book or box in his hands across mid body .... I felt no fear. I felt as if a friend had called .... I had the feeling, although there was no outward sign of it, that inside the habit of this thing there was an immense heat or pressure of some kind ... that it could take one away, just like walking from this life to another ....'

On Mr Daniel's sketch of the 'book' there is a pattern he says was inlaid. He describes it as an 8 lain sideways and appears not to know it is the symbol for infinity.

Also during this period both Mrs Daniel and Keith's sister say they observed UFOs hovering over the house during the middle of the night. But they cannot recall more details.

It was soon after these incidents, in about 1967, that young Keith began to have peculiar dreams. They were '... extremely vivid .... I dreamt I had been abducted aboard a UFO by little men. This sounds ridiculous, but it is the truth as I remember it.'

Keith was a fan of the Rolling Stones rock group, and his father was not happy about his 1960s hairstyle. He insisted that it be cut but, as teenagers tend to do, Keith rebelled. Then he found himself being taken from his bedroom into 'a strange yellow room with a batch of other kids'; there were odd men in green and yellow uniforms, and one was telling him to get his hair cut. Another put him into a glass tube, and pain coursed through him. Then he was led out, and 'I was a little green man then.' The experience was a turning point in his life. He got his hair cut the next day!

Naturally, this dream certainly *was* a dream. Its childhood imagery is obvious. But it was important to Keith and may have reflected inner knowledge that his subconscious possessed. The allegory of being captured by aliens because they wanted to make him one of them should be pondered. It is little different from adult reports of genetic experiments on mankind to produce a sort of hybrid (as suggested by the Villas Boas case, the Mrs Verona abduction and many of Budd Hopkins' current stories). Was Keith's mind trying to tell him something?

Soon after the first of these vivid alien abduction dreams (others involved flying in out-of-body states towards UFOs), he had a very odd daylight encounter. It was still 1967, after school at about 4.30 p.m. It was gloomy dusk as autumn turned to winter (meaning that it could have been around the point of the late October/early November 1967 great British wave).

Keith was walking to a friend's house just round the corner. There was a classic English pea-souper fog and he was enjoying cutting through it. As he reached the drive of his friend's home, there was '... the most incredible rushing noise overhead. It was so loud I thought a plane was crashing. I even dived to the ground and covered my ears.' This act did not stop him hearing the noise (showing, incidentally, that it was probably internal rather than outside in the air somewhere). Then it stopped. He ran into his friend's house and repeated the tale, but he was disbelieved. Not only had his friend heard nothing but (as he took great delight in showing Keith) there was no fog. There never had been!

By the age of twenty Keith had gone to see a psychiatrist, because 'I fell into a terrible depression over my "strange abilities", sure in the knowledge they were genuine, yet not seeming to be able to obtain solid proof that would make people sit up and see for themselves.' The psychiatrist was totally out of his depth and had no explanation or remedy, and Keith realized that he had to learn to accept his encounters as a fact of life. This he has now done.

The experience which drove him to that medical confrontation came in the summer of 1971, when he was aged eighteen. He was hiking in the Delamere Forest, south of Chester. It was between 28 and 30 June and at about 3 a.m. He was hitching along the A41 with someone he had just met (name Steve, not traced). Suddenly 'an electric blue light' began to '... dance down the road .... Its movements were extremely slow and erratic. It went among the branches of trees and began to dart all over the place.' His companion made a run for it, but Keith walked in a daze straight towards it.

He says: 'Before I had gone twenty paces, I found myself walking calmly back .... I felt I was doing this against my will and had been ordered to "go away" .... The object flew up a mud track and disappeared into a sort of garage .... I spent some time afterward searching, but there is no garage there.'

We do not know if there is a time lapse here, but it seems very suggestive of one. Steve refused to talk about it afterwards, behaving rather like Dawn's American friends after their encounter (p. 102). But Keith suffered a most enlightening effect: 'I spent several hours just hallucinating things that were not there .... I was really disorientated.'

Keith is most impressive as a witness, meticulous and without presumption. He even suggested that I use a pseudonym so that people would not get the idea he was trying to gain attention for his prospective book. I have used his real name, but this offer shows his basic integrity.

He says: 'I cannot judge what is genuine and what is not. I can only say what I personally think to have been true as I experienced it.' These 'ideas' that have flowed into him after his 'contacts' are worth looking at.

He sees two conflicting trends: 'the flowering of psychic abilities' in mankind, and our dangerous stockpile of nuclear warheads, 'waiting for some goon to start playing darts with them'. These resolve together because, 'If this awful holocaust does take place, man might need his psychic abilities when he returns to the caves .... Maybe more people are being born with actual psychic ability in these times because they're going to damn well need it when the crazy generations have killed each other off.' His inner conviction that Armageddon may be imminent seems wrapped up in his experiences. He has grown 'apathetic' but adds that, although '... nobody wants to die horribly in a nuclear holocaust – me included – if it brings better things for those to come ... maybe Armageddon is the only answer.'

Keith stresses he is not a religious nut and, having received some letters from readers of my books who would fit such a description, I can only endorse that. Yet his visions of nuclear horrors (a vivid recurrent dream of an explosion over the River Mersey, for instance) echo rather too well the claims of so many abductees.

When you hear it once, you dismiss it. When you hear it dozens of times, from many witnesses, you start to wonder. When you personally have frequent nightmares of Armageddon in the 1990s (and I must reluctantly admit that I have for most of my life), *then* you start to worry.

Perhaps there *is* a message behind these very strange encounters.

Abduction: The Guardian Angel

This series of case histories gradually builds up, from a straightforward time lapse towards more bizarre encounters. Yet none is an abduction full and proper. It is important not to view the next three cases in isolation. It would be easy to do that, but in truth they form part of a continuum. No solution would be satisfactory if it failed to take that into account.

This next case forms a neat bridge between contact stories that might be abductions and abductions which are clearly that.

There are three main components to the story, and by now they should be predictable. Peter Hough and I went to interview the witnesses because of the 'psychic' phenomena involved, and then found there was a UFO encounter, which in turn seems to hide abduction memories as well.

Karen is the chief witness. She does not want publicity, for reasons that will become obvious. Born on Merseyside (whose strong accent and sense of humour she still preserves), she became a cook, working for a cake company in Great Sankey.

Briefly, her psychic experience took place in September 1976, when she was aged eighteen. She was on the night shift and walking home at about 5.45 a.m. Taking a regular short cut through a partly completed housing estate, she heard a distinct female voice call out her name very slowly. 'It sounded a bit like my own voice, but was longer and sweeter, as if coming down a tunnel or something. It was **dead weird**,' she added.

This recurred a number of times over the next two weeks, always when she passed the same unoccupied bungalow. Other people were with her on occasions. They heard nothing. She checked behind the stone garden wall but there was nobody there. After a while she became frightened. 'I could hear this voice so clear. And it echoed. It was in my head.'

Karen was spared having to find a new route by leaving the

job. But two weeks later, after a night out with the girls, she was dropped by a taxi near this spot and had to go past it to reach home. A youth leapt from the shadows and grabbed her by the neck, pulling her into the garden of the same bungalow she had been 'warned off'. He almost strangled the terrified young woman as he attempted a rape.

Karen was rescued by another strange event. 'I was grasping round trying to find something to fend him off ... then suddenly I felt something come into my hand as if someone had put it there .... I just whacked him on the back of the head with what turned out to be half a brick. He was a big bloke, but he just flopped to the floor. I thought I'd killed him, but he got up and staggered away.'

The police caught the attacker, who was known to Karen. She was unable to speak for two months, such were her injuries, and she is certain, 'If I hadn't got that brick from somewhere, he'd have killed me.'

Karen left the north after these horrible events and moved to Newquay, where she worked in a hotel for the summer. Here she met Gary, who is now her husband. In September she and Gary went for a walk after their evening meal, along a country lane at Pentire.

A big glow appeared behind hedges ahead of them. 'We could hear like a low humming noise,' Karen said. Gary added that there was also a rustling as they got closer, but this could have been the grass in the field. Thinking at first that it was a tractor, they walked towards it, curious as to who should be working at that hour. Then, 'as if we had disturbed the thing', there was a 'whoosh' of displaced air, and a blinding, streaming light shot past them, coming within ten feet.

Gary said: 'We just turned and ran, although I remember thinking we should report it. It felt like when you are standing on a platform as a high-speed train rushes past. We really felt it.' They arrived back at the hotel at about 11.30 p.m., which possibly implies a few missing minutes from the reconstruction of timings. But on such a stroll the hour of day was hardly important, and they really were not certain of this.

Karen and Gary returned to the north to set up home at Dukinfield, Lancashire. A few months afterwards she found that she was pregnant. On 16 September 1979 she had a terrible dream. 'I had the baby. It was talking to me in a raspy, evil voice. The baby was like a devil. I knew something was not right.'

The dream recurred and Karen became frightened. She told her family that something was wrong with the baby. On 26 December that year she miscarried. 'When I saw the blood, I was relieved,' she admits.

Soon after the interview with Karen I had received an advance copy of Budd Hopkins' book *Intruders*, but since it was not published in Britain then, there is no way that Karen could have known the extent to which it linked with her story. Astonishingly, in his book Hopkins discusses a number of mysterious pregnancies terminated by shows of blood. Female abductees have reported these to him. They have also had what he calls 'wise baby dreams', where they see the baby as intelligent and feel it is alien, or not right in some way. He is convinced that these are the result of women being impregnated during abductions, then having the experimental foetus taken from them during a second abduction, to be brought to maturity elsewhere.

This theory is extraordinary to say the least, but Hopkins records a number of cases, and Karen's story is presented exactly as she offered it before there was any possibility she knew of these theories. Two other witnesses featured in the British Catalogue also suffered miscarriages soon after their encounter. (I have not named them because they asked this to be kept confidential). The pattern is disturbing.

At the time of this miscarriage, Gary and Karen met a very strange man in the streets of Hyde. He wore weird clothes, walked past them and smiled. Then he vanished. Gary made a perceptive remark at this point: 'The only time anything ever happens to me is when I have been with Karen, deeply in love.'

Karen certainly is the focus of these experiences, which have been occurring since birth. She recalls a vivid dream when she was six and living in Speke. All she remembers of it was that a 'dark shadow figure' turned up in her bedroom and 'wanted to take me away'.

Many of Karen's recent dreams are of her floating to a bright and strange land. Here is one from January 1987: 'I saw a big, long light in the sky. It was at the end of a sort of tunnel. I floated like I had no weight at all. Then I went through this tunnel and was in this place … green grass, blue sky. I knew it wasn't right. But I felt like it was real. It was like I was actually there. Then the tunnel recurred and I floated down it, and I was back in bed. I saw my body on the bed and climbed into it.'

Karen appears not to realize that this is a marvellous account of an adventure many others have shared, often called 'the Near Death Experience'. As the name implies, it tends to be associated with people in a very stressful state who almost die by accident or during an operation. Psychologist Dr Margot Grey in her book *Return from Death* offers a scientific review of this highly relevant topic, to which we shall return later when looking for answers. Peter Hough and I have been seeking Dr Grey's advice on cases like Karen's, and it is fair to say that she was previously unaware of this untapped data source.

Karen and Gary's child Laura was born in 1982, and after Karen had described the floating dreams, Gary chipped in: 'The other morning Laura said to me, "I was flying last night, Daddy. It wasn't like I was a bird. I was over the bed and I could see myself." '

In the summer of 1984 Karen had the strangest of these dreams. She said: 'I know this sounds silly, but I feel to this day that it was *not* a dream. That it really happened to me.'

She felt she was in her bedroom in Dukinfield. 'There was this low humming noise, the same noise that we heard behind the hedge in Newquay. I got out of bed and went over to the window. There was this little white thing hovering right outside. Then a door opened up and I saw this woman standing there .... It must sound absolutely stupid.'

We assured her it did not and Karen drew the UFO (egg-shaped with a dome on top) and described the woman. She had a very familiar description which, after reading previous stories, one ought to be able to predict: 'She was about six feet tall and had these beautiful pale blue eyes. They were very long and slanted and she had long blonde hair and skin that was extremely white. I remember thinking how it looked like china or porcelain. This was all *so* vivid.'

Karen paused for a moment to breathe in the memories, then went on: 'She was immaculate, snowlike. She wore a long gown. She held out her hands and wanted me to go to her. I felt that I had to. So I opened the window and climbed through. I asked her about Gary – "Should I go and get him?" – but she told me that he would not wake up and I should not tell him about this. I still had my nightie on. I walked up into this thing and it was cold … very cold. She took my hand and said, "Do not be frightened." Then I don't remember anything until I am stepping back through the window into my bedroom. I could see the pink wallpaper. I could see Gary in bed. It was *so* real.'

Karen is unable to recall details of what happened on board, except, 'There were little lights. I remember that. I felt very calm. I was not frightened. I think she was hypnotizing me. I wanted to go. I just remember looking at her eyes and I wanted to go.'

The next day Karen remembered the dream clearly and, 'I had this peculiar feeling that something important had happened. I just knew it.'

Bearing in mind that this happened in 1984, it is worth wondering about the most recent event Karen described at this April 1987 interview. She has not seen any connection, and there may be none.

'I was asleep. Then I could feel a little hand hold my wrist. They were tiny fingers, like a three-year-old child. Too small for Laura. They were holding on to me. It was nice. Then I was "out", and the hand was still holding me. I woke Gary and told him to switch the light on. As he was about to do so, I saw a tiny ball – like steam – rising up and vanishing through the ceiling.'

Gary denies any memory of this, but Karen was adamant. 'I don't believe it. You must remember. It was so real. I am sure it happened.'

She also says that recently she has found herself suddenly awake in the middle of the night, '… feeling like I have been awake for ages and certain that somebody has been in the room'.

Again these are things that Whitley Strieber reports in his book. But Peter Hough and I again recorded this interview *weeks* before Strieber's book was published.

There is so much food for thought here.

Abduction: The Long Drive Home

After police officer Godfrey's encounter was explored under regression hypnosis, this opened up the field for regular British investigations of that type. *None* of the stories in these case histories so far has involved that step, which you might feel to be rather odd, but the status of hypnotic regression is far from clear – there are some researchers who see it as such a factor that it can make a case more confusing rather than less so.

However, Harry Harris and his team worked on a number, such as the encounters of Linda Taylor and Jenny reported in the British Catalogue. This next case offered them the best opportunity of a real breakthrough because it featured three women who appear to have been abducted at the same time.

On Thursday 16 July 1981 they had been for their regular night out at Tiffany's in Shrewsbury, Shropshire. Consuming only coca-cola, as was apparently their custom, the women left at about 2 a.m. (on the 17th) for the twenty-minute drive along the A5 expressway to their homes in the Dawley area of Telford New Town.

Driving her own Hillman Avenger was Viv Hayward, aged twenty-seven. Beside her in the front seat was mother-of-three Rosemary Hawkins, also twenty-seven; behind them, in the back, was Valerie Walters, one year their junior.

It had been a normal convivial evening and their conversation was bubbling as they passed the village of Atcham, heading for Norton, Uppington and home. But then something strange happened. The conversation dried up. They all later remarked on this 'conditioning process', where their mood altered drastically for no obvious reason, and they went into a sort of limbo state where they just sat very quiet.

And then, across open fields beside them, they saw some peculiar red and white lights. Rosemary wound down the passenger window for a better look. There were four white and two red lights, seemingly attached to an object that was dimly visible in the summer pre-dawn. Rosemary looked at her watch and saw that it was about 2.10 a.m. They were no more than ten minutes from home, so they were not unduly worried – until the lights began to pace the car.

Viv Hayward glanced out and saw the white lights in a circle with the two red lights closely spaced together at the focus. A round object seemed to be behind. She decided to put her foot flat on the accelerator, but nothing happened. 'It was like we had no power, as if the thing was draining it from us.' As her frantic efforts to escape conveyed themselves to her friends, the feeling of panic rose inside the car. They were now near the deserted Shamrock Café with the brooding slopes of the Wrekin (Shropshire's only hill of real note) as a distant backdrop. Not a single car or passer-by offered them comfort. They were alone.

But then the lights dimmed and, according to Rosemary, the thing just vanished. Valerie Walters had a better view from the back of the car, being able to look behind her as they falteringly cruised past the now stationary object. She says that it had a row of windows on the side and that lights were on the base, tilted towards them. By the time she saw the dimly glowing lights climb into cloud, all three women *knew* it was a UFO. What else could it have been?

With the car now free of its restraining influence, they drove the few remaining miles into Telford and called immediately at Malinslee police station. During this drive the women felt '… a most odd sensation … it seemed to take absolutely ages to get to Telford. We know the journey so well. But this drive was unexpectedly long.'

Soon after their sighting the women wrote to me outlining the story as above. I asked UFOIN investigator Stephen Banks to drive over from Stone in Staffordshire, and he quickly compiled a thirty-four-page case report covering every conceivable angle. Then he left to begin a university degree course in sociology.

Stephen was very experienced in looking for hidden clues in cases and was impressed by the fact that, 'All three women seem to be psychic or suggestible and have a history of reporting other visionary experiences.' This was no more than either of us expected. Also Valerie appeared to be susceptible to entering altered states of consciousness ('going into a trance', as she put it). She had had a childhood UFO sighting and had always had the belief that '… one day I will be contacted.' Was it coincidence that *she* saw the UFO more clearly?

One important piece of information which Stephen uncovered during his work concerned the timings. The women say that they arrived at Malinslee police station at 2.55 a.m. (according to Rosemary's watch), but Stephen was able to confirm with the police that they had logged the report at 2.40 a.m. – fifteen minutes earlier. Does this imply that Rosemary's watch was wrong? It may. However, the 2.40 a.m. arrival still provides a time discrepancy of about twenty minutes.

When I summarized Stephen Banks' notes in 'Time Distortion on the Telford Road' (*Northern UFO News*, No. 90, November 1981), I made the following point: 'This is a fascinating report, very well investigated ... we have decided to continue investigation.' That continuation could only really follow one path, the hypnotic retrieval of memory. As it turned out, Harry Harris read the original case report and, having concluded his work on the Godfrey case, decided to proceed with this one. He did video-film sessions with Rosemary and Viv, when they were separately put under regression hypnosis on the same day. These sessions were in Manchester and, to their credit, the lawyer and his colleagues (close-encounter witness Mike Sacks and senior police officer Norman Collinson) spent large sums of money organizing this experiment. They also presented excerpts from the videos to the UFO community at an international congress organized by BUFORA in August 1983. But the case has never been adequately documented in writing. Because it is so interesting, I will summarize the results of the hypnosis sessions, which were followed by others with further doctors (the last of whom succeeded in getting a story out of Valerie, after she had long resisted telling it).

It is not clear how much separation of witnesses occurred during the original sessions. These involved Dr Joseph Jaffe, who ran a clinic in psychiatry at the North Manchester General Hospital and had a private practice in the city centre, and Leslie Davies, a homoeopathic doctor.

Jaffe's technique of inducing hypnosis came in for some criticism after these 1982 experiments, and he was accused by his peers of using a number of suspect methods. Davies worked quite differently and effectively *shouted* the patient into an altered state of consciousness.

Whilst on the first occasion Rosemary and Viv were hypnotized and interviewed separately (mostly by Harry Harris), they were together in the same room, and obviously they had plenty of opportunity to discuss their experiences before the next sessions, months later. Valerie's eventual breakthrough came after a year, so must be treated cautiously. The women had also had several months before the first experiment, when (as good friends) they must have talked about the UFO sighting and the missing time, without any conscious intent to cheat.

None of this is meant to deny the veracity of their recall under hypnosis. It is merely intended to point out that what *seems* to be an important series of corroborations has problems beneath the surface which cannot be ignored.

Taking Viv's recollections under hypnosis from the point when the car is impeded, it is noteworthy that she commented that, when they all went 'quiet', she had 'gone into my own thoughts', meaning that she had switched off attention to external reality and was tuned internally. I think we see the Oz Factor here.

Then suddenly: 'I feel funny … like I'm floating. I feel my body is very light.' Under hypnosis people tend to murmur as they drift with their mental images and describe what they see. The use of the present tense tends to indicate that they are actively re-experiencing the event.

Viv now says: 'The car is being taken up' and claims that it is floated into the air. 'I can't see the road any more. I see white cloud.' (This was also recounted by the witnesses to the Aveley abduction.) Her two friends are mysteriously not with her as the car enters the UFO, roof first, through 'two big doors opening' in the underside.

Inside she is vaguely aware of being in a room and says: 'I can feel these aliens holding me down.' They have taken her out of the car and put her in a reclining chair (like the one she was in at the doctor's). 'They are holding me down. They feel very strong. They are trying to find out things from me. They want to know how we are made.'

She describes the figures as four feet tall, without hair and ugly. They have deep-set dark eyes, very thin arms and strange-looking noses, and they are 'ugly'. They are wearing green cloaks.

These entities are very like the examiners in the Aveley case and the creatures whom Whitley Strieber says he has met. As such, they are most unusual in British cases, and it is possibly relevant that the only time these entities are 'seen' appears to be during hypnosis experiments. Conscious memory cases most often reveal the tall, blond, blue-eyed figures we have met several times in this book.

One of the creatures transmits a voice into the mind of Viv, and she reproduces it, deep and gruff: 'Don't … be … afraid,' it says extremely slowly. This precedes the almost obligatory medical examination.

'I feel as if they are taking something from my body,' she says. 'There is a lot of pain in my legs. They are putting their hands inside my legs and pulling at my bones.' She is asked if they know she is in pain: 'I keep telling them!' Viv cries. All these small figures continue to do is tell her not to be frightened, as one might tell a cat to which one is doing something painful for its own good. The grip of the entities releases, and Viv is then 'scanned' by a 'big light' that studies 'my top half and then the rest of my body'. Then she realizes that she is paralysed and is being carried back to the car. It is on the road again, but that is the last thing she remembers before driving off.

How would Rosemary's story match with this? It began promisingly. She reported first the Oz Factor: 'It's so strange ... There's no sound.' Then she realizes that the lights are 'attached to a spacecraft of some kind' and she is then taken from the car. 'I feel strange. I am floating. I'm not in the car any more with Viv or Val. I feel big and bloated.' This certainly seems to support Viv's account, where she said (if you recall) that she was *alone* in the car when it was floated up.

Rosemary now described being inside a room that was bare except for a bed, 'like a long table on a stand'. She is alone and feels it acutely. 'I don't know why I'm in this room,' she calls out. 'I don't believe this is happening to me .... Things like this don't happen to me.' But she has got onto the table, 'I don't know why I got on. I don't know why. It's something I've seen on a film.'

Her next memory is of suddenly feeling calm: 'I don't feel so frightened now.' And then she hears a noise and a metal object rolls in on wheels! 'It's about four feet tall. It's round on top with a round body and round legs.' More of these 'robots' arrive and she cries, 'They haven't got a face!' She wants to know where Viv and Val are. 'Why aren't they with me?' she asks. But she is oddly calm and relaxed in the presence of these figures. 'They don't seem nasty ... and they feel friendly. I like them.' She is convinced that she is just being held in a sort of waiting area and can see a larger room off this one (where Viv is being examined?).

There was no medical examination on Rosemary. She said: 'They just want to have a look.' That was all that she was told. Then she remembers floating and being back in the car. Her friends are there and, she explains, 'We are trying to get away from it.'

It was Dr Albert Kellar, a consultant practitioner, who finally coaxed something out of Valerie Walters. Whilst the two accounts above can be said to be at least partially corroborative and independent, that cannot be said of Valerie's claims.

In the Kellar session Val cries: 'It's coming towards us.' The doctor is monitoring blood pressure and heart beat and these shoot up at this point. 'The lights are hurting my eyes,' she calls out. 'I feel funny.'

Still inside the car with Viv, Valerie feels dizzy. But Rosemary is missing. This fits in with the other two tales, of course. Rosemary did say she was 'beamed out'. However, Valerie reports that the car is stationary, with the doors open. Despite a pain in her head, she decides to get out and try to find Rosemary. Viv would then be left alone, as she had claimed.

Outside, Val is surrounded by blackness and cannot see the UFO: 'I can feel it's here but I can't see it.' Then the bright beam of light hits her again and she staggers with the pain. A voice in her head tells her not to be afraid, and she 'floats' into a room. Two entities (one male and one female) enter.

Whilst Val describes these aliens as wearing the long green cloak reported by Viv, her account of the entities is very different. But not unfamiliar. They are six feet tall, with dark, shoulder-length hair, vivid blue eyes and extremely white skin. We seem to have come across them before.

She was told that the aliens only wanted to examine the women 'to see what we are like'. Viv had been selected out of the three of them to be medically examined. Rosemary was just held so that they could watch how she responded. As for Val herself, the two human-like figures seemed very intrigued by her clothes. The female entity supposedly took off Val's high-heeled shoes, put them on and tried to walk in them!

Val does not recall returning to the car and says that, when she asked who the aliens were, all she was told was: 'You are not to know. You would not understand.' She is convinced that something else very important happened on the UFO that night. In 1983 she insisted that it was '… gynaecological in nature … but I don't know why I know that'. This was long before any researcher in Britain was aware of Budd Hopkins' research supposedly demonstrating alien gynaecological experiments on selected Earth women. Indeed, his theories were stimulated by a case which occurred in June 1983. The Telford case was recorded on tape well before then, although unpublished, so Hopkins would not have known about it.

What do we make of this case? The women insist that they never expected the story to go so far: 'We thought it was over when we reported it. But when we were told there was twenty minutes of our lives missing, of course we had to discover what had happened.'

But Valerie made an interesting comment. She, if you remember, was the one who had been anticipating a contact. She said that before the UFO appeared the three of them '... had been wishing something exciting would happen'.

Of the doctors involved, Jaffe was very noncommittal and refused to be drawn but Davies was more specific, insisting the women were telling 'the truth as they saw it'. Dr Kellar went even further in discussing his session with Valerie: he told how her pulse jumped from 70 to 136 during the hypnosis, indicating severe trauma and generating responses that could not be faked. In his view she was in 'absolute terror'.

Abduction: The Man Who Wasn't There

This Australian abduction might not seem very dramatic compared with the previous case, but it may be very important, because it offers a major clue to our understanding. That clue will become obvious in due course.

Judith Magee of the Victoria UFO Research Society investigated the triple encounters of Mrs Maureen Puddy, a twenty-seven-year-old mother from the town of Rye. Her account was published in *FSR* only weeks after the first events, which were consciously recalled in their entirety.

At the time, Maureen had an invalid husband and two young children. In June 1972 the boy, aged seven, suffered an accident which hurt his leg and caused him to be hospitalized at Heidelberg, near Melbourne, taken there by air ambulance. So when, in the evening of 5 July 1972 Mrs Puddy was driving on Mooraduc Road between the towns of Frankston and Dromana and saw a blue light following her car, she thought it might be another air ambulance helicopter. She stopped and got out to have a look. The object that confronted her was no helicopter!

Above her was a disc formed by two saucers placed one atop the other. It was radiating blue light from all over and hovered with just a faint humming sound. She estimates it was a hundred feet in diameter and only twice as high as the telegraph poles along the road – that is, perhaps thirty or forty feet. Forcing herself back into the car, she set off and was horrified to find that the glow travelled with her. The chase lasted eight miles along the deserted road and then the object shot away. She went to the local police and reported the incident immediately.

Twenty days later Maureen was driving the same route back from visiting her son in hospital. It was again about 9.15 p.m. and completely dark (July being winter in Australasia). Again the blue glow appeared. 'Oh hell, not again!' Mrs Puddy exclaimed. So she bent forward and pressed on the accelerator. Nothing happened. Exactly as Viv Hayward was to find nine years later and half a world away, control of the car had been taken away from its driver.

The vehicle was dragged onto a grass verge and halted, bathed in blue light. As Maureen peered forward, she could just see the rim of the disc hovering above her. She felt as if she was in the centre of a vacuum. It seems that she was describing both a pressure loss and an isolation feeling, very similar to the Oz Factor again.

During this period Judith had a mental communication 'beamed' at her from the UFO. The voice seemed to be 'translated from a foreign tongue' and said three things. Firstly it said: 'All your tests will be negative', which she has never been able to comprehend, as no medical tests were in process – although she seems not to have considered the idea of 'nuclear' or weapons tests.

Then the voice said, 'Tell the media ... do not panic ... we mean no harm', which she understood, although 'media' (in the sense of press, radio and television) was not a word she would use herself and was much less widely used fifteen years ago than it is today.

Finally the voice told her: 'You now have control', at which point the car engine returned to life and she drove away. The vacuum and glow vanished and she again went straight to the police.

This time they were more helpful and put the Royal Australian Air Force on to her. They are charged with responsibility to investigate such cases and checked for aircraft movements (finding none), then politely advised her that she should say nothing to anyone. However, Mrs Puddy had interpreted the voice literally. If she did not 'tell the media', the UFO might come back. So she called several television channels, most of whom laughed and said, 'You must be joking, my dear.'

There were a few lights in the sky seen in the area on that night of 25 July. Maris Ezergailis, a twenty-one-year-old engineering manager at Mount Waverley, reported a blue streak of light '... like a meteor trail, but an unusually broad one, travelling horizontally'. Maureen Puddy was quite excited when she heard this, because she had described the disappearance of the object on the first night in very similar terms. But Maris saw his UFO at 10 p.m., providing a forty-five minute gap. If he *did* watch the disappearance of the UFO on the 25th, is there a missing three-quarters of an hour in Maureen's recall?

However, it is the events of 22 February 1973 that are really enlightening. All day, Mrs Puddy says, she heard a voice in her head saying, 'Maureen ... come to the meeting place.' After first going to the door to see who was there, and then dismissing it as imagination and going out shopping, she realized it was not about to stop and decided the aliens wanted to talk to her again.

Maureen Puddy telephoned Judith Magee, who had investigated her experiences the previous year. Judith and fellow investigator Paul Norman agreed to meet her on Mooraduc Road at 8.30 p.m. As Mrs Puddy's car arrived, she jumped out and said, 'I nearly ran off the road back there!' Judith calmed her down and then got into Maureen's car to drive to the precise spot where the previous events had taken place. As she clambered aboard, Judith Magee claims, 'I was experiencing a tingling sensation like a mild electric shock. It shortly passed off.'

Maureen Puddy explained as they drove that on her way to meet the investigators a figure had materialized inside her car, seated between the two front seats. It was totally encased in a gold foil suit. It quickly disappeared.

As soon as they reached the location on Mooraduc Road,

Paul Norman, who had been following in his car, got out and sat in Mrs Puddy's back seat. The three went over this story of the alien materialization. Suddenly Mrs Puddy grabbed Judith's arm and said, 'There he is! Can't you see him? He's in the same clothes.' Judith shook her head, Paul Norman too. There was nobody there. 'But you *must* see him!' she insisted. The investigators had to placate her by suggesting that her perceptions must be acting like a closed-circuit television and that only *she* could see what was happening.

Mrs Puddy said the figure was walking towards the car and had stopped by the left headlight. Paul Norman got out and walked around the front of the car, passing the exact spot where Maureen said the alien figure stood. She explained that the entity had stepped back a bit to let the investigator go by!

This bizarre abduction continued. Mrs Puddy said the entity was beckoning her to go with it. 'I'll come too,' Judith offered, but Maureen was clasping the steering wheel, adamant she would not move. At this the entity allegedly got annoyed and disappeared behind bushes. Moments later Maureen was screaming that she had been kidnapped!

Whilst still in the driving seat of her car, and with two astonished UFO investigators only inches away, Maureen Puddy was describing the *inside* of the UFO which she claimed she was now aboard: 'I can't get out. There are no doors or windows!' she yelled.

There was a large object like a 'mushroom' in the room, she said. Inside was like a jelly that was moving about. 'He wants me to close my eyes,' Mrs Puddy said. Almost immediately she relaxed into a semi-catatonic state. Here she described the room again, more as one would under regression hypnosis – with one rather obvious difference.

The experience did not last very long. When the figure left, Maureen said simply, 'He's gone. I can tell. It feels different.' The startled investigators gave her something from a thermos to soothe her and then drove her home. She gave more details of what she saw 'on the UFO', describing the 'mushroom' as like a compass resting on a suction cup, but the true nature of the events of that night is still a mystery.

There are many questions we might ask, based on what we know of other cases in this book. For example, did Mrs Puddy have a history of visionary experience? What has happened in the fifteen years since? Sadly these details do not seem to have been obtained, and Judith Magee reported in 1978 that Maureen, then aged thirty-three, had become widowed not long after the third contact and had since remarried and moved out of the state.

It goes without saying that this case poses many questions about other abductions. If there had been an outside observer in the car with the three Telford women, or police officer Godfrey, or indeed any of the Type III witnesses, would they too have seen the 'abductee' in a trance or cataleptic state whilst mentally believing he or she was inside a UFO?

One thing Judith Magee is adamant about. During the 'abduction' Maureen Puddy was *not* consciously fabricating. She said, 'I put my arm around her shoulder to try and calm her, and could feel tears on my hand. She really was upset.'

7 Abductions Around the World

It is time to look further afield and examine the evidence from other places where abductions happen.

Thomas ('Eddie') Bullard, with a doctorate in folklore from Indiana University, is doing the most exciting work in abduction research at present. He has compiled a statistical survey of over 200 time-lapse and abduction cases culled from reports. This incredibly detailed review was designed to test a number of hypotheses for his grant-aided project, notably whether these accounts should be viewed as objective, subjective or updates on folktales handed down through the ages.

I am most grateful for his kind assistance in my own work and for providing me with copies of large sections of his data. I shall refer to these several times in the pages to come, as they provide a scientific study conducted alongside the compilation of this book.

If a 'league table' of abduction cases is compiled, it is apparent that Eddie and I (from sources that overlap to an extent but which also have many differences) agree on the countries which are placed first, second and third according to the number of cases. The USA has far and away more abduction reports than anywhere else – more than fifty per cent of those in his survey. Britain comes third in both samples, although it is important to remember that the Bullard data is unfiltered, whereas I was rather more selective, rejecting many cases he uses if I was not satisfied with the investigation or the amount of data available. This may partly explain why my first three geographical groupings are much closer together in case totals than he found.

It is also necessary to bear in mind that we are not talking about the number of cases that have happened but the total that have been reported, investigated and then documented (normally in the literature of UFO research). There could be good sociological reasons why some regional totals are artificially low.

South America

Of course, South America (second to the USA in both surveys' totals) was where it all started, with the Antonio Villas Boas case. Remembering the warning to beware some of its media tales, I have still based this section on forty-two cases. They range from twenty in Brazil, through twelve in Argentina, five in Venezuela and scattered reports from Chile, Colombia and Mexico.

The anomaly here might seem to be Mexico. With a population of 73 millions, it is second in size only to Brazil, yet it is thin on the ground with abductions. Why? Because Brazil and Argentina are much larger in geographical area, and because Mexico has a population three times that of Brazil and Venezuela and four times that of Argentina. The one factor that these events appear to require is a region of low population density. (The British cases do not happen in the middle of London but in much more isolated spots.) Mexico may not be ideal on these terms, but if abductions were a purely sociological phenomenon, would there not be more cases there, because there are more people to report them?

Another immediately arresting fact about the South American cases is that they almost exclusively involve male witnesses. No fewer than ninety-three per cent of those claiming experiences were men. The average number of witnesses per case was also only 1.22 in my sample. This means that, with near unanimity, only the abductee was involved. In fact, thirty-six of the forty-two cases had one witness only.

Very few reports come before the Villas Boas case, although quite a few before it was published in South America. The breakdown into case types is also interesting: there were only two time lapses, and seven each of the entity and contact variety, but twenty-six cases were full-blown abductions, showing this to be the norm in South America.

Many of the 1950s and early 1960s cases were very much akin to the 1947 Villa Santina story from Italy. The aliens were clearly not interested in abduction. They effectively put up a sign saying, 'We do not wish to be disturbed.' Just as the unfortunate geologist in the Italian mountains suffered for his curiosity, so did many in early South American cases, often at the hands of a type of entity that seems to appear only in such reports: the hairy dwarf.

Typical is the case of two nineteen-year-old hunters, Lorenzo Flores and Jesus Gomez, who were at a quiet spot on the Trans-Andean highway in Venezuela late on the night of 10 December 1954. A disc-like object landed near them, and four figures got out. They were only about three feet tall and seemed to be covered in hair. Their one intent appeared to be to drag the young men aboard.

Not surprisingly, Lorenzo and Jesus were far from keen to oblige. Lorenzo hit one of the creatures with his rifle as it was pulling his screaming friend away. He said later: 'It felt like I hit a rock. My gun broke.' Jesus had by now fainted and Lorenzo was so concerned with helping him that he failed to see what happened next. The two men struggled to the police, who assumed they must have been attacked by animals as they were covered in scratches.

Be that as it may, another Jesus, in parkland near San Carlos, met a similarly intent dwarf as he walked off the road for a moment to relieve himself. Fortunately his friends came to the rescue and took him to a local hospital, in severe shock. This was just six days after the Flores-Gomez case. The hairy dwarfs seem to have faded from the scene after these failures. They rarely crop up in the later reports.

In the following chronological flip through some of the more interesting cases, note the excellence of medical follow-up in certain examples, which more than makes up for the press sensationalism. Abductions in South America also really 'took off' around 1968, just after the same thing occurred in the USA.

7 August 1965 – San Pedro de los Altos, Venezuela

This very important case was remembered immediately and was examined at once by experienced UFO investigator Horacio Gonzalez Ganteaume, but it was never publicized (so notoriety was not a motive). Only in 1969 was it published in detail by the investigator – in *FSR*, Volume 15, No. 2.

The witnesses were three men – two businessmen and a highly respected professional gynaecologist. They were at a thoroughbred horse stables thirty miles south of Caracas, discussing horses and investments in the late afternoon sun.

Suddenly, out of the blue comes a blinding flash of light. The men look up amazed and puzzled and watch as a glowing sphere, churning out yellowish light, drifts down. They can hear a soft humming that is inside their heads and is most peculiar. One of the young men turns to flee, but the doctor grabs his arm, saying, 'Don't run. Let's stay and watch!'

The sphere is now hovering slightly above the ground but at a comfortable distance away. From the side a beam shoots out, angled to the ground, and floating inside this, as if on an invisible lift, are two very strange beings, seven feet tall, with long, golden-blond hair and large, round eyes. Their suits shine as if made of metal. By now the men are all petrified, rooted to the spot by terror. The figures are walking towards them and a voice, inside their minds, is repeating slowly 'Do not be afraid. Calm yourselves.'

The aliens seem to perceive that the men are disturbed by this, and say, again in that voice, 'We are speaking to you directly.' Whilst his friends remain stupefied, the gynaecologist is determined to seize the opportunity and asks a series of questions aloud. All three men hear the answers in their heads.

The information which the entities offer is long and detailed. 'We come from Orion,' they say. They are here 'to study the psyches of humans to adapt them to our species'. They are also 'studying the possibility of inter-breeding with you to create a new species'.

There are other visitors besides themselves, three-foot-tall creatures 'that originate in the outer dipper', whose purpose is less clear. The men from Orion are friendly souls – they could have brought 'a wave-compressor capable of disintegrating the moon' had they wanted to; instead they brought only a few portable ones, 'powerful enough to halt a plutonium explosion'.

After more philosophical discussion, the memory of the witnesses becomes hazy. The next they know, the entities have gone.

The fact that this conversation comes prior to any of the current set of genetic engineering and inter-breeding cases makes one speculate whether, right at the start, a gynaecologist was deliberately told what was being considered. Also, the idea of two alien races would make a lot of sense out of the apparent confusion. Do we have six- or seven-foot-tall beings with blond hair and blue eyes and white complexions, or do we have ugly three- or four-foot midgets with huge eyes, slit noses and tiny mouths? According to this case, we have *both* sets of visitors, from different abodes.

Another visit by the tall beings was reported by retired airline pilot Alfonso Rey of Tres Arroyos, Argentina, in November 1972.

Rey said that he was watching television and reading when the set 'went funny'. He got up to fix it and began to feel strange (possibly the Oz Factor). As he went back to his seat, he saw the figure of a tall man wearing a green metal coverall seated in the armchair. He had 'Oriental eyes'. The visitor never spoke but during several minutes gestured once with his hands and refused a glass of water that Alfonso offered. When Alfonso touched it, the being felt insubstantial, as if made out of foam rubber. Alfonso followed the figure as it went out into the back garden. Here it looked at the sky and vanished instantly.

This ghost-like behaviour is very interesting, because it seems peculiar to these large entities. This was how Reg, the Keighley ambulance driver, reported the tall beings who appeared in his home in 1976, and this Argentinian case has remarkable similarity to Cynthia Appleton's living-room visitors in 1957.

Let us keep an eye on the behaviour of these two types of entity as we come across more cases in this book, bearing in mind that, if they were the products of imagination, there is no reason to expect them to follow a logical pattern. But if they seem to have a distinct mode of behaviour and features that are peculiar to one type but not the other, what does it mean? It might justify belief that two types of entity are abroad in this world with their own rules and game plan. The small ones come in UFOs, the tall ones often do not.

28 October 1973 – Villa Bordeu, Argentina

A detailed report in *FSR*, Volume 26, No. 4, 1980, shows how exhaustive medical investigations can be.

Just after 1 a.m. on the morning of 28 October 1973

twenty-five-year-old truck-driver Dionisio Llanca was fixing a wheel on a lonely road when he was struck by a yellow beam of light that paralysed him. Nearby was a hovering disc from which three entities, including one female, approached.

They had fair hair and large, slanted eyes and wore tight-fitting grey coveralls. Whilst he said only that they were of normal height, they are clearly the familiar 'tall' beings. Speaking in squeaky voices, they took a sample of blood from his finger, and he passed out, recovering consciousness about an hour later. Having no memory and being shaky on his feet, he was taken by a passer-by to the municipal hospital at Bahía Blanca.

The hospital records read: 'NAME – Not known ... SITE OF ACCIDENT – Highway 3 beyond El Cholo ... CAUSE – Says a very powerful light blinded him; that it was a flying saucer and that he remembers no more. Saw two very blond men and one woman ... LESIONS – Traumatism of the skull and right temporal forehead, with total amnesia.' Assuming that Dionisio must have had a crash or been hit by a car and knocked senseless, trauma specialist Dr Ricardo Smirnoff was called in.

Smirnoff said later: 'At first I thought he had been knocked down. In this business of flying saucers there are two attitudes you can adopt: either you believe or you don't believe. But I am obliged to admit that this case of Dionisio Llanca is very strange ... very extraordinary.

During the ten weeks spent attempting to resolve the truck-driver's problems, a consultant surgeon, two psychologists and four psychiatrists were involved. One of the psychiatrists, Dr Eduardo Mata, explained how, 'We tried as devils' advocates to *disprove* Llanca's story. But we failed.'

To attempt to relieve the memory, sodium pentathol (the so-called 'truth drug') was administered, and Dr Eladio Santos performed hypnosis. Dionisio recalled being in a bright room and being warned that the Earth was in danger of suffering a terrible catastrophe if people did not change their ways. He was told that the aliens had been coming 'to make a record for posterity' because they did not have any great faith in Earth people's survival potential. Since 1960 they had switched tactics and were now attempting to see how 'adaptable' people were, so that, if they messed things up here, the aliens might be able to rescue some strand of the race and transport it elsewhere.

Could a truck-driver really create such a plausible outline, especially one that seems to match so well what other cases show?

5 January 1975 – Bahía Blanca, Argentina

A clue as to what might have happened to Dionisio Llanca comes in the case of a railway employee, the father of a young child, twenty-eight-year-old Carlos Alberto Díaz, who claims he was taken aboard a UFO and remembers much more.

According to Pedro Romaniuk's investigation, Carlos was returning from a part-time night job as a waiter providing extra money for his family. It was approaching 4 a.m. Suddenly there was an intense hum. He was blinded by a beam of light, paralysed and found himself floating upwards. He lost consciousness to awake inside a strange room, with air coming through holes in the floor. As he tried to move away from them, he felt giddy and sick. A being approached that was normal in height and covered by a suit that hid everything (a balaclava-style helmet, rather like the one seen by the Day family in Aveley just three months earlier but completely unheard-of when Romaniuk investigated this case). The being was using a suction device to take pieces of hair out of the young man's flowing locks. He felt no pain. When he touched the entity, it had a texture like rubber (again a feature reported before).

The next memory Carlos has is of waking by the roadside. It was now 8 a.m. His watch had stopped at 3.50. Thinking the dazed man had been run over, a passing motorist took him to the nearby Railway Hospital at Retiro. When he realized this, Carlos was astonished. Retiro is near Buenos Aires. He had been found over 300 miles from where the light beam had struck him!

Mrs Díaz was already frantic, and she was very relieved to hear that her husband was safe. The police were called in by the hospital staff, but they could find no suspicious circumstances. As the team of doctors and psychiatrists worked on Carlos, his wife travelled to him by train. It took her the rest of that day, illustrating the distance of the young man's transportation.

The doctors found that the hair that was missing had been taken from Carlos's hair roots. They could not explain it. One doctor said he had naturally been incredulous when Carlos arrived, claiming he had been in Bahía Blanca just four hours before. But his scepticism evaporated when Carlos showed a copy of that day's *La Nueva Provincia*, a newspaper which he could have bought only in the early hours in that distant city.

Carlos Díaz refused all suggestions of publicity, but he would happily tell his story to investigators 'for free', so there is no way a charge of monetary inducement can be levelled. He said later: 'I don't know if you will believe me. If someone were to tell me, I surely wouldn't. The only thing I know is that this happened to me.'

25 April 1977 – Putre, Arica, Chile

This next case received extensive investigation at the time, and Chilean UFO researcher J. Antonio Huneeus gave an update briefing at the 1987 MUFON conference in the USA.

It is 3.50 a.m. on the cold, inhospitable desert plateau 12,000 feet above the small town of Putre. Here an army patrol of six conscripted men commanded by a regular soldier, Corporal Armando Valdes, is watching the night. Suddenly Pedro Rosales, the young soldier on sentry duty, spots two violet lights that are descending and bathing the ground with a glow. Is this an exercise or an attack? He alerts his commander, and immediately Valdes orders the men to screen the camp fire with blankets.

The object is now ahead of them, down a slope. It comprises a large central light with smaller lights at each side. The corporal calls to God for protection, tells his men to cover him and steps over a stone wall heading straight for the object. Soon he is swallowed into the blackness. The object disappears.

The despairing soldiers hold their ground, peering into the night. Then, fifteen minutes later, Valdes reappears – behind them – walking as if in a trance. He is muttering to himself, 'You do not know who we are or where we come from, but I tell you we shall return.' Then he collapses into unconsciousness by the camp fire.

The men care for him as best they can, as a cold dawn rises over the mountains. In utter amazement they can see that Corporal Valdes has suddenly developed a heavy beard growth out of nowhere. It looked as if he has not shaved in days. His watch has stopped at 4.30 a.m. but the date on the digital read-out says 30 April – five days hence!

The conscripts hustle their commander down to the town, where the local school teacher, Professor Araneda, immediately tapes an interview with the bemused man. Journalists flock to him, until the Army issues a command that Valdes must not talk.

Six years later a newspaper tried to revive the case. An Army communiqué confirmed that the events happened as alleged, but General Julio Canessa, Vice-Commander in Chief of the Chilean Army, advised that the only way to talk to Valdez was by order of President Pinochet. The paper gained permission, but all Valdez would say was, 'I do not recall anything of those fifteen minutes. They are a void in my mind. I do not even recall the words I spoke when I returned, but the kids in the patrol maintain I said them.' Then he added wryly, 'We must wait a little while. But I shall talk one day.'

We may never know what happened to Corporal Valdes, or whether it has any relevance to the abduction phenomenon, but the trend set by the previous cases and noticed independently by Hopkins in his American reports (and, indeed, if we are to judge by cases such as Karen's, in Britain) seems to have taken root in South America. That trend is for abduction for sexual procreation.

3 March 1978 – Fragata Pelotas, Brazil

On 3 March 1978 eighteen-year-old José Alvaro claims he was struck by a blue beam as he walked to a house in Fragata Pelotas, Brazil. He was on his way to check that it was locked for the night, because the owner (his father) was away. He never arrived, waking up in a daze sometime later, with the words 'The task is accomplished' racing through his head and strange images of war running like a picture show in his mind. He slapped himself and found it was now 4 a.m.

Two weeks later, after UFO investigators, including Luis do Rosario Real, had heard the tale, two hypnosis sessions were set up with psychologist Dr Palmor Carapecos. During these José 'remembered', being led into a room where a silver-haired, tall female entity with large eyes rubbed him down, forced him to have sex with her and then told him he would have another task to perform later.

Before she was told of these sessions, José's mother said she had had an odd dream. In this she was *told* that her unmarried son was about to become a father, but the child would be born on another world.

Much more interesting is that, before UFO researchers published details of the case, two stonemasons, living in the only building in the deserted area where José met the UFO, reported seeing a strange light above their houses that night. Additionally, a passer-by admitted he had seen the young man prone on the ground at the spot where he later claimed to recover consciousness. The traveller had walked past, assuming the youth was drunk or asleep.

15 October 1979 – Ponta Negra, Brazil

In a detailed investigation Irene Granchi provides one of the best reports of this type of case, involving two witnesses. One was a twenty-five-year-old male student who had visited Saquarema earlier in the day and left his driving licence there, causing him to travel back down the coastal highway from Rio. He was accompanied by Luli Oswald, the stage name of Margarida Henriquieta Marchesini, mother of seven and a well-known Brazilian concert pianist. She has also worked at a clinic for mongoloid children and is noted as a psychic healer.

On the way out along the coast road, the night has fallen. It is 9.30 p.m. and the rain clouds have cleared. For conversation Luli decides to ask the young man what he might do if he saw a flying saucer. At that precise moment, out at sea, three lights appear on a dome-shaped object.

Driving on in astonishment, they see the lights pace them into town. Are they stars or the moon, they wonder? Surely they cannot be a UFO? It would be too coincidental. Even so, they agree, on the return journey to Rio it would be best not to take any chances: they will follow the inland road instead.

But it does not work out that way. The man, who is driving, makes a wrong turn and they arrive on the coastal highway with little choice but to continue. It is now 11.30 p.m., and they want to get home as soon as possible. Suddenly, out of the sea lights climb, pulling the water into a towering mushroom that cascades down below. The car is faltering. The occupants are terrified.

Above the mountains to their side is a large pencil shape with orange windows on the edge. Three dazzling balls of white light roll down the slopes, heading straight for them, illuminating everything as they pass by. They look around in panic, trying to decide if they will be safer inside the car or getting out and hiding underneath. The decision becomes academic, as memory fades and they remember nothing more.

The two frightened travellers recover their senses still in the car, but it is further down the road, on a side track near a farm. In need of something to calm their nerves, Luli recalls a petrol station nearby that serves coffee until late. They go and order some from the attendant, but he points out that he does not serve *that* late. It is 2 a.m.

Five days later Luli contacts Irene Granchi, to whom she has been recommended by a local priest. As it happens, the MUFON investigator Bob Pratt is there at the time and becomes involved in the case. The car, a Fiat 147, shows heavy magnetization on one side. Luli's watch is virtually useless, gaining many minutes every day. For two days after the encounter her eyes have burned and she has been unable to urinate, suffering a burning sensation internally.

Luli Oswald agrees to be hypnotized, and Dr Silvio Lago carries this out at his office in Niteroi. An amazing story emerges.

As they drive along under the gaze of the UFO, they suddenly find that it begins to pull the car up in a brilliant beam. Luli screams and finds herself inside a room, with the car alongside. Standing by them are ugly creatures, with long, thin arms, grey skin and pointed features. Their mouths and noses are just slits. They are only about 4½ feet tall.

The figures are examining the now naked woman with lights. The beams in her ears hurt. Hair samples are pulled out, and there is a complete gynaecological examination. She is told (by telepathy) that they have contacted her because of her ESP. However (perhaps because she was past child-bearing age), she is of no use to them. They are interested only in the man – for 'research', they explain. He lies on a marble table looking white 'as though he is dead'. They are examining him sexually and taking samples. These aliens come from 'a small galaxy near Neptune', Luli is told, although she knows this to be absurd. 'It isn't real, but it happened all the same,' she reports to Irene Granchi later.

You may regard these cases in whatever light you choose, but it is hard to ignore them. There is an eerie consistency and a morbid kind of logic to these 'alien experiments'. It would not be difficult at all to put the jigsaw pieces together from such sample reports and form a general picture of what is 'going on'. Would that picture be so complete and uniform if these were merely individual fantasies?

Remember that we do not have only the South American data to rely on – this we shall see much more clearly as we continue – but in South America the evidence nonetheless continues to mount.

29 November 1982 – Botucatu, Brazil

Thirty-eight-year-old João Valerio da Silva says that he got up in the early hours of 29 November 1982 to get a drink of water from the kitchen tap and was struck by a beam of light and floated aboard a UFO. Strange creatures were there and he was approached by a naked woman who touched his cheek. He passed out. His family found him at dawn, flat out and naked on the floor. His clothes were in a pile next to him. His watch had stopped at 4.20 a.m. and he had red marks all over his skin.

João's wife and twenty-year-old daughter cared for him, and doctors were called in. But the investigation was complicated by poltergeist effects around the house (including saucepans rising into the air on their own).

Dr Luciano Stancka was insistent: 'It would have been impossible for him to have invented a story so rich in details as the one he related.' His penis had strange lesions on it, never noticed before.

14 December 1983 – Chapeco, Brazil

The most recent case reported, as I write, comes from Dr Walter Buhler and concerns a former Radio Chapeco announcer (now a cattle rancher), Antonio Tasca. He was abducted on the night of 14 December 1983 by the same pale-skinned beings with Oriental eyes (this one claimed she was called Cabala, from the world known as Agali). He had been chosen to spread the word because he had a 'cosmic mind'. A message 'you will never forget' had been planted in his subconscious by machine.

Antonio has no interest in notoriety and has lost all concern for material things since his encounter. He had marks on his back and was studied medically by Dr Julio Zawadscki, who said: 'The mysterious burns are inexplicable, causing no pain, erythema, fever or other symptoms of first- or second-degree burning.' They remain a mystery.

North America

Despite the differences between the USA and Canada, these two nations share the same continent, language and culture, so it would be difficult to separate them in this context.

My sample was virtually the same size as that for South America, as already explained, but there are many cases (at least a hundred) where I did not have enough information to feel confident in using them. Eddie Bullard does include some in his survey.

A number of general points are worth making first. The reliance on hypnotic techniques to retrieve memory is much more evident in both US and Canadian cases. This is due to the existence of a number of specialists who practise hypnosis and concentrate all their UFO activities on abduction research. Artist Budd Hopkins is the best-known due to his involvement in the Strieber affair and his two books on his investigations, *Missing Time* and *Intruders*. But he was not the first. Psychologist Dr Leo Sprinkle, at the University of Wyoming, called into the Herb Schirmer case by the Colorado University research project in 1968, has probably investigated more cases since then than anyone else in the world.

The average number of witnesses per case is also greater than in South America: 1.43. (For comparison purposes it should be noted that in samples of ordinary UFO sightings without entities this figure usually stands at around 2.5 witnesses per case.) The sexual distribution is very even, 50/50 male and female, within the limits of error.

Again for comparative purposes, note that the average age of abductees is around twenty-six in both South and North

American samples, suggesting (as Alfred Burtoo in Britain and Luli Oswald in Brazil discovered) that once you are past about thirty-five your chances of being abducted are pretty slim.

The cases which pre-date the 1961 Hill abduction have all been discovered since its publication. They usually involve witnesses who have reported subsequent abductions and, under the sort of intense life profile which Hopkins carries out, also claim previous childhood encounters.

7 October 1955 – Nebraska, USA

I am grateful to Dave Stewart and case investigator Don Worley for the tape of this session, reported by Jennie and explored under hypnosis by a female psychologist who did not wish to be named. Here is the story of the teenaged girl's abduction as it emerged later.

Jennie is in her bedroom when 'the explorer' comes. He is floating outside her window and telepathically wills her toward him. 'I really don't want to listen to him,' she says, 'because I'm trying to think I'm in a dream.' She asks how she can follow, but he glides back across the air to a 'laboratory' shaped like two 'dessert bowls placed together'. 'I can't see it really. It's not really there. It's in my mind, but I can't really see it with my eyes,' Jennie cries.

In her nightgown (a scene weirdly similar to Karen's bedroom encounter in Britain), Jennie floats out towards the UFO. She sees dirt and cobwebs inside the house wall as she passes right through it! The man tells her as they drift, 'We have business.'

The UFO is bizarre. It fades in and out of visibility, periodically allowing the car-park below to be seen. 'When it goes, you can almost see inside,' Jennie says in confusion. She glides in through the wall and immediately curls up at the cold. The Nebraska night air is chilly, but the inside of the UFO is like a freezer.

Jennie is now desperately trying to fathom out the way this man talks to her: 'I feel it .... He doesn't do long sentences .... He does words, thoughts … like 'not fear' … 'no hurt' .... If I said it like him, you wouldn't understand me.'

The man is '… tinier than four feet, but bigger than three .... The others inside are a little smaller. He has a tight white swimming cap on, with material like parachute nylon .... I don't think he has hair! The head is shaped like an egg .... The face is waxy ... real pale, pinkish, greyish .... It's like if you touched him you'd hurt him. The nose is just a tiny bump, like two black slits. The mouth is a slit. The eyes are like long slits with nobody home. He's being very stern ... but he's not angry. He means business.'

Jennie is told to get on a table of silver metal. 'I ask him where we're going and he says "Nowhere".' Clamps appear. She is trapped!

A helper alien arrives and hair samples are taken, then blood is sucked up through a little capilliary tube. 'I tell him it hurts and he's pretending he doesn't care. But he cares. He's smiling because he knows I know it really doesn't hurt. I only *think* it does.'

She returns to her room, and the alien goes. Next morning, when Jennie wakes, she remembers this as a vivid dream. 'Then I look out of the window and the elm tree is burnt. Pop says it was hit by lightning. But it wasn't.'

That is the sort of case which typifies American abductions, although it is not famous and has not even been published to my knowledge. Whilst the entities are clearly identical with those in most of Hopkins' cases and are precisely what Whitley Strieber says he saw, none of those things has effected Jennie. This session was recorded in 1984, long before Strieber came on the scene.

3 May 1968 – Westmoreland, New York State

Parapsychologist Professor Hanz Holzer records a fascinating case, similar to Jennie's, which involved a nineteen-year-old female nurse's aide, Shane Kurz.

Shane saw a UFO, and then woke in bed with her mother shaking her. Muddy footprints led up to her room from outside, and naturally Mrs Kurz was puzzled. This was at four in the morning of 3 May 1968, although it was 1974 before Shane wrote to the professor – that decision had been prompted by the aftermath, during which she had suffered nightmares, migraines and strange red rings on her abdomen and had not been menstruating for nearly a year. She was passed from Dr Roger Moore of Clinton to Dr Chantry, a gynaecologist in Utica, who was at a loss to understand her problems. Happily in February 1973 all suddenly became normal again.

In January 1975 Dr Holzer performed hypnosis on Shane in New York. This was six years before Hopkins published his first book and well before knowledge of gynaecological elements in abduction encounters became public. Holzer had published the case in limited form by 1976 (*The UFOnauts*, Granada) but it was barely known.

The hypnosis memory was a classic of modern cases. Shane is kidnapped into a room by figures that are small and have off-white skins and probing eyes but no hair. They insist that she get on a table, which she does not want to do (but has no choice). 'He knows me. How does he know me?' Shane asks, echoing a question many abductees pose. Then ova samples are taken through a long needle, and the being tells her she has been chosen to give them a baby. 'We are studying ... we want to see if we can,' they say.

Are we to assume that the rape which followed created the loss of her periods? Was this a hysterical reaction after the terrible trauma that was induced? Or is the repetition of the same hidden theme in another obscure case coincidence or the sign of a very strange form of psychological disturbance sweeping the Earth?

American cases have many other features found in global patterns so far: weird places of origin ('the galaxy of Guentatori-Elfi', according to what the tall, blond entities told one woman taken from a car near Norwalk, Connecticut, in 1973) and warnings about the Earth's future (a security guard and hospital technician abducted, again by the tall ones with long, thin faces, from Palos Verdes, California, in August 1971, and then treated to a holographic picture show of how the Earth might blow itself apart if the aliens don't prevent it).

6 January 1976 – Stanford, Kentucky

In a virtual duplication of the Telford abduction three women from Liberty, Kentucky, were taken from their car near Stanford.

This was one of Dr Leo Sprinkle's hypnosis cases. Forty-four-year-old Louise Smith offered few memories (as if she was held in a sort of transit state). Forty-eight-year-old Elaine Thomas was observed by the four-foot-tall beings. The youngest, thirty-five-year-old Mona Stafford, remembered much more. She was on the usual bed with her arms clamped down. The beings in white gowns were prodding and poking all over her body. 'My eyes hurt so bad,' she said. 'My feet are being bent backwards ... twisted.' She also felt something blowing up her insides, which very much suggests that gynaecological examinations went on, possibly ova sampling again.

None of the women referred to this aspect. They were all devout Christians and insisted on lie-detector tests. Detective James Young, the senior operator for the Lexington, Kentucky, police, performed the tests. He was vice-president of the association of operators and was highly skilled. Afterwards he was forced to admit: 'It is my opinion that these women actually believe they did experience an encounter.'

There are some famous cases in the USA, even before that of Whitley Strieber. The two that made the biggest headlines around the world were probably those at Pascagoula, Mississippi, and Snowflake, Arizona.

11 October 1973 – Pascagoula, Mississippi

The Pascagoula case occurred during the same wave as that which produced Mrs Verona's 'rape' in Somerset. It involved two fishermen, eighteen-year-old Calvin Parker and forty-five-year-old Charlie Hickson. There were many classic features, such as the floating sensation and medical exam by a giant eye device. However, the men remembered details without hypnosis and went straight to the local police after being deposited back on the dock. Their captors were small and were described as having horrible wrinkly skin, although this may have been some form of uniform.

The two men were left alone in the police station for some time, unaware that hidden microphones were recording them. It was anticipated that this would catch them discussing the hoax. Instead it caught Calvin Parker praying! In all the conversation between the two men, no hint emerged that what they were reporting was anything other than a horrifying abduction. Sheriff Fred Diamond and Captain Glen Ryder, who investigated, said afterwards, 'If they were lying, they should be in Hollywood.' Later the two were given lie-detector tests by the Pendleton Detective Agency in New Orleans. Operator Scott Glasgow was determined to prove that they were faking. Instead they passed easily. 'This son of a bitch is telling the truth!' Glasgow exclaimed afterwards.

Parker found it hard to cope with the pressure and ended up under psychiatric care with a nervous breakdown. His older companion seemed better able to handle things. I saw him in the USA in June 1987 and he struck me as a quiet man, grateful to his family for rallying round and being understanding. 'I had to learn to accept what happened,' he said, 'because I saw what happened to a man who could not accept it. This thing almost destroyed his life.'

Charlie Hickson has not made money and was insistent that, 'I make my living with my hands. I had a chance to make a million dollars like Whitley Strieber back in 1973. I was offered all kinds of money to let them do a movie. I declined. I am still declining. Making money is not what this experience is all about.'

5 November 1975 – Snowflake, Arizona

The other case is the Travis Walton abduction, controversial because of newspaper prize money awarded later, when it was voted the 'most evidential' report of the year. Was this a motive?

Travis was a twenty-two-year-old forester in a group of men on a commission near Heber. Time was running out before penalty clauses for late delivery of timber cost them dearly. Sceptics later alleged that this was one more reason to invent an incredible excuse for their failure.

Supposedly, on 5 November 1975 a UFO appeared over the woods. Travis leapt from the truck to investigate, and his companions fled when a blue beam shot from the disc and knocked the young man senseless. Returning minutes later, after recovering their composure, there was no sign of Travis.

There was a massive search when his disappearance was first reported to deputy Sheriff Chuck Ellison ninety minutes after the abduction. He took a search party back, including Duane Walton, brother of Travis, who was one of the foresters. Three of the party *refused* to go into the woods that night. According to Ellison, 'One of the men was weeping. If they were lying, they were damned good actors.'

Crew chief Mike Rogers refuted all the claims of the sceptics, notably aviation journalist Philip Klass, that they had cooked up the tale to extend their contract. He says they actually lost money because many of the trees they had already felled had to be damaged when they tore the woods apart looking for the lost man.

Five days into the search the six eye-witnesses insisted on taking lie-detector tests with the Navajo County Sheriff, Marvin Gillespie. They were tired of the local rumours that they had murdered Travis. Cy Gilson, of the Arizona State Office of Public Safety, carried out the tests on 10 November. One man was too worked up for it to be valid, the other five were good subjects. Gilson said: 'I think they *did* see something they believed was a UFO. I gotta say they passed the test.'

Travis Walton returned late that same night, claiming he had been dumped some miles from the forest by the highway into Heber. He recalled many details of being inside a room, examined by five-foot-tall beings who looked like 'an overdeveloped foetus' with mushroom-coloured, hairless skin, domed foreheads and large eyes (very familiar captors). There were many memory blanks in his story, which had all the usual features.

Later Walton took and passed a lie-detector test. He was also studied by Dr Gene Rosenbaum, a psychiatrist of Durango, Colorado, whose conclusion was firm: 'This young man is not lying. There is no collusion involved. He really believes these things.'

There do not seem to be any important differences when we look at cases from Canada. Of course, considering that these American stories must be equally influential north of the border, this is barely surprising.

16 October 1971 – St Catharines, Ontario, Canada

Jack is an electronics expert and member of a rock group, born in 1955. After reading Budd Hopkins' *Missing Time* he set up sessions with New York psychiatrist Dr Aphrodite Clamar and later with behavioural therapist Dr Susan Schulman in Toronto. Investigation was by the group CUFORN (a detailed report appeared in *FSR*, Volume 29, No. 3, 1984).

An amazing array of experiences appeared: aged two, Jack is taken from his push-chair by beings with 'big black eyes'; inside a room he is put on a table, examined by his thoughts being siphoned and told this is a test to determine if he is suitable for some purpose.

Then he and his father are abducted together in 1961. (The father was put under hypnosis by Dr Schulman and he recalled the story as well.)

At the age of ten Jack and a friend, Jim Voss, are taken from Twelve Mile Creek near their homes. The beings are four feet tall, with cream skin, a slit mouth, small nose and large head.

But this is only a prelude to the October 1971 events when the rock group are returning from a party at 1.30 a.m. Suddenly lights appear ahead. They think there is a road accident. Then the van is pulled out of control to the side of the road, where one of the entities urges them to get out. Some of the six resist, and in the confusion one of the entities knocks the drum kit over and it rolls out of the van. By telepathy the entity asks for an explanation of these puzzling instruments.

The small creature explains they want to test the youths, but they have time and facilities for only three. The others are to be left in the van whilst Jack, Sam, the drummer, and Calvin, the bass player, are taken aboard. In a sort of drugged or controlled state Calvin is led into another room, and Sam and Jack are made to take their clothes off and lie on the familiar table or bed (Jack calls it a 'cot'); then they are examined by small instruments and lights. Hair and blood samples are taken, and the aliens answer a few questions. Where do they come from? 'A long way away ... if we told you, you would not understand.' What is the correct religion? 'There is no correct religion on Earth.'

Before being escorted back to the van, the aliens are interested in Jack's bag in which he carries his recorders. He explains how they work and offers a small one which, to this day, he believes to be somewhere not on Earth. One wonders if the aliens have learned how to play it.

This experience by musicians is noteworthy, because there have been several others by musicians.

A woman in Virginia reported her encounter to me, when she

and her young child lost time after being hit by the ubiquitous beam of light from a UFO. She went on to write and record music about love and peace for a group called 'Phoenix'. She believes this comes from the abductors.

A British New Wave group, A Flock of Seagulls, argues similarly. They have had chart success with songs such as 'Run' and '(It's Not Me) Talking', which recount their supposed contact experiences. Middle-of-the-road group 'Hot Chocolate' had a number-one hit 'No Doubt About It' describing their close encounter.

It is interesting to notice just how many very successful modern musicians are involved in UFO ideology. Kate Bush writes hits about the paranormal and has been president of a West Country UFO group. David Bowie has even played an alien in the film *The Man who Fell to Earth* and has written hit tunes about UFOs, such as 'Starman', reflecting quite accurately the problems of the abduction ('There's a starman waiting in the sky .... He'd like to come and meet us but he's scared he'll blow our minds'). Bowie once worked for a UFO investigation group and helped put together its magazine. Another group, Glasgow's CE IV, have even named themselves after the abduction phenomenon (the close encounter of the fourth kind). They write lyrics which concern UFOs and result, so group leader Brian McMullan tells me, from several close encounters, the most interesting being on 13 July 1985, the day of the 'Live Aid' famine-relief concert.

A detailed look at these cases and more of the evidence for a link between abductions, contacts and music were published in my article 'All spaced out on cosmic rock' (*The Supernatural*, April 1987). Within days of its publication, Rikki Peebles won the British heats for entry into the Eurovision Song Contest with his tune 'Only the light', which he says describes his own close encounter. Afterwards he developed ESP and had lyrics dictated to him by the aliens! This is so exactly what I reported in my article that one might be tempted to envisage collusion. Perhaps Peebles read my piece and made his gimmick up? Not so: the song was entered months before my article was published and clearly *is* about a UFO encounter.

Peebles was promised by the aliens that he would win the competition for Britain when it was staged live in front of 100 million television viewers during May 1987. He came thirteenth, showing that another feature of these abduction cases was repeated once again: alien predictions are unreliable.

Africa

The North American cases were very much like those from South America. They included all the standard features and differ in really only one major way: there are far fewer sightings of tall, thin aliens. In fact, ninety per cent of the reports refer to the small, ugly, large-headed figures, the type Spielberg chose for his movie – *because* of this stereotype and not to create it.

This again reinforces suspicions of a real phenomenon. If it shares so much across cultures, is this because it is essentially the same thing being observed around the globe? The true test of that comes now, as we look much further afield to where American civilization has had less influence.

Do they have abductions in Africa? On a glance at the map we might expect it to be ideal. There are huge areas of desert and forest where no habitation is possible. Elsewhere, especially by the coast, there are quite large cities. Countries such as South Africa (31 millions) compare in population size with many European and South American nations, but most of the people who live there are indigenous Africans whose distinct cultures have their own traditions. Thus if we assume that abductions are subjective, a product of ourselves (that is, a form of psychosis), they will either be absent or very different, because of the gulf between folklore, history, lifestyle etc. If they are not …

The first thing to note is that African abduction reports are rare. Eddie Bullard found only three for his study. I doubled that total, but it is still far from spectacular. In the case from Dar-es-Salaam, Tanzania (p. 23), the classic small entity was supposedly seen many years ago (but reported much more recently), but the witness was a British woman then living there as a child. Other entity sightings are known (from South Africa, for example) involving Europeans living in Africa, but there are also ordinary UFO reports, some quite impressive, witnessed by indigenous Africans. Mostly these come from South Africa, Zimbabwe, Egypt, Libya and Morocco; some of the events, which occurred around oil fields in the northern half of the continent, have attracted interest from US security services, who have compiled dossiers on them.

The problem is that contact with the USA and Europe might affect the data.

Spring 1951 – Drakensteen Mountain, South Africa

A good example of this sort of case happened in spring 1951, according to the witness, but was not reported to and published by investigator Juan Benitez until 1978. It involved a British engineer working at Paarl, just inland from Cape Town in Cape Province, South Africa.

Having trouble with his car, the man took it for a late-night drive up a mountain, the Drakensteen, to test out his home-made repair job. Half way up, in a deserted spot, a man emerged from the shadows and insisted, 'We need water.' Since there was only what was inside the car's radiator, the engineer offered to take the stranger to a mountain stream he knew.

On the drive he realized that the man was unusually small, just under five feet tall. He wore a brown coat, as if he worked in a lab, and seemed to have no hair at all on his smooth-skinned face, and domed head. He also spoke with an odd accent.

Collecting water in an oil can, the engineer drove the mysterious stranger back to the pick-up point. Here he now saw a disc-shaped craft hidden in the shadows of the mountain. He was invited inside and shown a table or bed, on which lay one of the entities. He had supposedly been burnt – hence the need for water. For the man's kindness, the aliens allowed their benefactor to ask questions. Naturally he wanted to know how their UFO worked, but the reply was not helpful: 'We nullify gravity by way of a fluid magnet,' they explained. So where did they come from? They looked at the sky, pointed and said melodramatically, 'From there!'

This tale is not exactly convincing, but it is typical of what we might call voluntary abductions, where there is no forced entry into the UFO. The absurd regularity with which the aliens seem accident-prone and can find their way across the universe but cannot navigate in the dark to a mountain stream has an air of plausibility. Who would invent such a daft thing, especially when it recurs so often? It featured in the Cynthia Appleton case from Birmingham, where the entity burned a hand and wanted water to bathe it in, and then in the USA when, in 1961, Joe Simmonton received 'cardboard' pancakes in return for water given to aliens. All these cases were in the pre-abduction phase and seem to have been 'set-ups'. It is very much as if they were tests on witnesses. Or was it just the way the delusion then operated? If so, why has it altered so drastically, to become steeped in sexual and genetic experimental overtones?

There have been cases that fit the description of an abduction, most notably that investigated by Carl van Vlierden on 31 May 1974 (*FSR*, Volume 21, Nos. 1 and 2, 1975).

1974 – Umvuma/Beit Bridge, Rhodesia (Zimbabwe)

The witnesses were a twenty-three-year-old man named Peter and his wife Frances, who was making the long desert drive overnight from Salisbury, Rhodesia, (now Harare, Zimbabwe) into Durban, South Africa. Both are Rhodesian born and bred.

Between Umvuma and Beit Bridge their car was taken over by a strange force after they saw lights in the sky. It glided without being driven past scenery that seemed not to be real. This illusionary journey has been found in other cases – for example, the Oxfordshire abduction (p. 87). Later the Rhodesian couple realized there was a time lapse, and that the drive had used far less petrol than it should have.

Frances seems to have slept through all this, and the suspicion was that the sleep was induced. Peter was clearly the key. He had undergone a close encounter at the age of thirteen, when taking time off school to go with his father, a truck-driver, on a delivery run. At Shabani a UFO appeared, and on arrival at their destination it was found that all the electrical equipment they were ferrying had been destroyed by a power surge.

Peter had also undergone frequent floating dreams and what we would call out-of-body experiences, which have often cropped up in these stories. He compared the memory of these (which ended after his teenage years) with the 1974 abduction: 'It was like I was travelling in a dream .... I had lost trace of time. I felt as though in a coma .... I can remember nothing. I seemed mesmerized by the solid, unending stream of road .... It was like driver's hypnosis.'

This last remark shows that he was familiar with the fact that, when one is driving on long, straight roads with no passing traffic or other visual stimulation, it is quite possible to travel miles as if in a trance and not recall it. He saw both the similarities and the differences.

The silence of this Rhodesian car ride was clearly the Oz Factor, showing that Peter was in an altered state of consciousness at the time. This led to regression hypnosis in December 1974 by Dr Paul Obertik of Durban. It produced a fairly normal abduction story, although with some differences. The being 'beamed' into the moving car and then showed Peter the UFO by manipulating his mind. He saw a 'laboratory' where they put humans they took aboard. The beings said they came from 'the outer galaxies' and that they appeared in whatever form the mind of the witness was capable of accepting. Their form, as he saw it, was that of a human with hairless skin and no reproductive organs.

Peter was also told a great deal about alien purposes on Earth. There are thousands living among us, but they never interfere directly – usually they simply 'influence others'. But they have 'changed the Earth' in the past, and will do so again, to end war and introduce 'their way of doing things'.

Interestingly he was also informed that they do *not* travel across space but across time. The speed of light restricts space flight, so 'They come back in time to get to the Earth.' Then, in a typical contradiction, there was a quite nonsensical story from the 'aliens' about coming from 'twelve planets of the Milky Way'.

There are sufficient grounds here for comparisons with other cases, but why do we have so few reports? I am grateful to Cynthia Hind, MUFON co-ordinator for Africa and undoubtedly the most skilled investigator on that continent. She answered many of my questions.

'In Africa, it is often difficult for me to contact the remote villagers who might have had an experience which would be of interest, and it is generally only when some European or more sophisticated person comes in contact with someone from the village that I hear about the experience.' She explains that often these stories are then reported in traditional terms, linked frequently with ancestral spirits and so forth, and are obvious as a UFO event only in her eyes. 'Could it be that many sightings never come to our attention because in their country of origin they are explained away in a totally different concept?'

Without being racist, she points out that Africans are often difficult to interview: 'I have found them quite terrified of supernatural involvement. They have *never* tied it up with anything from another planet or dimension. It is something beyond their understanding.'

But she does have completed investigations, such as the following.

15 August 1981 – Mutare, Zimbabwe/Mozambique border

Central southern Africa is covered by dense forest and is far removed from Western civilization. On 15 August 1981, in the early evening, about twenty foresters were returning to the village from their day's work when they saw a ball of light drifting across their path and light up the La Rochelle estate. It climbed a disused fire look-out tower and then suddenly flared up. At that point most of the foresters fled, but the head man, knowing his duty, stood firm. He was Clifford Muchena, and Cynthia Hind made the long trek to interview him and later the estate owner, who was as puzzled as the foresters.

The ball reverted to just a glowing disc and then proceeded to float around the estate. Such was the light emission that Clifford rang the fire alarm. Then three tall beings appeared, silhouetted against the glow. The forester thought they were estate workers, but they wore strange suits. Clifford walked towards them and called out. The beings turned towards him, and there was a brilliant flare of light that hurt his eyes. A terrible force struck him down. Crashing to the ground, he was dazed and paralysed but recovered his senses an unknown time later. Looking up, he saw no men and no ball of fire.

Clifford vividly describes the paralysing light beams often reported in pre-abduction cases (for example, at Villa Santina in Italy), yet he had no way of knowing about these. He spoke a local dialect, Mashona which lacked words for the key concepts. He recalled crawling on hands and knees after being struck but could not describe the colour of the odd suits worn by the figures. He picked up a silver coin and pointed to that – his language had no word for silver.

Cynthia Hind found others who saw the beings. They

described a 'torch' they had held, but no torch she could shine at the trees was bright enough to match it. They knew nothing of spacemen, and she could not even convince them that men had walked on the moon – 'only God does that', she was told.

Cynthia took a break from her globe-trotting in October 1987 to advise me of latest developments in Africa. She stressed the complexities of different styles of government in so many different tribal nations bordering on each other, with often less than friendly intentions, which makes life very tough for a UFO investigator.

She was following up a new abduction claim from South Africa, involving fifty-six-year-old Jean Lafitte, from Roodepoort, who alleges contact over the past thirty years. He says that his abductions began in 1956 when he was paralysed, taken into a room by beings with large heads and no hair and medically examined on a table. Then they implanted something into him to activate his psychic abilities. They said they came from the Pleiades star cluster and that there was only one other alien race visiting Earth, who were from Alpha Centauri. They are not hostile and are here only to study us – indeed they lent a helping hand, minimizing the effects of the 1986 Chernobyl nuclear plant explosion in the Ukraine, by 'mopping up' excess radiation.

Cynthia was also quite surprised to find that there has been a sudden wave of bedroom contacts. The wife of an army man from Bulawayo, Zimbabwe, claims to have been taken to a strange room and shown how the aliens are manipulating life on Earth. They did not like some of the things they had to do in the process, but these were 'necessary'.

In another case a woman from Harare was pregnant at the time of her visit, but no longer. Cynthia hopes to study the woman under hypnosis.

But the most evidential case so far concerns a woman from South Africa who was sitting drinking coffee one day when a strange man appeared, dragged her into a tunnel that suddenly appeared in her wall and took her to a clinically white room where she was paralysed, put on a table and lost consciousness. Next day she was covered in bruises where her arms had been restrained.

It may not be very long before the African evidence is as extensive as that from other continents. It is already large and has features identical to cases seen so far, so that it must give cause for concern.

Asia

Asia covers a very large part of the world and includes countries such as China and India with enormous populations. Yet abduction cases are almost non-existent there. Eddie Bullard seems to have just one case and recognizes the problem this creates. He refers to 'the Cinderella factor' – the fact that versions of this popular fairy tale occur all over the world, albeit with crucial differences, proves that it is just a folk tale. If the same were true in UFO abductions, we would have significant reason to assume that no real events lay behind them.

It has been difficult to find more than pointers that there *are* major similarities with the African data. My Asian sample is about the same size (six cases), so it is not valid in any statistical sense. It is merely suggestive of patterns. Fundamental once more is the question of why there is so little evidence.

Is it because UFO abductions do not happen? If population size were the only criterion, there ought to be thousands of them.

Perhaps a real alien race interested in breeding experiments does not want non-Caucasian stock. We cannot rule out such a seemingly absurd idea. One wonders, for example, if Clifford Muchena had not been an African, would he have been 'felled' as he appears to have been, or 'picked up'? The miniscule number of non-white people who claim UFO encounters is undoubtedly important, because it even occurs in societies such as America and Britain where there are significant numbers of immigrants. Surely the odds say that some ought to experience abductions? In this lurks a key to the whole mystery, because either the abduction is a product of the mind of Western white people or some intelligence behind the abductions prefers to contact such people. That it may be the latter possibility is suggested by the fact that there *are* cases of non-whites meeting UFOs. Also, the Hill case featured both a white and a coloured individual, as if the two were being evaluated side by side.

Cynthia Hind's point about remoteness applies in Asia too, as does the general lack of English language. For instance, I have worked several times with Jun-Ichi Yaoi, a Japanese television producer who is also a UFO investigator. He assures me that a number of abduction cases do exist in Japan, and by and large they are similar to British stories.

One curious taste the Japanese have is for television shows that feature their citizens in wild hysterics. I was a little disturbed, but not astonished, to observe the Japanese television method of handling a UFO abductee: stick him in front of an audience, wheel on a hypnotist and get the witness to relive the trauma in the typically vociferous fashion of his countrymen. The tape I saw depicted one such experiment, with the clearly terrified young man, in his twenties, leaping and thrashing about as he screamed that the light was shining at him. While I picked up little of what went on, it was impossible to avoid comparing the poor man with British witnesses I have seen first-hand, suffering the same terror.

Here is one Japanese case for which we do have details, thanks to another investigator, Jun-Ichi Takanashi.

3 October 1978 – Sayama City, Japan

It is late evening and twenty-nine-year-old snackbar-owner Hideichi Amano has decided to talk by CB radio to his brother. So he drives to the top of a mountain where the air is clean and reception good. In the car he takes his two-year-old daughter, Juri, for the ride.

Suddenly the interior of the car begins to glow. Hideichi sticks his head out of the window but sees nothing. Looking back, Juri is flat on the seat with an orange beam shining on her abdomen. In a moment of terror he registers this and the pressure of a metal object against his right temple. He looks up and stares straight into the eyes of a weird being under five feet tall with almost no nose.

High-pitched noises scream at him. His head fills with thoughts and images like a rapid-action slide show. He is totally paralysed.

An unknown period of time passes and the glow fades. The figure has gone and the car and radio (which failed while the encounter took place) suddenly spring back to life. Hideichi's watch had stopped at 9.37 p.m. In panic he flees down the mountain without even looking back at Juri. At the foot of the slope he suddenly remembers her and turns. 'I want a drink of water, Papa,' she cries, thankfully none the worse for the experience.

Later, after Hideichi has gone to bed with a pounding headache, he recalls that the aliens have planted something into him which will 'vibrate' when they need him again. They *have* promised to return.

This case follows the standard pattern. But we must decide why it is one of so few known from the two billion inhabitants of China, Japan and India.

One bizarre Indian case was investigated by BUFORA's Mike Wootten but unfortunately the Indian businessman who was involved refused permission for the taped interview to be publicized. He had good reasons. All I am at liberty to say is that it involved an incident in a rural area of the country late in 1958, when he and another witness saw a UFO land in broad daylight. Four entities emerged, just three feet tall and walking as if they had difficulty. Two boys who had been playing in the same rocks were then found to have disappeared. One was discovered dead with several organs removed as if by 'expert surgery'. The other was found in a catatonic trance and survived five days in hospital, before he died without speaking. Mike Wootten saw no reason to disbelieve this story, and it is a pity more cannot be said about it.

China is another country where no definite abduction cases are known, but contact cases occur there. An example, reported by one of the few Chinese investigators, Shu Jia Lin, would not seem out of place on a British or American road.

13 October 1979 – Lan Xi, China

It was 4 a.m. on 13 October 1979 when twenty-five-year-old truck-driver Wang Jian Min nearly ran into a parked car as he drove towards a hill near Lan Xi in Chekiang province. The car driver explained that he had just seen a strange craft and was too scared to drive on. Bravely leading the way, Wang took the two vehicle procession up the slope and confronted a blue glow and a dome straddling the road. Beside it were two small figures, under five feet tall and dressed in silver. They had bright glowing lamps or torches on their heads. Wang stopped and turned his headlights off, thinking perhaps they had created an illusion. The object was still there, so he rooted around beside him, found a crowbar and leapt into the night. But the UFO and figures had gone.

14 February 1975 – Réunion, Indian Ocean

Yet another indication that contact is not desired in the Third World comes from the story of Antoine Sévérin, a twenty-one-year-old shop assistant on the small island of Réunion in the Indian Ocean. At 1 p.m. on 14 February 1975 he saw a domed craft in a field at Petite Ile. Some small figures about three or four feet tall clambered out and knocked him senseless with a white beam. Then the entities made off with soil samples.

Antoine was left without speech and with poor vision for several days. He was studied by the local police and by Dr Henri, a psychiatrist, who decided these were hysterical reactions to a terrible shock. Commandant Legros and Lieutenant-Colonel Lobet of the police published their findings in the French journal *Lumières dans la nuit* a few months later. Lobet said: 'It turned out that [Sévérin] is normally a well-balanced, well-behaved individual of excellent character, and not given to the perpetration of hoaxes .... None of the persons who have testified to us believe Antoine Sévérin to have been hallucinating, and they all take his statements seriously.'

There may be some cases of Asian abductions for sexual purposes. A story reported in *FSR* in 1971 tells of a twenty-seven-year-old called Machpud who met a strange, beautiful woman in Bandjar, West Java, Indonesia, in June 1969. She took him to her 'house', which turned out to be a large room which glowed 'with an abundance of light'. The woman clearly wanted intercourse, and Machpud was in no mood to refuse. But then he lost consciousness and woke in Gunung Babakar forest with his clothes on a tree. He was dazed, disorientated and helped by a passer-by to the local equivalent of the psychiatrist, a medicine man. Machpud was none the worse for his exploits.

One of the few Asian researchers of such cases is veterinary surgeon Ahmad Jamaludin, from Pahang, Malaysia. Ahmad kindly gave me his thoughts on the phenomenon.

He does not believe that the amnesia in abductions is caused by the entities. He thinks it is a result of a time difference between the reality in which we live and the reality in which the abduction occurs. 'If in our time fifteen minutes are missing, how would you accommodate a two-hour abduction into one's life? ... It is impossible, so is automatically cancelled out.'

Ahmad had not found a single abduction case involving the stereotype aliens reported in other countries, despite widespread searches among the Malaysians, some publicity and a number of examples of UFO sightings. But there are several reports which he believes to be the Malaysian version of the same phenomenon. These are known locally as kidnap by the 'Bunian people'. As he explains, 'They are very much like humans (although small), and during the abduction process only the victim can see the abductors. Others nearby usually cannot see these mysterious entities at all.' He thinks that whilst in the West the entities step out of UFOs in Malaysia, the same inter-dimensional creatures just step directly out of their reality into ours. He summarized one of his cases for me.

June 1982 – Malaysia

The witness was a twelve-year-old girl named Maswati Pilus (children are frequent victims of Bunians it seems). It was June 1982 and she was going to the river behind her house at 10 a.m. to wash some clothes. Suddenly she was confronted by a female being about her own size. All the sounds of the village nearby disappeared, and it seemed as if only she and the entity existed. The strange creature invited her to see a land – which Maswati had no option but to agree to. She felt no fear and found herself in a bright and beautiful place (she recalls little more). It seemed as if time had whizzed by. She was discovered by frantic relatives on the ground, unconscious, not far from her home and right where they had been searching, but two days had slipped by.

Not only are there indeed many parallels with UFO abductions in this story, but it is also oddly like the disappearance of Bernard and Angela in Britain and the Chilean soldier at Putre.

But then again it is also rather akin to the folktale of Rip van Winkle, who fell asleep and woke to find that years had passed by. Perhaps he was abducted too!

Australasia

Australia and New Zealand are fascinating places to study because they are in 'midway' states. Between them they have only twice the population of London (some 18 millions), yet Australia in particular covers vast areas. They also share a good deal on a cultural level with Britain and America (British heritage and language and US-based currency and customs). So what type of abduction pattern manifests here?

We have already looked at the story of Maureen Puddy (p.126). This was a sort of 'mind' abduction, and that is interesting, because the watchword of Australasian ufology is certainly that there are psychological answers to these cases. Practically all research is conducted with that premise to the fore. This is totally different from the situation in the USA, where the belief that abductions are proof of alien contact is so dominant that it would not be unfair to call it an obsession.

In June 1987 I gave a paper to a conference at the American University in Washington DC, where abduction cases were discussed in depth. I spent many of the sessions with industrial chemist Bill Chalker, an investigations co-ordinator. I was interested in his reaction to the almost wild and semi-hysterical zeal which greeted abductees such as Whitley Strieber and Kathie Davis (a terrified young mother who is the key witness in Budd Hopkins' book *Intruders*). In one session the packed audience of many hundreds cheered out loud at the very mention of the name Strieber and literally jeered and hissed, as if he was some pantomime villain, when sceptical journalist Philip Klass was mentioned. Bill and I could not help but wonder if all sense was being sacrificed. This was certainly not how abduction stories would be handled in Australia, he assured me.

A perusal of Australian literature failed to reveal any typical abduction cases, although there are some borderline examples, and Eddie Bullard included eleven in his study. Some of them are very doubtful though. One, reported by Professor Holzer, alleges rape by a handsome alien, but it is so unlike any of the other reports and so scanty on detail, that there seems every reason to presume it a hoax. The young Melbourne woman who claimed it reported it to a New York journalist, which is by no means the normal response of these witnesses.

30 October 1967 – Mayanup, Western Australia

Keith Basterfield reported on this case in *UFO Research Australia Newsletter* (*UFORAN*). It is a good example of a possible abduction, well investigated.

Mr Harris is married with three children, in his early thirties and a wool-classer by trade. After paying off some of his crew, he is driving at night to another outpost. Suddenly his car loses all electrical power. 'My machine just stopped!' he exclaimed. 'Motor, radio, everything went dead. I had no feeling of deceleration ... the car just instantaneously came to a stop.'

Above him in the sky is an oval object projecting a blue tube of light onto the car. It hits him full on, and this creates the sensation that he is being watched. As he grips the steering wheel tight, he is aware of, and puzzled by, the Oz Factor: 'Everything around the place was dead quiet. There wasn't a sound of any sort.' Suddenly the light switches off, the car is moving again without transition, and he drives into Boyup Brook. His Omega watch is mysteriously several minutes slow. He also begins two weeks of intense headaches.

There is no real prospect that this story, familiar as it is, could be based on prior abductions. Although Mr Harris wished no publicity, he did see his doctor because he considered he might be ill. Our knowledge is based on a twenty-three-page transcript of the investigation by this man and Dr Paul Zeck, a Perth psychiatrist. They looked for evidence of temporal lobe epilepsy (which can cause brief lapses of consciousness). They found none, but of course this would not have accounted for the effects on the watch. Dreams and hoaxes were also considered and rejected for sound reasons.

One thing that was *not* done was regression hypnosis. In 1967 such an idea was unthinkable in Australia. We might speculate whether this case would have provided hidden memories.

Lack of abductions in the record might be caused by undiscovered cases such as this. In other words, they *are* there.

The memory simply never surfaces beyond a certain point. It is widely held amongst researchers that the number of abductions lurking in the data might be staggering.

We have some interesting reports from Aborigines and Maoris, the true natives of Australia, and New Zealand. At Awanui, in New Zealand, on 22 February 1969, one Maori met several of the tall entities with the thin faces, very white skins and long fair hair. They were in a wood beside a big glow. The Maori had no idea what was happening, so he fled and carried out a local ritual for warding off spirits. This seems to have consisted of running around in a circle whilst urinating.

Back in Australia, at Kempsey, New South Wales, a thirty-four-year-old Aborigine might have been abducted the hard way. It was 2 April 1971 and the town had been inundated with UFO sightings. At 10 p.m. the man went for a drink of water in his kitchen when a small being appeared outside the window. Immediately the man felt a force that sucked him into the air, and he blacked out. He was discovered cut and shaken on the ground seven feet below the window, which was smashed. An iron bar across the middle of the window was unaffected, and how this reluctant abductee got through the thirty-two by ten-inch hole remains a mystery.

Thanks are due to New South Wales researcher Mark Moravec for his help on this section. He has provided one very enlightening example of an Australian abduction.

It happened on 27 September 1974 at Jindabyne and concerns a professional musician, aged nineteen, and a boy aged eleven, out hunting animals in the Snowy Mountains. There was a big white light on the horizon emitting a low humming noise. Apart from that, everything was deathly quiet. Not even the animals uttered sounds.

That was the size of the story, until 1983, when the now adult second witness began to have dreams in which he relived the experience and remembered more details. He had also become 'very psychic'.

In these dreams he saw himself being pulled towards the object in slow motion, floated inside and laid on a table. Instruments were attached by tall, thin, grey beings to 'gauge how electromagnetic fields related to my body'. The older man had tried to resist and was carried away. When later he was returned, he appeared 'drugged'. The youth also recalls seeing a desolate landscape which he took to be the aliens' home world, and he had a feeling of being 'used like some specimens and dumped'. Interestingly, he told Mark Moravec, 'We were not afraid but we were not really conscious either.'

The Jindabyne case is so similar to other abductions in so many respects that one might suspect a reason why few are reported from Australia. Regression hypnosis is almost never used to try to relieve memory blocks. This might prevent all but the occasional case of spontaneous abduction memory or dream recall.

Why is it not used? Because, as Mark Moravec says, Australian researchers do not consider it reliable. He has many excellent reasons, some of which we shall look at later. One of them especially relates to the Jindabyne case. The night after the 'abduction' the two men were still at the site and saw 'the UFO' again. A big white glow on the horizon was there for 1½ hours and was almost certainly a bright star or planet. Had they seen something different the night before? Or, as Mark believes, did this misperception of a very mundane object trigger a psychological experience?

Europe

In continental Europe there is a large number of countries geographically close together but separated by different languages. This is a lot of ground to cover, as Europe is relatively rich in material.

Since the Le Verger case of 1944, France and Belgium have produced some very sophisticated UFO research. There is a definite tendency to consider abductions as extreme psychological events and to seek mythic and fictional relationships. Apart from *Lumières dans la nuit*, there is also a journal called *Ovni Présence* (*The UFO Presence*), a deliberate play on words stressing the internal origin which many French-speaking researchers accept). This often contains in-depth interviews of a philosophical nature.

Because they are hard to penetrate unless your French is very good, few people in Britain or the USA truly understand why these views are adhered to. It is doubly ironic because France is the home of the only *admitted* Government-funded UFO research establishment. The team is based at the space centre in Toulouse and does not employ psychiatrists or psychologists. Its use of engineers and astronomers seems to imply that officially there is less scepticism of the physical reality of these cases. Judging from the voluminous published work and the many lectures given by leaders (for example, the present one, Jean Velasco), they spend time on very tangible aspects such as landing traces. Abductions, at least on the face of things, are virtually ignored.

This problem is compounded because the few cases from the French-speaking world which receive promotion abroad tend to be absurd. A major Paris abduction was given global publicity because the witness vanished for several days and then turned up again. Both the Government team and independent UFO researchers quickly saw through the hoax, but its unprecedented promotion by the press creates the belief that all abductions are as devoid of reality.

In 1987 there was amazing hype for one of the very few Swiss UFO cases, the claims of a farmer Eduard Billy Meier that he has met aliens, had long discussions with a beautiful flaxen-haired space beauty and taken hundreds of photographs of their craft. The hype began with a book by journalist Gary Kinder, *Light Years*. This had originally been contracted as a serious work. Why Kinder fell for this audacious and highly controversial story would perhaps be more worthy matter for his fellow journalists. And, of course, the promotion of this wild story fosters delusions about the real evidence.

Despite huge media publicity in the USA and Britain (including magazine cover stories), it is simply *not* true, as was claimed, that Meier's photographs have baffled the experts. A glance at them shows just how many are taken pointing straight at the sun, a very obvious way to obscure detail. Original investigators found models in Meier's possession identical with the objects on his pictures – he claimed that he made them after taking the photographs. Finally, William Spaulding conducted computer enhancement on the photographs in Arizona, using technology developed out of NASA's deep space probes. He claimed that these show the string holding up the models. I have seen the computer images, and that is certainly what they look like to me!

What is disturbing is not that so-called sincere journalists and reputable sources promote this junk. That is sadly inevitable, so long as the idea remains fixed in media circles that fake claims are not news, while promoting them as real makes people happy. Less easy to accept is the illusion this generates. Other abduction tales are *not* the same. For the sake of the thousands of victims, the press had better start realizing that very soon and stop treating the subject as fodder for sensationalism. It requires the sort of press treatment that would be given to serious crime: hard research.

There is no visual evidence such as the Meier photographs. No one – and this has to be stressed – no one has ever taken a photograph that shows UFO entities or a UFO on the ground. Not one photograph has passed the tests and been accepted by committed UFO researchers. Of course, this is extremely important when we come to consider what might be going on. But I refer to it here to emphasize how cautious abduction researchers are. Neither they nor the witnesses are making extreme claims. The responsibility for that falls on the shoulders of others who see no harm in making a story out of falsehoods at the expense of the truth.

The real truth lies only in these confusing, contradictory and baffling cases which cry out for understanding. There are many good ones in France.

July 1965 – Valensole, France

Maurice Masse, a forty-one-year-old farmer, was up at dawn tending his crops when a whistle announced the landing of an egg-shaped craft. At first he thought it was a new Air Force helicopter. Then some 'little boys' got out. They were four feet tall with 'pumpkin' heads, thin mouths, big eyes and white skin. It should be appreciated that they were described *before* the Betty and Barney Hill abduction was published in the USA (late 1965).

Masse went to confront them as they were picking samples of his lavender. One took a tube from its side and fired a beam, whereupon the farmer collapsed onto the ground, paralysed. Later he slept for much longer than normal (a quite common after-effect).

This again shows the pre-abduction pattern found all over the world: Masse was rejected in identical fashion to hundreds of others not required by the abductors. But *was* he not required? His subsequent admissions to researcher Aimé Michel are revealing: 'I did not tell all. But I have already said too much. It would have been better had I kept it all to myself .... This would not be understood. You have to undergo it to understand it. I have not told anybody. Not even my wife.'

In a letter to me, Aimé Michel hinted that this was indeed an on-board abduction, for which Masse simply does not want publicity. If so, then it begs the question of how many other cases where the witness appears just to have been 'zapped' hide a deeper experience?

A good example of the astonishing consistency of these entities and their actions is shown in the following Belgian case.

7 January 1974 – Warneton, Belgium

A thirty-one-year-old businessman is returning from a refresher course on a wet border highway one evening. He is playing his new radio cassette when it, the car engine and the headlights all fail. Annoyed, but assuming it to be no more than a dead fuse, he cruises to a halt. As he is about to get out, he spots a strange craft with a dome on top sitting by the road.

Two figures come towards him from the object as he stares in disbelief. They are about 4½ feet tall; each has 'a pear-shaped face' with greyish skin, a small nose, slit mouth, large eyes and long arms. One approaches the car and points a tube-like thing at the driver. He describes hearing a high-pitched whistle and a feeling like 'an electric shock at the base of my cranium'. The next he recalls is seeing the entities scurrying back and the object rising and then just popping out of existence. It has gone as if at a magician's command. Perhaps the arrival of another car on the road has disturbed them. The driver rushes over to the potential abductee. He is still paralysed in a position of holding the door whilst about to get out. Gradually he recovers his senses, and then he continues his journey.

The second driver *saw* the UFO. He explains that he lives nearby. 'I will go home, bring friends and search for proof,' he tells the still shaken victim. 'If I find it, I will talk. If I find nothing, then I will stay silent because nobody would believe a word of this.'

Lest it seem that complete abductions do not occur in France, with its ultra-sceptical researchers, here is a case that proves they do.

11 June 1976 – Romans, France

Twenty-year-old Hélène Giuliana worked as a maid in the house of the mayor of Hostun. Returning after midnight from seeing the celebrated movie *One Flew Over the Cuckoo's Nest* (about mental delusions), her Renault failed as she crossed the bridge at Romans. A big orange glow poured from the sky and then suddenly vanished. She drove home – but it was now 4 a.m.

The mayor told the story, and investigators arrived. When Stéphane Dey conducted hypnosis five weeks later, Hélène 'remembered' being carried into a room by small figures with big eyes and ugly faces, clamped on a table and examined, particularly around her abdomen. Sound familiar?

Because so few cases have been translated into English, it is difficult to know the full extent of abductions in Europe. There are bound to be more than in Eddie Bullard's study (twenty-one) or my data (thirty-two). They are fairly evenly distributed across France, Spain and Italy. There are a small number from Scandinavia and from the USSR and other Communist states (where, for obvious reasons, much less is known). The one anomaly appears to be Germany, where there are very few good UFO cases and where I could not find a single reported abduction. We might speculate endlessly on the reasons, but if there really are UFOs, Germany (heavily dominated by troops and at the front line of military surveillance) might not be on their 'tourist schedule'.

There is one quite amusing Austrian case claimed from September 1955 by twenty-seven-year-old Josef Wanderka. His encounter was with the tall, thin ones and he literally drove his moped up a ramp and straight into their arms! After he had apologized for his intrusion, the aliens explained (in fluent German) that they had arrived 'from the top point of Cassiopeia' and then insisted he tell them how the moped engine worked.

Josef was much more interested in lecturing them on anti-Nazi politics, and they appeared to get very bored and dumped him back out again, after suggesting he create a movement to lead the world into equality.

Whilst the French cases are certainly homogeneous, the Italian sample is characterized by a number of recent cases of 'tall monsters'. These are unknown elsewhere, have received a lot of publicity and, I suspect, may well be dubious. Removing these, we are left with two very clear sets of data that again describe in perfect unity the tall, thin entities and the small, ugly beings.

Typical of the latter is the case of a peasant woman, Rosa Lotti. At dawn on 1 November 1954 she was journeying into Cennina, as it was her day off from the farm. She was carrying her one pair of shoes and stockings so as not to get them muddy on the trek through the woods. Suddenly she came upon an upturned egg and two beings about three feet tall with huge eyes. They grabbed her, took one stocking and a bunch of flowers she had picked and threw them into their craft, 'jabbering in Chinese'. She was paralysed by a beam but then found herself running away. This suggests a time lapse. Some village boys had intruded onto the scene and saw this last part, including the entities and the UFO.

The tall beings appeared in July 1968 to a twenty-five-year-old man at the Grodner Pass in the Dolomites. He noted their domed heads, beautiful Oriental eyes and telepathic communication. They also had a small robot working for them. The contact was very benign, with useful information passed on, such as 'We come from a planet in a far galaxy' and 'Everything is God.' They also issued the dire warning that a pole shift was due soon, the Earth's crust would crack, and life would be in great danger. These bits of friendly advice from outer space typify the actions of the tall, thin ones.

Everywhere in northern Europe the pattern is the same, from Finland to Poland and Sweden to the Soviet Union.

23/24 March 1974 – Lindholmen, Sweden

Håkan Blomqvist published a report for AFU, a Swedish research team, on the case of a young man, Harald Andersson (a pseudonym). He was getting some fresh air when a voice inside his head made him walk in a certain direction. Then a blinding light appeared and he threw himself to the ground, shielding his eyes. The next memory he had was of standing on his front-door step confronted by his wife, who was scared because his cheek was burnt.

Dr Ture Arvidsson at the Danderyd hospital performed hypnotherapy during April and May after the physical effects had subsided. Here are some verbatim extracts from these sessions: 'The light! Light! … I'm blinded. There is no light such as this. I throw myself in the snow. Now I am lifted straight up … they take me!' Blomqvist points out that the man was screaming and kicking in terror under hypnosis whilst he described these tall, hooded figures. Then he tried to fight them off as they attempted to put a device against his forehead. 'They put an instrument [on me] … I am not allowed to say [anything].' But he cannot escape. They press it on his head, and there is a burning sensation. Then the entities promise they will see him again, and he passes out, to awake on his doorstep.

After the events, Andersson began to have premonitions and disrupt electrical equipment simply by going near it. Dr Arvidsson said of his work with the man: 'To me it is completely inexplicable.'

Moving across the Iron Curtain, Zbigniew Bolnar reported to the Center for UFO Studies in the USA (*IUR*, November/December 1983) a study of farmer Jan Wolski, who saw something at Emilcin, Poland, on 19 May 1978. Jan had never heard of UFOs and described his experience in simple language. His horse and cart were stopped by beings with slanting eyes. They took him up into a 'bus in the sky', which hovered slightly above ground level and was reached by a 'tube'. The entities helped him to undress and were fascinated by the workings of his belt buckle. Then they performed a medical examination and let him go. Whether it was sheer accident that this case came out and it was considered safe to allow such an uneducated man free memory, we do not know, but Wolski remembered the whole episode in full detail and needed no hypnosis. He was examined by sociologists and psychologists at the University of Lódz, who found that he was apparently telling the truth.

A few days later, during what appears to have been an Eastern

European wave, one of the few known Soviet abductions was reported by Anatoly Malishev, a high-ranking officer in the Red Army. Needless to say state suppression of UFO data being what it is, the report given to Nikita Schnee, one of the few Soviet scientists allowed to discuss UFO cases with the West, is most unlikely to be hoaxed, so it is well worth studying.

May 1978 – Lake Pyrogovskoye, USSR

Anatoly was walking on the shores of the lake when suddenly two entities appeared in front of him and spoke by telepathy. Unhappily we have no details of their appearance, except that they wore dark, cellophane-like suits (seemingly very akin to those in the Cynthia Appleton case.) The aliens talked to him for a long time, refusing his request that they help him fight the evils of the world, such as capitalism. 'It would not be of any value if we helped the poor,' they claimed, 'because then we would have to help the poorest of the rich and then everybody.' This was part of their reason for not interfering. They told him that they came from another galaxy and were biding their time until the Earth was ready for full contact. Finally he was given a drink which he said tasted like lemonade with salt in it. Several other witnesses have described an identical liquid, and it appears to be an amnesia-inducing agent. Anatoly asked why an advanced civilization such as theirs did not drink alcohol and – in what may be the only example of an alien joke – they said, 'Perhaps if we did, we would not *be* such an advanced civilization.'

When he was deposited back by the lake, Anatoly's memory was hazy. Returned home, he felt as if he had been 'in a dream' but recalled parts of it. He was advised by his wife to say nothing '... or they will put you in gaol' but he had to tell the authorities, because the memory block had caused him to forget his assigned duties. The authorities were naturally unconvinced and thought it an excuse to evade court martial, so he was examined by psychologists, put under hypnosis and given lie-detector tests. No evidence that he was fantasizing or lying came to light. He described things more fully, and they had to let him off.

2 April 1980 – Pudasjarvi, Finland

Aino Ivanoff was driving her car in the early hours of 2 April

1980 when it was surrounded by mist and she found herself in a room. She was then examined on a table by small entities. They explained that war was evil and that she should support peace groups. They also sadly recorded that they were unable to 'beget our own children'. Once again the gynaecological angle is stressed to a female abductee in a land far removed from American hysteria. This case was obscurely published soon after it happened and was certainly not known by any of the witnesses in Britain or the USA now relating tales of alien genetic experiments to breed hybrid children.

As a final emphasis of these points, let us look at the Spanish data. I am grateful to Vicente Juan Ballester-Olmos for all the time and trouble he took on my behalf preparing reports. Vicente is a financier for the Ford motor company in Valencia, although qualified in physics at university level. Over the years he has undoubtedly been the leading Spanish investigator, producing numerous scientific papers and several excellent books. Indeed his 1987 *Encyclopedia of Close Encounters with UFOs* (prepared with Juan Fernandez Peris) is illustrative of the sophistication of research in his country. It is a mammoth catalogue, detailing several hundred cases and providing every conceivable statistical analysis. Even IFO (Identified Flying Objects) cases are separately catalogued and assessed. I can think of no other country where it would be economically viable to produce a mass-market book of that complexity.

Of his cases, about forty contain UFO entities, thirty-five per cent being the small ugly ones and fourteen per cent the tall, thin visitors (the rest were described as of normal height but mostly relate to the smaller-stature entities). Analysis of the time of day when these events occurred showed that the vast majority centred on the period from 11 p.m. to 4 a.m., which a quick scan through this book will show is amply verified virtually everywhere else in the world. Abductions are a nocturnal experience by an overwhelming margin.

Ballester-Olmos adds a weighting factor to his cases, a percentage score formed by multiplying the number of data bits by the witnesses' reliability and then by a probability score for its potential to be explained. One of the highest values for an abduction is awarded to the following case.

28 January 1976 – Bencazon, Spain

Just after midnight twenty-four-year-old farmer Miguel Carrasco was walking home from his girlfriend's down a dark lane when he saw a powerful beam shoot from the air where a strange craft hovered. Miguel began to run but two tall, thin entities emerged, blinded and paralysed him with a beam and he then awoke on his front-door step at 2.30 a.m. He was banging and screaming, 'The men from the star will come back – let me in and shut the door!'

The police were called and they brought in the local doctor, Francisco Calero. Seeing a strange burn on the farmer's cheek, he immediately summoned a taxi and drove with Miguel to the Hospital de San Lazaro in Seville. Here Dr Mauricio Geara observed and treated him. The marks turned out not to be burns at all and faded after about seven hours. Later the puzzled physician said: 'We don't really know what they were due to.' Note the considerable parallels with the case from Sweden reported previously.

5 February 1978 – Medinaceli, Soria, Spain

In another case – of which Ballester-Olmos is more sceptical although colleague Antonio Ribera supports it – a thirty-year-old vet named Julio said he was out with his pointer dog during the early hours of 5 February 1978 when he suffered a time lapse. Dozens of sessions followed with a psychologist, a hypnotherapist and Dr Jesus Duran, a psychiatrist. From these quite a tale emerged, involving Julio's being blinded by a light, led into a room and calmed by a voice in his mind that reassured him.

The aliens are the tall, Nordic type, and they want to borrow his dog for an examination. The dog, Mus, is more concerned with doing what dogs do naturally – all over the UFO! Eventually the dog is calmed and the aliens tell Julio that they may as well examine him too, since he is there. A full medical involves taking blood, gastric juices and semen samples. Then he suffers a black-out and finds himself back in his car, where he sits for hours.

Julio's eyes hurt – he has been told that the large eyes of the aliens cannot cope with the bright light of our sun, which is why they usually come out at night. Their world is a dark, spoiled place. Ours is a wonderful treasure trove, a rare oasis of life in the mostly uninhabited universe. It is this rarity that is attracting them here to experiment and take samples before we make a mess of things as they did. However, they are not the only visitors, Julio was told. There is also a bunch of small, ugly brutes who are somewhat less interested in the finer things of life and the beauty of earth. They have a strange idea about biologically reprogramming humans and seem determined to do it whatever we think.

It may just be coincidence. Julio may have been very well read and made it all up, fooling the doctors who studied him, but this supposed alien scenario of two races visiting us, from different worlds, with their own individual way of doing things, fits remarkably well. It mirrors the extraordinary case material we have found throughout this book – in a very disturbing manner.

8 The Abduction Pattern

It is now time to see where we stand with all this mass of confusing data. Do the cases agree or disagree with one another in enough detail to offer hints about an explanation to account for them? Major disagreements and lack of pattern would, of course, support the idea that the abduction phenomenon is a kind of story with inevitable individual variations. Major similarities would be hard to explain in this way and might imply that an objective experience of some sort was responsible.

Eddie Bullard found that seventy-nine per cent of his cases began with the sighting of a UFO (the others usually started with a beam of light). But how common are UFO sightings and what do people think about them? We can answer this by looking at several Gallup poll surveys conducted into the question.

Most of these surveys have been carried out in the USA, but it is interesting to compare them with one 1987 Gallup survey conducted in Britain. This found that only about sixteen per cent of women and twenty-three per cent of men accepted the existence of UFOs, and that only about five per cent admitted to having seen one. That is still over 2 million British citizens (although, because nine out of ten UFO reports turn out to be misperceptions of one form or another, this and all other similar results should be stepped down a decimal place).

Even so, 200,000 unexplained encounters with UFOs in one small country would be staggering enough. As most UFO sightings are never reported by the witness, that total has support from the known size of existing archives – for example, those held by the major national organization BUFORA (about 15,000) and those retained on the files of the Ministry of Defence since 1962 (believed to be about the same number, if one reasonably extrapolates from figures recently given in the

House of Commons, following questions by Conservative MP Sir Patrick Wall).

Of course, very few of these are abductions. But abductions might well be far less likely to be reported, basically because they are so extraordinary. Without any form of proof to support them, the witness could well feel great reluctance to reveal an experience. The very high percentage of known abductees who prefer anonymity, compared with witnesses to simple UFO sighting, seem to endorse that view.

Gallup survey figures for the USA exist over several years. The average of 1973, 1978 and 1987 surveys (there were no major changes) shows about ten per cent claiming a sighting and fifty-three per cent accepting their reality (with only twenty-nine per cent not accepting it, the rest being unsure). One very interesting finding here was that, the higher the calibre of education, the more likely the person was to accept the existence of UFOs. That might not be what one would anticipate.

In 1984 Budd Hopkins offered some clues towards the number of abduction cases in the New York City area. There were sixty-eight cases, twenty-five of which had been fully studied and shown to be abductions. Eleven other cases he had researched under hypnosis turned out not to be abductions, showing quite clearly, as the British Gaynor Sunderland case revealed, that abductions do not always come to light simply by taking a UFO witness back to an event under the influence of hypnosis.

Hopkins' figure was gathered by quite intensive searches and provides the suggestion that there might be one abduction for approximately every quarter of a million people. This would assume that he has discovered every case there is to discover in New York, a most unlikely premise. But juggling with those sums would give us, for instance, thirty-two abductees in London, about 220 abductees in Britain, and 1000 in the USA. Even these minimum figures are quite disconcerting, and they may have to be up-rated considerably if the views of some investigators are justified.

Abductions do appear to hide within seemingly innocent sightings at times. It is perfectly possible that thousands more exist in countries such as Britain and the USA, where even the witness does not suspect anything.

In Eddie Bullard's major folklore study of over 200 abduction events, he tried many ways to test the data. He found very large degrees of consistency, but he also found differences, notably in the types of entity observed. To try to combat this, he created a 'top fifty' abduction list based on the detail of the case, the calibre of the investigation, and the reliability of the witness. From this he was able to determine the most trustworthy abduction profile. It would not be sensible for me to reveal this in detail, because it remains an invaluable research tool for the future, to test against reported cases. Three things Bullard was particularly interested in were the way in which events differed nationally, their changes across time, and the internal format of the abduction.

What he means by this last point is that there is a very specific order to an abduction story. It begins with the capture, moves on in many cases to the examination, passes through several phases, often includes some form of communication of a message and ends in clearly defined ways. Obviously, the capture has got to come before the return, but if, for instance, abductions were nothing but invented stories, there is no good reason, it seems, why the order of other elements should not vary. Why not have a chat with the aliens, then be medically examined, for example?

In fact, this pattern is exceptionally consistent, far more consistent than chance could possibly decree, Bullard finds.

So what about the changes across time? Two things are important here. If the cases are just stories, they should even out into a stereotype theme, as folklore does. 1987 abductions ought to be much more homogeneous than, say, 1967 abductions. They are not.

The other key is the influence of well publicized cases. In 1988 we might imagine that new abductions would naturally draw upon the Strieber case as the model. In the past, prominent cases like the Betty and Barney Hill saga or the Pascagoula abduction should effect stories that come after them. In fact, there is virtually no detectable influence.

Finally, the national spread. Here there is rather more ground for dispute. Bullard did find, and the data in this book largely concurs, that the American standard alien (the little ugly man with the large bald head) was rather less standard elsewhere, and Britain was notable for its taller entities (almost non-existent in Bullard's US sample). Beyond that, however, the similarities vastly outweighed the differences. Culturally the abduction does not vary, as it should if it is simply a form of folk tale.

Bullard said of his work in this area: 'Advantage has always gone to the story prospect where possible. If abductions *are* stories then unreliable reports should compare with reliable reports as one and the same, but they (largely) do not. If abductions *are* stories then the accounts should branch off into a different national version for each geographic area, but they do not. If abductions *are* stories the investigator should be able to impose an individual style on them ... [that] outcome does not occur. If abductions *are* stories they should change according to an expected pattern over time, but their history is steady instead, even to the point of opposing external influences.' He believes that, 'The story hypothesis shows itself to have struck out at every turn.'

As a folklorist this naturally perturbs him, because it has obvious implications. However, as he told me in a recent letter, 'The high number of human or tall-humanoid occupants among reports from England [sic] and South America ... are differences particularly difficult to square with the hypothesis of an objective abduction .... The fact that most elements of the abduction story are alike everywhere casts doubt on the traditional story hypothesis, the fact that some differences appear calls the objective hypothesis into question.' Neither answer fits very well.

Let us attack the question from the data in this book, for it seems to offer some important clues.

The entities seen all over the world settle into two groups (less than ten per cent of cases do not fit into one or other). We have met these many times over past chapters, but let us consider them more specifically.

There are the small, ugly beings. These are between 3½ and five feet tall, have large, pear-shaped heads, big, round eyes and slit noses and mouths; they are usually hairless and often wear greenish uniforms; skin is sometimes said to be grey or wrinkled. Many witnesses have used their own words to describe these beings – for example, 'like a little five-year-old lad' (Alan Godfrey, Britain), 'like an overgrown foetus' (Travis

Walton, USA), and with heads variously described as 'like a lamp', 'like a raindrop', 'like a mushroom' and so on. An identikit of these beings is easier to compile than it would be from a group of witnesses to a burglary. The lack of variety is staggering.

Then we have the tall, thin ones. They are almost always said to be six feet tall or more. They have very pale skins but are often said to be oddly beautiful. Calling them Nordic or Scandinavian is not uncommon, possibly because of the long blond hair often observed. They have eyes usually said to be 'Oriental' or 'cat-like', not infrequently blue or pink in colour. Clothing tends to be silver or grey suits. They are normally described as much more human in appearance than the small aliens – perhaps that is why they are sometimes called 'normal'.

This truly remarkable division into just two types of entity is possibly the most amazing fact of all to contemplate. If these cases *are* the product of the human mind, the scope for aliens would be as wide as the range of entities in science fiction. Why are abduction cases so restrictive?

Of course, one obvious possibility would be that there *are* just two types of entity who are doing the abducting. However, the small, ugly creatures sound rather familiar from folklore. They are the gnomes or the elves. The taller ones have more in keeping with magicians or 'wise ones'. The comparisons are not exact or without their problems, but they are noteworthy.

There is more useful information to be gained by looking at what these beings do in the cases cited. Whilst there are again similarities (both occasionally abduct people to carry out medical examinations, for instance), there is a very definite behaviour pattern common to each type, and that pattern does not change around the world.

In a staggering eighty-two per cent of the cases involving the small, ugly beings, the normal first response is to paralyse a witness with a beam of light. This is often from a hand-held implement and commonly produces unconsciousness. Many cases go no further than that, but we might suspect that this is just the first phase and that later abduction sequences might be found if we probed for them. It may be that the differences in American cases (where more medical examinations are known) are apparent only because the investigators have been persistent enough.

Commonly in these cases the small beings are said to be not

exactly friendly (although rarely particularly hostile).. They can be likened to scientists dealing with animals in an experiment, with no wish to hurt them but with no special privileges being offered either. Messages of any sort are rarely given. It is all usually a case of getting down to business, taking samples of this and that.

The behaviour patterns of the tall, thin ones are dramatically different. Only twenty-eight per cent of these cases involve attack by a light beam and resultant paralysis or unconsciousness.

These beings are characterized by their magical properties. They are often said to materialize inside rooms (for example, in the Cynthia Appleton case) or to abduct in an out-of-body state (as with Karen in Dukinfield), Instant disappearance and the demonstration of such tricks as projecting images onto walls are also frequently reported, as are the awakening of psychic abilities in witnesses after the events. It is not uncommon for witnesses to confuse the reality status of these dreamlike incidents.

The tall entities come over as kindly and 'god-like': they enjoy talking about philosophy and conveying messages. Some of those messages can be treated as tongue-in-cheek, such as the typical story of the home planet, which is usually complete nonsense. Again they sometimes say that we would not understand if they told us where they did come from. Their other messages are of more concern, as they refer to despoiling the Earth and the hazards of nuclear war. They seem to convey a concern for us and, although direct intervention does not appear to be their way, tips and advice are sometimes given. Very interesting are those reports where the tall ones seem aware that the small, ugly beings are also coming here and do not share their way of doing things.

These two scenarios may involve reading too much into a few hundred cases, and there may be an alternative to accepting them as proof that two types of alien being are coming to visit us. They may, for example, represent two different 'necessary myths' within the human psyche, although, the likelihood of that is barely aided by Eddie Bullard's findings. If there *are* two types of being, this would almost certainly go a long way to reconciling the few differences he found in his research. That might make it overwhelmingly probable that abduction cases are more than simple stories.

9 Discovering Abductions

During the weeks in which I have been writing the final draft of this book, researchers in Britain have discovered three new abduction cases. In their different ways they teach important things about the phenomenon.

One case, from Altrincham, Cheshire, is being investigated by Roy Sandbach and myself with the local team at MUFORA. It involves a graphic designer – who naturally has a very good visual imagination. This ability to shape images in the mind seems important, if we consider the number of people in artistic professions who experience abductions or examine the often quite delightful handwriting of many abductees.

Details of this Altrincham case are not important at this stage, as investigation is just under way, but the witness, apparently without any background in the subject, has seen one of the small, ugly chaps in his bedroom on two occasions, once having a message fed directly into his subconscious mind. Because he is a highly intelligent man, he has analysed these experiences (which occurred in October and November 1984) very thoroughly.

Two illustrations of this are helpful. First, he is short sighted, yet had to screw up his eyes to see the figure just as he would if it were real. As he, quite logically, explained, 'I thought about the possibility of this being a hallucination. But hallucinations are surely routed past the eyes and are internal things. So why did it follow all the rules of my distorted eyesight?' A good question, as is his contrary observation that, when the figure vanished, it disappeared in a flash and, 'If it had been a solid body, it would have left a vacuum of displaced air. This gap would have sucked more in and this should have created noise. Yet it was totally silent.'

Another case came to our attention in a quite different way. There was no suspicion of alien contact on the part of the witnesses, nor, when I received the original report a few days later, did I suspect anything either.

29 April 1987 – Swansea

On 29 April 1987 a twenty-six-year-old model, now mother of four-year-old Hannah, was returning to her home near Swansea from a night out with her boyfriend. It was 10.30 p.m. As he put the car away, she heard Hannah say 'ghosties', her word for anything strange or frightening. When the child's persistence caused her mother to look, there, low above the garden, was a grey oval shape surrounded by windows or lights. It was seen for only seconds before it blinked out. The boyfriend saw nothing except bright reflections on the car bonnet.

I suggested to BUFORA's South Wales co-ordinator of investigations that he look into this, and Tony Mann did so. His brief report noted that the woman had admitted she was 'a little drunk', as they had stopped at several pubs on the way home. So we were really left with just Hannah's story. Tony quite rightly said the case ought not to be rated highly.

However, there were some hints in the case which cried out to me because I was working on this book. Whether they would have done so in different circumstances, I do not know.

First, Tony had checked with the local police. Nobody else had seen anything. The way in which close encounters are so isolated, even on a popular housing estate, is a clue to watch out for. Secondly, Hannah seemed the main witness. She had observed the UFO for two minutes before her mother deigned to look at it. Far more interesting was the fact that she sketched it immediately afterwards, separate from her mother, and the two pictures were extremely similar. When Tony Mann's report explained that there had been paranormal incidents within the family (essentially the boyfriend had seen apparitions), I thought it worth contacting them and talking further.

They impressed me. There was no interest in publicity. Indeed they wished now they had never spoken publicly about the matter. The mother had lost a part-time job because she had reacted to the disbelief of her boss by squirting him with a soda siphon! But then their accounts of the story added a whole new dimension to the affair.

The boyfriend had undergone several UFO experiences as a child in north London. On one occasion he spotted a green mass in the sky whilst walking with his mother, but she could see nothing. On another he was camping out in a tent in his garden, at the age of nine. Although he recalls nothing, his grandmother woke in the night and went to the window attracted by a light. A glowing object was hovering above the tent projecting a beam straight into it. He has also experienced a number of time lapses where it was suddenly much later than it ought to be. Yet, as he told me, 'I would never tell the press about all this.'

Hannah's story was far more interesting too. When she first saw the object (at roof-top height), she was entranced. She began to walk forwards, talking to it! Neither the girl nor her mother knows what was said, but on several occasions between 29 April and 14 August, when I telephoned the family, Hannah had woken in the night after vivid dreams where lights and figures had been seen. When comforted, she has said, 'The ghosties have come.'

The mother admitted to me that she would love 'to be taken off by one'. A few weeks after the sighting (in early June) she too had a vivid dream. In this, 'I saw small creatures with funny, large heads and big eyes.' They were inside the house but were not being nasty. They told her that they wanted to help.

In many senses it is a shame that this family do not wish to be more involved, hence my decision not to name them, but it is perfectly understandable. The social pressures of living with the aftermath of a possible abduction are often worse than the experience itself, thanks to people who are largely ignorant of just how real and traumatic these events can be. How often I have heard those words, 'I wish I'd never said anything!' Even family and friends can be cruel in their lack of understanding of this often shattering experience.

How many cases are there which on the surface seem just boring lights in the sky, but beneath that façade hide something much more disturbing? This example certainly supports the idea that we learn about only a tiny part of the total abduction experience. It also shows that right up to the production of this book they were still happening. It should also make us question the ethics of investigating these stories. That is often a major problem in this work.

The third current abduction is being studied by Philip Mantle and Andy Roberts, BUFORA investigators in Yorkshire. Again, no publicity is desired by the young woman who claims repeated and at least partially conscious memories of being taken into a room by small beings who have then impregnated her. Later the foetus has been removed.

How does one handle a story like that? UFO researchers are totally out of their depth. Indeed, it may fairly be said that most people would be. The investigators, quite naturally, want to adopt the tried and tested technique of hypnosis to relieve the woman's memory block. She seems to want this herself. But will she feel the same way if this process reveals something unpleasant?

Canvassing the views of scientists is useful here. Dr Michael Swords, a natural history professor at the University of Western Michigan, is becoming very intrigued by this phenomenon. He asks, 'What *is* our proper response to this phenomenon as outsiders, as researchers, observers and caring human beings?' He is not sure he knows, but adds: 'The detail in abduction cases is so rich as to be a researcher's dream. However, the detail is also so frightening as to be a researcher's nightmare .... They are too good to be true, but also too bad to be true.'

Another recent convert to the mystery is Dr David Jacobs, associate professor of history at the Temple University, USA. He cast aside years of work on a mammoth historical treatise on UFOs because he considers the abduction an 'intellectual breakthrough'. Now he is working with groups of people who display symptoms, such as a strange time lapse or recurrent dreams of alien beings, who might therefore be potential abductees. He always cautions them before they start to explore a case: 'This decision to find out is quite possibly the biggest decision of your life .... This is one of the few times where the witness will be able to say yes or no to an absolutely life-changing situation. It will put them into a different perspective with their family and friends. They will have a different idea of themselves and the world.'

So, obviously, this cannot be taken lightly. I asked British clinical psychologist Dr John Dale if he would consider getting involved in a case such as that of the Yorkshire woman but he would not. His basic point was: 'Either these cases are real in some way, in which case the trauma amnesia is there for a purpose to block out painful memories, or it is a psychotic delusion of some sort, in which case stimulating the fantasy by hypnosis might be extremely harmful.'

And yet, these witnesses generally *want* to know what happened to them. Psychologist warnings that it might be better if a witness did not know generally wash over their heads. Dr Jacobs says that he gives his subjects time to decide, but once they face up to the choice the overwhelming majority *need* to go ahead. Certainly I have noticed that most people in Britain who suspect hidden memories come to me hoping I can help them find a way to remember.

It is a very hard choice. At a conference in Washington I was approached by several members of the huge audience who had come because they thought they might be secret abductees. I talked for some time with one man who was using me as a sounding board as he wrestled with the decision, 'If I go into hypnosis, will I be better or worse off afterwards?' he asked. And how could I answer? In the week I write (in October 1987) a reporter on a science magazine in New York telephoned for confidential advice on behalf of a friend. That woman had '... this terrible choice between needing to find out what happened, but being terrified of what she might learn and what that discovery might do to her reputation, credibility and sanity'. Counselling such as this is becoming increasingly important but I, as a ufologist, do not feel properly qualified to handle it. Yet who is there *with* those qualifications who is prepared to help?

This problem is much more difficult in Britain. There are so few doctors and clinical psychologists prepared to study this phenomenon. It is no good working only with Harley Street or St John Street practitioners whose main eye is on the bill they can charge at the end of the day. But, as Dr Jacobs recognizes, the lack of support by professionals creates a serious threat: 'Diving into extraordinarily personal aspects of [peoples'] lives is not something anyone can do. We are starting over. We are getting our feet wet learning how to do it. But there is a terrible danger of everyone going home and trying to do it as a parlour game. This is serious business.'

There is also the worry about what hypnosis does to a story. Indeed, is the state of hypnosis itself responsible for the abduction memory in the first place?

We know very little about what hypnosis is. Some psychologists call it an altered state of consciousness. Others think it is just a diffusion of one's ego. A few suspect it may even be a con trick, fooling people into believing they are somehow different when all they are doing is imagining things.

Certainly experimental hypnosis has shown that it can induce memory recall. This has been done by, for instance, regressing an adult back to a schoolroom and getting them to describe where he, she or the other children are sitting. This is not something any of us will consciously remember, but if it is there in our subconscious, and it can be checked against available school records, useful data emerge. It turns out that some things are remembered better, others creatively altered, whilst several are reported just plain wrong. These come out as pure imagination. Since all these things are possible, hypnosis is a tool which must be used without great confidence and as something rather less than a magic wand. Such factors as personal prejudices, the way the hypnotist phrases questions and, of course, the level of expectancy during the session, necessarily affect the results.

This helps explain why regression hypnosis is used sparingly in criminal prosecutions (for example, to extract deeper memories from the mind of a witness). Exactly the same caution – indeed, perhaps much more – has got to be applied in abduction situations.

On the other hand we have already seen Hopkins' report on a large number of cases where hypnosis revealed no abduction, despite all the pressure on the witness to do so. In British cases the same pattern has occurred, and I have sat in on two Harry Harris abduction experiments with likely candidates (one a former RAF pilot whose sighting had several suggestive features), both of which failed to produce abduction memories.

Also it should be apparent from reading the case histories that there are almost as many abduction cases which are not revealed through hypnosis as those which are. Sometimes the recollection is in the form of dreams (Karen from Dukinfield). Sometimes it is a completely conscious memory (Alfred Burtoo in Hampshire). On other occasions there is a more subtle or subconscious belief in contact (for example, the cases of influence by way of music, which one might choose to interpret as a clever alien plan to reach millions of young people without having to abduct each one).

Eddie Bullard's data comprised one third that had a full-conscious memory of the experience. There were a few differences, most notably in that the hypnotic cases were twice as likely to produce memory of medical examinations. But all other crucial features and the all-important order of phases within the abduction were almost identical *however* the story came about.

So it is simply not tenable to claim the hypnotic state as a cause for the abduction experience. Indeed, the differences that were found could possibly be important. Perhaps witnesses who are medically examined are more likely to suffer amnesia than those who are not. That would certainly be consistent with human psychology. It is most unlikely that a fantasy would adhere to such logic.

However, I have explored ways around the continual use of hypnosis. This is best demonstrated by an example case, one of several where this method was tested during the writing of this book.

I am extremely grateful to Mrs Elsie Oakensen of Church Stowe village in Northamptonshire for all her patience and assistance on this experiment.

Church Stowe is very close to the site of two other Northamptonshire cases referenced in the British Catalogue, and this particular experience happened just a few weeks after the release of Ian Watson's previously discussed science-fiction novel reviewing abductions, *Miracle Visitors*. Although Ian Watson lives in another village just a few miles from Church Stowe, he did not know about this case, and Mrs Oakensen had no idea of his writings or of the two other cases at Little Houghton.

Whether all of this is important or just a great coincidence, I have no idea!

22 November 1978 – Church Stowe, Northamptonshire

Mrs Oakensen was head of the teachers' centre in Daventry. (She is now retired). At lunch-time on 22 November 1978 she felt a strange tightening sensation around her forehead, like wearing a hat which was far too small. It passed quickly but was unusual enough to remember.

At 5.15 p.m. she left the centre for the six-mile drive home, noticing that a sidelight was not working so she had to travel with dipped headlights all the time. In an account written immediately afterwards, she said: 'When I reached the traffic lights at Weedon, I turned right onto the A5. Ahead of me I could see two very bright lights immediately above the road .... The left one was red and the right one was green. My immediate thought was that this was a very low-flying aircraft which would zoom over my head. However, it seemed to be stationary and I drove towards it with my nose practically pressed on the windscreen.' She then drove straight underneath it and observed '... an hour-glass or egg-timer shape with a light under each circular end. This thing was no more than 150 feet up.' There was no sound, and the object was directly over the point where Mrs Oakensen had to turn off into Church Stowe village.

This was at about 5.30 p.m. on a very busy main road. Thousands of motorists should have seen this object. Yet, despite a story at the time and the kind assistance of the *Daventry Weekly Express* in this research, not a single traveller has come forward to report seeing anything, even that the lights *were* an aircraft.

Fascinated, Elsie drove up the road towards Church Stowe, which lies atop a hill. She looked back several times during this half mile ride, and the lights were still sitting there over the A5. It was then that it all happened.

Mrs Oakensen turned right into the village, driving as usual in second and changing up to third gear. 'The next thing I knew, my foot was hard on the accelerator pedal, which was flat on the foot of the car. There was no sound from the engine at all. My lights were still functioning but the engine was dead. The car was slowing down and had almost reached the point of stopping.' She did not switch it back on but, feeling surprisingly calm, changed back to first and depressed the accelerator – the car started normally. She drove another hundred yards and there was a second, more pronounced, jerk in reality.

Mrs Oakensen describes what she saw: 'The car was

stationary. Everything was in absolute blackness. My engine had stopped. My lights were out. Suddenly, piercing brilliant white circles of light about a yard in diameter came from nowhere, on-off, on-off, starting at the left of my car, round in front of it, to the right, back again and the last one disappeared into the air ... when the lights hit the ground they lit up the farmyard to my left, the road in front of me and the path and garden of the house to my right ... [otherwise] it was absolutely black. I could not even see the houses at the side of the road.'

Elsie spoke aloud: 'Good gracious!' Then, again without transition, she was moving again. She says: 'I did *not* switch on my ignition. I did *not* put my car into gear. I did *not* depress my accelerator pedal. I did *not* start the car. I just found myself driving along normally.'

She drove into her garage just a few hundred yards away and noticed the sidelights on the car now working. It never failed again. The village was also as it normally is, quite well lit (there had not been a power cut). Looking at the time, she was surprised to realize it was ten or fifteen minutes later than it ought to have been. Driving the route every day, she had a very good idea of how long it takes, but she checked the next night just in case. There was definitely a period of time missing from her memory. That was the whole case, except that at about 7.10 p.m. that same night the tightening sensation occurred one more time.

Of the time lapse Elsie said: 'While the incident was on, time seemed to stand still. It passed unnoticed, like when one is asleep.'

Recognizing immediately that this was a promising case the local UFO group and BUFORA co-ordinator Mark Brown went to investigate. They soon found a vital new lead: another case had come to them which had not been publicly reported. This occurred at 7.20 p.m. on the same night, at virtually the exact time Elsie was feeling that subsequent tightening sensation.

This second case involved four young women driving by car to a meeting in Northampton. They had left Byfield and were travelling near the village of Preston Capes at the time. This is only four miles south-west of Church Stowe. They first saw a parallel-sided beam of light shoot out of a cloud across the sky.

This was repeated a few seconds later. Then a red and green light side by side appeared and crossed the road directly ahead of the car, which suddenly began to lose power. The driver had to change down from top to third gear to maintain engine revolutions, as the lights paced the car to the south. The women then drove into the village, and the lights merged into one and 'switched off abruptly like a light bulb'.

The coincidences here – there was certainly no collusion between the two sets of witnesses – is quite astounding. It would not be difficult to imagine this as two attempted abductions of women from travelling cars.

On 6 August 1987 I spoke to Mrs Georgina Laurie, driver of the second car. It was a Ford Granada, only seven months old. She struck me as eminently sensible and had obviously tried hard to forget the whole thing, though she had considered all sorts of possible explanations. The women had not talked to each other about the incident, nor did they appear interested in Elsie Oakensen's story. It was 'best forgotten', Mrs Laurie told me, but she added, 'The car was perfectly OK after that night. I have no idea why it suddenly lost power when the lights appeared.'

Desperate for help to retrieve missing memories, the BUFORA team arranged for researcher Graham Phillips to conduct a hypnosis session. This occurred on 18 August 1979. Elsie relived the sighting only partially, although during the two days after the session much flowed into her mind 'as if popping out of my subconscious'.

Elsie felt the tightening as the car slowed down the first time. 'I got hotter and hotter .... The pressure hurt my head.' Then a brilliant 'pure white light, very bright' hit her full on from the front. It throbbed with circles radiating out from the centre. 'The pain in my head was intense .... I felt no reaction in my legs ... I was very frightened.' Then two shapes appeared, silhouetted against the glow. Both were grey. They were hazy but from her drawings could be taken as 'people'.

Afterwards Elsie Oakensen said she felt as if she had been 'selected, scanned, promised a return visit, then ultimately rejected'.

Because the hypnosis had been so ineffective, I suggested she try my idea of reliving the experience whilst alone and quiet, simply letting it unfold in her mind's eye. She should note whatever came out even if it was different from conscious memory. She did this by actually following the route on 17 September 1987, stopping at each strategic point and reliving the events. This greatly helped her to get a clear recall. (In fact, if controlled visualization such as this is proved valuable in other cases, we may be able to avoid the use of hypnosis altogether. The present use of hypnosis offers sceptics the chance to claim that the trance itself induces bizarre revelations.)

Elsie Oakensen now wonders if the initial tightening was a preliminary scan earlier in the day. As the car came under the influence of the UFO, she was put into a limbo state. It was taken to a position right outside a farm (where she later discovered the owners were away at the time). Here the lightshow involved beings from the UFO and beams scanning her. When they were not satisfied, they left and she was brought back to full consciousness a little further down the road.

All I can say is that such an interpretation does not infringe either common sense or what we have discovered about the abduction phenomenon. But two points are worth remembering, for very different reasons. First, many of the symptoms Elsie Oakensen describes (tightening pain, flashing lights etc) are suggestive of migraine. But lest you write the case off as a migraine attack, you should remember the UFO in the first place, the effects on the car, the totally independent second sighting and the fact that Elsie suffered from migraine for several days afterwards and can tell the difference. She believes it was brought on by the bright lights.

Secondly, if Elsie, who was past normal childbearing age, was rejected, what are we to think about the younger women in the car?

10 The Search for Answers

It would be nice if there was a simple solution to this very strange mystery, but if there were, it would hardly qualify as the mystery that it is.

Very few are inclined to take the most obvious reductionist view – that *all* these cases are hoaxes – but one man well on the way towards such a hypothesis is the aviation journalist Philip Klass, who has written a series of fervently argued sceptical books. In his 1983 offering, *UFOs: The Public Deceived*, he provides the classic line of the debunker: 'One possible explanation for the mushrooming number of abduction cases in recent years is that the UFOnauts are growing bolder .... The alternative explanation is that people have discovered how easy it is to fool famous ufologists with tall tales and to become instant international celebrities via the pages of sensationalist tabloid newspapers.'

He adds, rather curiously, that it is puzzling that no witness has ever reported their abduction to the FBI, who are responsible for kidnappings in the USA. I scarcely find this strange. Many abductions *were* reported to the police or Ministry of Defence. If you lived in the USA and endured what abductees endure, would your first thought be to call the FBI? Is there any evidence that this would be productive? Yet Klass argues that the true reason for this failure to report is that false claims can produce a $10,000 dollar fine.

This demonstrates the pretty dismal nature of most sceptical thinking on abductions. Remarkably few abductees are interested in becoming overnight celebrities. Most pretend (or wish) that their experience had never happened. Of course, there are exceptions. It would be utterly naïve to suggest that no abduction cases are ever hoaxed. Some must be, for reasons of self-aggrandizement or other rewards, or perhaps because the witness simply enjoys a joke or is an undiagnosed psychotic.

Where thinkers like Philip Klass make their grand mistake is in trying to explain everything by way of a few selected examples. The vast mass of abduction evidence categorically refutes the idea of hoaxes.

Indeed, by far the best critical thinking comes from people within abduction research itself. Very few are running headlong into an acceptance of alien reality. Those that are often do this with great reluctance.

Researchers such as Vicente-Juan Ballester Olmos from Spain argue (in a paper he prepared especially for me with colleague José Fernandez): 'It seems like respected abductions have come to be a substitute for discredited contacts; a sort of transmutation from old style naïve, early space-age stories to contemporary, sophisticated, techno-age stories ... as if the UFO novelty has been exhausted and an even more dramatic type of incident was needed to replace it .... In Spain all abduction cases have been explained (to our satisfaction) in terms which do not defy present-day knowledge, e.g. conventional scenarios deeply rooted in psychology.'

American Mark Rodeghier, the scientist who took over the research side of CUFOS after the death of Dr J. Allen Hynek, argued in an August 1987 letter to me: 'Some explanatory mechanism is required. The reports can not be brushed off lightly .... Abduction cases offer the UFO community the first good chance in years to co-ordinate a massive research effort that just might pay dividends, if only in our understanding of the human psyche. An international conference *is* required.' He went on to propose a central repository of abduction cases for study by academics in the correctly qualified fields.

If this is the result of 'famous UFOlogists' being 'fooled' by 'tall tales', then all I can say is: we need more fools.

In Australia Mark Moravec is yet another who favours the psychological school of thought. In his September 1987 letter to me he explains why, including the ambiguity of physical evidence (which he argues could often be coincidental or spurious) and the clear links with mythology which suggests an answer rooted in the mind.

Moravec sets out the choice: 'The explanation for UFO

abduction reports comes down to three basic possibilities ... (i) A physically real contact with extra-terrestrial intelligence ... (ii) A psychological or hallucinated experience, most likely occurring during an altered state of consciousness, on which is superimposed personal and cultural beliefs ... (iii) A mixture of the physical and psychological.'

In the latter he is referring to a real stimulus of some sort that triggers an hallucination. But it seems necessary to add a fourth option, albeit a bizarre one: that the combination of physical and psychological is the other way around. A psychological experience somehow produces a form of real event.

We shall look at these suggestions in turn.

Hilary Evans is a British theorizer who has pondered the abduction and come down clearly on the side of a psychological experience. He kindly sent me a copy of his 1987 paper *Abductions in Perspective* in which he summarizes his argument. He says: 'In one sense or another abduction reports are real; what is in doubt is whether that reality is the everyday reality of the physical world, or the private reality of the witness's mind.'

Evans quite correctly points out that there are no known cases of uninvolved people watching an abduction, just as a bystander chances upon a bank robbery. If abductions are as common as some researchers claim, this either proves their subjectivity or demonstrates remarkable selection or mind-bending powers on behalf of the abductors.

There are some cases which come close, such as the Rosa Lotti case in Italy where two village children saw the UFO and entities, and the Alan Godfrey case in Britain, where three other police officers saw a UFO head for the spot where minutes later Godfrey says he was abducted. Then again there are cases, such as that of José Alvaro in Brazil, where the witness was apparently seen during the abduction – he was flat out on the ground. A very similar thing occurred in the Gaynor Sunderland case in Britain: during her bedroom abduction her mother chanced to go into the room and saw her still on the bed but in a most unusual trance-like and very deep sleep.

Evans acknowledges the emotional power of an abduction as one of its most important factors, but he cautions against viewing this as evidence for its material reality when it need not be: 'This shows he had something to be emotional about, [but] we must not jump to the conclusion that the abduction experience was the cause; it may have been part of the cure.'

Of course, there is one major barrier to the acceptance of the psychological answer: how can the cases share so much detail in common?

In BUFORA's twice-yearly research journal, *JTAP*, in March 1987, Bob Digby reported on an interesting experiment ('The witness as a subtle and complex instrument of observation') and showed a slide of a very specific model UFO shape for an exact number of seconds. This was done in front of two southern English audiences of professional business people (one all male, the other all female). They were then asked to sketch what they had seen and estimate how long it was visible for.

These are standard questions asked during field investigations, but the results were remarkable. Almost no two drawings were even closely identical. They varied in size, orientation, number and presence of windows; some were far rounder or squarer than the image, and so on. And the duration estimates were as inaccurate: the men's varied from five to sixty seconds; the women's were better, ranging only between five and twenty-five seconds (the actual figure was close to the middle of the female range).

This difference between male and female sets is supported in a separate test conducted by Peter Hough and myself during November 1986 and September 1987, whilst teaching children aged between ten and twelve in Cheshire schools. We obtained 200 drawings in response to the request 'Draw what you think a UFO looks like.' The way in which they varied widely but kept within a broad overall concept of a disc-like craft shows the powerful effect of a stereotype even within young children's minds. But, as in Digby's experiment, the girls took the task far more seriously and made fewer remarks about ET and spaceships when they added a description to the sketch explaining what they believed UFOs to be.

Obviously this demonstrates that precise witness accounts of what the UFO or its occupants look like are bound to vary. Why do they not seem to vary anything like as much as these experiments suggest they should? In real cases men and women describe the two types of entity which we isolated from the data in exactly the same manner.

To find out whether there can be a psychological explanation, we must inevitably turn to psychologists. I spent an afternoon debating these matters with Dr John Dale, a clinical psychologist who is sure a psychological explanation exists.

He demonstrated suggestibility by asking me to give the first word that came into my head when he said 'sun'. I replied 'moon', to which he said, 'Fine. I understand why you said that, but what if I were to tell you that I said "son", as in "daughter", not "sun"?' Then he cautioned me not to think about yellow dogs. 'What is the first thing that runs through your mind now?' he asked. And, of course, it was an image of a yellow dog!

From this he proposed that a group of people (friends, family etc) might have an abduction almost by association with the strongest-willed individual in the group. He or she persuades the others that they have seen a UFO, and this mind-set becomes sufficiently powerful to take over. Subtle cues make them see things, and those who do not are afraid to admit it because the majority are against them. The only way in which their lack of an experience might manifest is in a refusal to submit to hypnosis. On the surface they do not want to go against the crowd and admit nothing was there. Subconsciously, they *know* there was not a real abduction, so they decline hypnosis on a pretext.

It is true that in multiple witness cases it often seems to be true that one witness, or more than one, wishes not to be hypnotized. Usually we put this down to fear of what might emerge, but if Dr Dale is correct, it is actually guilt at recognizing, but failing to admit, the 'imaginary' nature of the experience.

In France, Dr Dale's equivalent might be Michel Monnerie, noted for his book which posed the provocative question in its title, *And What If UFOs* Don't *Exist*? He explained how he visualized the abduction in an interview for *Ovni Présence* (summer 1982): 'If the observer, in his inability to identify what he has seen, persuades himself that the affair is extraordinary – a UFO, for instance – autosuggestion takes over. This is nothing dreadful. I prefer to call it a mental accident, just as we can have physical accidents. One person, upon seeing the moon, will recognize it every time. Another might occasionally think it to be a UFO.'

Others feel that the psychology of the explanation needs to be found in more borderline areas, arguing that one cannot dismiss evidence as powerful as we seem to have for the abduction phenomenon just by claiming misperception of planets or the moon, although it must be remembered that some cases (for example the Hills) do seem to start that way.

One of the borderline areas most under scrutiny is something called 'the false awakening'. This is best illustrated by an experience of my own.

I was seeing my boyfriend off to work one very cold morning. It was early, I was tired, and the fire in the living-room was set too high. He drove off on his motorcycle into the icy conditions for a twenty-mile ride to Chester. Suddenly I saw him back in the living-room. He was so close I could touch him, and I felt great relief. I did not know why he had returned, but I was glad. The experience of his return was as real as anything could be, but it lasted only a moment. Then I found myself waking from a doze on the settee, where I must have fallen asleep.

There is no question in my mind that I recognized the false awakening as an hallucination only because of the sudden 'coming-to' and discovery that my boyfriend was *not* there and had never returned. But if I had visualized a UFO being, for example, I can understand the confusion that might have arisen, because, of course, I would have no way of knowing whether its presence in my room was possible or impossible.

Australian Keith Basterfield is one researcher who has considered this phenomenon in connection with abduction cases and believes it can account for most of them. ('Strange Awakenings', *Magonia*, winter 1978-9). He gives quite a few examples and says: 'We note throughout these cases that there is a recurrence of vivid illumination, figures materializing/ dematerializing, or the reporter falling asleep immediately after the cessation of the event .... Wish fulfilment, as in dreams, could be the main factor, the person genuinely wanting to see one of these UFO things.'

Wish-fulfilment it undoubtedly was in my case, but I can see scant evidence that it applies in UFO abductions. Who would wish for the trauma these involve? There is good reason to consider the Basterfield 'image' hypothesis valid in a few cases, specifically those involving bedroom visitors. Indeed, he makes the very telling point that such stories focus on the period between 1 and 4 a.m. That may not be odd, because it is when most people will be in their bedrooms asleep, but his point is that they centre on the deep sleep stages, not just sleep itself, from which the witnesses are awakened.

So we are faced with a possible psychological answer for a number of cases but not with a workable solution to the abduction phenomenon, as such.

However, we must take heed of these suggestions of hallucination. In a paper given to the 1984 Anglo-French UFO conference at Brighton ('It's all in the mind', reprinted in *Magonia*, April 1984), Peter Rogerson argues that what he calls 'profound subjective responses' are triggered by seeing an object mistaken for a UFO. This, in turn, generates a hallucination using imagery from the subconscious mind. But this is less '... the product of the imagination of isolated individuals. It is a social and cultural phenomenon.'

Rogerson has to say this to get around the very awkward problem of considerable similarity between cases. He is emulating the famous Swiss psychiatrist Dr Carl Jung, who proposed that the human mind shares archetypes (or mythic images) at a deep inner level. The difficulty is that such an idea tries to explain the abduction evidence by recourse to unproven psychological theories in a way that is tenuous to say the least, for it has no way of explaining the physical effects on witnesses, the problems suffered by time-pieces or the way in which the UFO manifests in the first place. Even Jung saw that and never tried to dismiss the phenomenon as purely psychological.

Whilst, in the main, psychologists have struggled to find a viable psychological theory, it is non-psychologists (Rogerson, for instance, is a librarian) who have championed the idea.

Only one truly developed theory, the so-called 'birth trauma hypothesis', has been consistently put forward. This by Alvin Lawson, a professor of English at California State University, Long Beach. However, because it stands alone, it must be looked at.

Lawson was interested in and involved with UFO research before he set up his experiment. This involved canvassing university students to find some who claimed no knowledge of UFO matters. Six were then hypnotized by Dr William McCall MD, who had conducted regressions on real-life abductees.

The idea was to get the students to imagine an abduction under hypnosis, using questions designed to extract a similar sort of story. For instance: 'Imagine you are seeing some entities or beings aboard the UFO. Describe them,' followed by: 'You are undergoing some kind of physical examination. Describe what is happening to you.' There is a blatant flaw. In arguing, as he did, that similarities exist between the real and imaginary cases, he misses the point that there are bound to be major comparisons. Lawson has actually structured imaginary stories by deciding in advance what an abduction should be like, based on the pre-existing real cases.

That error was so serious that when Lawson circulated his detailed paper *What can we learn from hypnosis of imaginary abductees?* (California State University, May 1977) most researchers dismissed it. They pointed out the mistake, plus several other glaring points (for example, only eight cases form his data base). That should have been an end to the matter, at least until others duplicated his work – which nobody ever did. However, Lawson published his results and, since many scientists preferred there to be an answer to get rid of this abduction problem, they received more credence than they deserved.

Five years on from his experimental research, Lawson published a theory based on them. The entire September 1982 issue of *Magonia* is given over to this ('The Abduction Experience: A testable hypothesis'). What Lawson here claimed is that during hypnosis, or conscious fantasy when hypnosis is not used, the subject regresses to the most traumatic event in his or her life. Because the subject has not really been abducted, substitute imagery generates the story. The one trauma which each of us has shared is birth, so this is where the images in the abduction come from, and this is also why the abductions are so similar all over the world. Birth is a very consistent phenomenon.

Superficially this sounds rather plausible. Travis Walton described the entities he saw as 'foetus-like'. Large heads and eyes are characteristic of unborn babies in the womb. And other features – for example, the clamps and head pains, and travel down a tube of light – all might fit the birth process.

But is this exciting solution truly viable? The abduction researchers think not. In an open letter dated 15 March 1985 (published in *FSR*, Volume 30, No. 5), Budd Hopkins challenged it on many points. For instance, he asks how '... a new-born infant knows what he looked like as a partly formed foetus ... or why he should have foetus imagery as he was presumably born as a full-term baby ... and what kind of warped logic lies behind a "birth recollection-UFO abduction account" in which the baby [remembered when] a fully grown adult – appears on the examination table surrounded by foetuses. What became of the doctors and nurses?'

Of course, Lawson might legitimately argue that there are *some* cases where the small, ugly beings are seen alongside others in surgical gear. But then again, researchers can counter that his entire hypothesis is based on the idea of abduction cases involving the foetus-like entities. As this book has shown, reported entities equally include the tall, thin ones, who naturally have no place at all in Lawson's theory and are summarily ignored by it. Even his own set of eight imaginary cases featured six different types of entity, including four categories that almost never turn up in abduction stories (for example animal-like beings).

Perhaps the best response came from D. Scott Rogo, who lectures in parapsychology at John F. Kennedy University in California. In his paper '*Birth Traumas From Outer Space*' (*IUR*, May/June 1985), he demolishes Lawson's ideas point by point, challenges him to set up the standard psychological procedure of a blind test and shows how those psychologists studying birth-process memories totally dispute the very idea of Lawson's alleged imagery.

A blind test would involve Lawson's giving comprehensive accounts and psychological profiles to psychologists who had no idea what the experiment was about. Some of these accounts would be real abduction stories and others imaginary data. If the psychologists were then unable to distinguish between them, he might have a case. This has never been attempted.

Finally, it must be said that in 1982 the BBC and an American television station made a science programme (screened in the *Horizon* series in the UK and the *Nova* series in the USA) entitled *The Case of the UFO*. I had some involvement in the fifty-minute documentary, made by BBC producer John Groom. It was a very sceptical look at the scientific evidence, and Groom had been keen to feature Lawson's then new birth-trauma theory. However, as Groom told me later, after filming material with the professor, they had to abandon all plans because they could not get a single psychologist who would appear on film supporting the idea. This was despite a general feeling amongst psychologists (who knew only what they had read in the sensational press about abduction cases) that there must be a psychological explanation.

It is surely very suggestive that no psychologist has been able to put forward a comprehensive, testable theory to explain these cases.

I attempted a small experiment for this book, duplicating and extending some of Lawson's work. Since it is clear that hypnosis is not essential (and many abduction reports arise without it), the same creative visualization technique used on witnesses such as Elsie Oakensen was recommended.

My standard questionnaire asked the subject: 'Imagine that you are out driving late one night on a country road. Suddenly a strange object appears above you. This, you determine, is one of those UFOs so often reported .... Describe what you see.' The only questions around which any framework was determined were: 'If the occupants of the UFO wished to take you on board, how would they do so? ... When on board what would the inside look like? ... Describe what the occupants would look like and what they would wear .... What would the occupants have brought you on board for? What would they do to you? ... Where would the occupants come from and why would they come?'

I set the test to a sample of twenty people, whose age, sex and occupation were recorded. Half had interest in, or clear knowledge of, UFOs. The other half professed no such interest and, so far as it was possible to check, this *was* verified. None had undergone a UFO encounter.

The full results are too complex to summarize here, and more data is needed before too many conclusions ought to be reached. However, as expected, the UFO-aware group produced results that were very similar to our real abduction data. Ninety per cent, for instance, reported the medical examination. Seventy per cent said they either did not recall the transition onto the UFO or it was accomplished by some form of hypnotic induction (a very odd feature of real cases). Fifty per cent reported the small, ugly beings and thirty the tall, thin ones.

There was a dramatic difference when the non-aware group was analysed. Here no one reported the small, ugly beings, no one reported a medical examination, no one failed to visualize the transition into the UFO, and sixty per cent said it was accomplished by force (for example, at the point of a ray gun).

These last results are so unlike genuine abduction data that they may be very important. I hope the test will be repeated in a controlled manner by psychologists reading this book. It also demonstrates the probable importance of screening abduction witnesses for prior UFO interest. This is something I certainly do during interviews (for example, finding an excuse to look at the bookshelves in a witness's home is a good place to start, and the framing of careful questions can be helpful too). Of course, the non-aware group must have come across UFO stories in the media or on movies, so it is not total lack of knowledge about UFOs which appears to be important. Somewhere here there could be the seeds of a valuable experiment.

In finding what clues we do have, it is often the non-specialists who have provided them.

Ken Phillips, a London mathematics teacher and research official with BUFORA, has worked hard to discover psychological characteristics in close-encounter witnesses. He has co-ordinated a project called 'Anamnesis', implemented by the BUFORA investigation team and supervised by Vienna psychologist Dr Alex Keul. This has carried out major life profiles and other psychology tests on over a hundred witnesses between 1984 and 1987. The work is proceeding, but latest results are reported in BUFORA's research journal *JTAP* (September 1987).

Phillips shows that there is a '... significant "social dissatisfaction" cluster* ... [that] dream reportage of UFOs and flying (floating) [is much greater] ... and, even more significantly, there is a high level of ESP reportage.'

Whilst this data is not based on abduction cases, it *is* based on close encounters that in many instances are potential

* Meaning that more people than chance predicts were found by the study to be dissatisfied with their treatment by society or to be 'loners'.

abductions. We have also seen plenty of evidence within cases cited of the ESP, UFO dream and floating elements. The one interesting new clue is the idea of witnesses having a greater tendency towards social dissatisfaction. But, the question must remain: Does this disenchantment in some sense precipitate the experience, or does it perhaps result from it?

The work is being continued in Britain by BUFORA, but is also now to be duplicated at the Framington Institute in Massachussetts and the University of Salzburg in Austria.

One partial replication is reported by Dr June Parnell, a psychologist at the University of Wyoming, who picked up her interest from abduction researcher Dr Leo Sprinkle. In her 110-page 1986 paper published by the university ('Personality characteristics on the MMPI, 16PF and ACL tests, of persons who claim UFO experiences'), she carried out these named tests on 225 witnesses. Their encounters ranged from lights in the sky to abductions and so were an unfortunately mixed bag. Nevertheless, she soon realized that standard UFO sightings tend to happen to everyone, not to any distinctive type of personality. So she looked separately at more exotic contact and abduction cases.

She describes the resultant subjects as '... having a high level of psychic energy, being self-sufficient, resourceful, and preferring their own decisions ... [with] above-average intelligence, assertiveness, a tendency to be experimenting thinkers, a tendency toward a reserved attitude, and a tendency toward defensiveness. There was also a high level of the following traits in these deep-encounter witnesses: 'being suspicious or distrustful ... creative and imaginative ...'.

We need much more of this research if we are to answer the question: can abductions be explained as a psychological experience? It must be said that the provisional conclusion so far has got to be 'probably not', with reservations that we shall look at in a moment.

Perhaps the single most important evidence in favour of that tentative conclusion comes from an epic research project conducted in 1983 and 1984 and once more paid for by UFO researchers, in this case the Fund for UFO Research in Maryland, USA. The full story can be found in one of the last articles written by the doyen of UFO scientists, Dr J. Allen

Hynek ('Abductees are 'normal' people', *IUR*, July/August 1984).

Budd Hopkins and his colleague Ted Blœcher set up the idea and accrued the funding in an effort to demonstrate the invalidity of the psychological theory. Ambivalent clinical psychologist Dr Aphrodite Clamar devised the methodology of the testing.

The idea was to take nine abductees, five men and four women, whose stories had already been intensively researched and which seemed to hold firm. They were then individually (and quite separately) sent to Dr Elizabeth Slater, a psychologist who had no knowledge of, or interest in, UFO cases. She had no idea what the nine people claimed, and during their sessions the witnesses gave no hints of any UFO connection.

Dr Slater simply felt she was testing these people to ascertain their emotional and psychiatric stability levels. This is something psychologists do as routine – for example, when vetting individuals for top security jobs. It entails the setting and analysing of many different tests. In this case Dr Slater used the following: Rorschach, TAT, Wechsler Adult Intelligence scale, Minnesota Multiphasic Tests and projective drawing. This forms a very comprehensive and credible patient study.

None of the nine abductees was publicly known. All had insisted on anonymity for their cases. So Dr Slater cannot have read about them. They ranged from the director of a chemical company through a secretary and salesman to a tennis coach. On each she prepared an extensive personal report and submitted this to a third party who had no connection with the experiment or the experimenters. Only once all of this was in writing was Dr Slater told the purpose of the experiment and that her nine subjects shared the belief that they had been taken aboard a UFO and medically examined by aliens.

In her report, written before she learned the truth, Dr Slater concluded some important things. They are even more important when compared with Dr Parnell's findings in Wyoming. The witnesses all formed a normal, stable group. They had: '... a richness of inner life ... relative weakness in the sense of identity, especially sexual identity ... vulnerability in the interpersonal realm ... there is little to unite them as a group from the standpoint of the overt manifestations of their personalities .... [But they did share] above-average intelligence ... one subject has an overall IQ score in the "very superior" range and five had overall IQs in the "Bright Average" range. Only three of the nine fall within the "Average" range, and they fall in the very upper end of that.'

In other words, they were extremely bright and perfectly stable. They were not alike in terms of personality, character, skills or interest and spanned a broad range. But they did share a degree of distrust of others, a tendency towards secretiveness, high caution levels and a fear of relating with strangers. They also had very vivid abilities to 'image' things, such that it '... can operate favourably in terms of creativity and disadvantageously to the extent that it can be overwhelming'.

I believe this superior imaging ability, coupled with the high ESP scores in other experiments, and the very clear incidence of paranormal experiences in abductees' lives, will prove to be the key to the entire mystery, for these seem to be the only things that make them in any way different from everyone else.

The test results were verified by other 'blind' psychologists. No one disputed that these were 'normal' people. After Dr Slater was told the news – which 'flabbergasted' her – she assessed the problem anew: 'The first and most critical question is whether our subjects' reported experiences could be accounted for strictly on the basis of psychopathology, i.e. mental disorder. The answer is a firm no.' She confirmed that none of the witnesses could be described as 'pathological liars, paranoid schizophrenics, or severely disturbed and extraordinarily rare hysteroid characters subject to fugue states or multiple personality shifts'.

More importantly, many of the features she found (for example, the defensiveness and secrecy, the tendency to avoid relationships and the sexual ambiguity) would make perfect psychological sense if we were to accept that these people really had been kidnapped by aliens and given a soul-bearing sexual examination. Dr Slater added: 'The closest analogy might be the interpersonal alienation of the rape victim, who has been violated most brutally but somehow becomes tainted by virtue of the crime against her.'

She was quite adamant about her final conclusion, which seems to be the last word on the psychological theory: 'There is no apparent psychological explanation for their reports.'

We do seem to have effectively disposed of the 'all in the mind' school of thought. We can even call upon folklorist Eddie Bullard's quite different blend of research, because he found that the story hypothesis simply did not work for all kinds of reasons.

One small point that stood out in Bullard's view was the existence of what he called 'doorway amnesia'. As we saw from my experiment in creative visualization (p. 204), people tend to imagine going through the door of the UFO. There seems no reason why one should imagine the rest but not that. Yet in real abductions the way into the UFO is a blank in the vast majority of cases. This smacks of reality.

Something else that points that way are the fascinating connections that weave between cases. They are not things which stand out or which are featured in media stories – that is what makes them all the more important. Imagine you were trying to decide if the same car was involved in two separate road accidents. Witness accounts of the sort 'It was big and blue and had four wheels' would not be much use, for that is standard for many cars, but if the two versions mention a tiny, ornamental pink frog hanging from a string in the rear window, we might sit up and listen.

Data of the 'pink frog' variety does exist. You only have to remember the salty lemonade drink. This featured in the 'Janos People' case, reported to me in the summer of 1978 and explored under hypnosis a few months later. In this book you will find the same obscure factor in one other case, that of the Red Army officer in the USSR. Whilst each was investigated separately and reported in time and space without prospect of one case effecting any other, in every instance the salty drink acted as a way to induce amnesia. It is incredible that both cases came within a four-month spell in 1978. It is hard to avoid the conclusion of a new procedure being tested out on abductees during this period. Coincidence appears totally out of the question.

But if the several clues like this imply that these abductions *are* real, what does that mean? Need it necessarily imply visitors from another planet?

Probably not. Dr Michael Swords, the natural scientist, has delved into the idea that the aliens may be so interested in us because they *are* us! He has extrapolated from changes in the form of human beings over the past few million years and concluded that the entities we see might represent future development. On this theory, *homo sapiens* many generations hence has devised a method of time travel.

Given the extent of time stretching into the future, and despite the paradox-problems time travel might introduce, it should be remembered that if time travel ever becomes possible in the entire history of our race, it is quite likely we would see time travellers from that future here right now. It would be their distant past, of course, but a crucial era in our progress, especially if there is something nasty just around the corner, like that nuclear holocaust abductees are continually warned about. The period between our discovery of atomic energy, our first steps into space and this major cataclysm could well be *the* place for future historians to travel back to, just as if we had time travel there are certain eras we would want to visit for scientific research.

Indeed, if we take these holocaust warnings seriously, we have every reason to ask how even super-intelligent aliens could know our future. But one group who would certainly know it are our own descendants. Indeed, they might have good reason to try to warn us.

What if time travel were possible, but intervention not. What if future historical records showed that just before the holocaust there was a spate of 'alien abduction' claims where normal, sane people told of kidnaps and warnings. There apparently were no aliens. History has shown that. But could you resist the temptation of trying to do something, by travelling back to study or warn people, disguised as those space travellers? That way you do not interfere because the spurious UFOnauts are already a part of historical record and as long as you stick to their party line, you can visit in safety. But we must not forget those paradoxes, beloved of science fiction, which ask what would happen if a traveller came back, changed our future (which would be their past!) and so effectively stopped themselves being born … which would, of course, make it impossible for the non-existent traveller to have come back and done anything. You see why most scientists reject the idea of time travel!

There are cases that might seem to fit this outline. And if it is correct, the time to start worrying will be when the abductions stop, because we might well believe the 'aliens' have stopped coming because it is now too near those dreaded events to risk miscalculation. The end really would be nigh!

The idea of time-travellers may fit individual cases, such as that of Bernard and Angela Shine, or what could look like repeat visits by the same observers (as in the Ranton, Poole and Sheffield cases in the British Catalogue). But it is deliberately provocative and far-fetched. I am not pretending there is any real evidence for the concept.

I offer the intellectual exercise for one main reason: to demonstrate that it is not necessary to accept aliens from outer space flying here in spaceships, even if you are committed to the reality of abductions. That may seem an obvious point, but I was disturbed – when visiting the USA to research this book – to learn just how many sober researchers view the ETH (Extra-Terrestrial Hypothesis) as the only viable option – in other words: they are certain we are being visited by aliens from another world.

Dr David Jacobs, for instance, is a remarkably astute man, an incisive historian whose recent conversion to the study of abductions is a great bonus. During a long conversation, which turned into a public debate and which ultimately drew quite a crowd of onlookers, I tried to explain some of my worries about the evidence for this theory.

True, the cases are very similar, but the presence of even a hint of difference between cultures ought to give cause to wonder about any physical reality. British data simply do not share the overwhelming proportion of small, ugly beings. Eddie Bullard arrived on the scene to support me, but our caution seemed largely irrelevant to those researchers without a global perspective on this subject.

Also I felt that the links with folklore and mythology could not be overlooked. At this point a Canadian television journalist who was making a documentary on the subject chipped in with similarities he had found in Indian traditions, and Bill Chalker commented on Aborigine shamanism and its features in common, such as trance states, time suspension and communion with sky gods. Can this pattern be irrelevant?

Then the question of the physical evidence arrived. Budd

Hopkins is very much persuaded by this. He says that in many of his cases mysterious scars have been found, often on the legs of abductees. These are to him the location where alien samples were taken, and he has published many photographs which seem to show similar (although not identical) unexplained wounds on different witnesses. Usually these people had not known the scars were there until Hopkins suggested they look.

I am certainly not disputing this evidence, nor Hopkins' sincere belief that we will obtain firm medical traces of the so-called 'implants' which many witnesses believe the aliens put into their heads. Several expensive brain scans have been attempted so far, all unsuccessful in finding anything. But the doctors concerned are not surprised: if the implant is there, it may be *very* small.

Naturally, if this work comes up with something, we are into a whole new ballgame. But right now I feel it is wise to be careful. I suggested a simple experiment that abduction researchers ought to try. What is the normal incidence rate of small scars which someone does not know they have? The only way to learn is to conduct what will probably be a somewhat entertaining experiment of checking out men's and women's legs! It is quite possible that many of us have marks, created by forgotten childhood accidents, for example. If so, the fact that they turn up in so many abduction cases could not be considered significant.

It is basic tests such as this which need to be done, but as yet are not getting done, because too few people are accepting that there might be a real phenomenon, whilst questioning the ETH just enough to tread carefully. However if hidden abductions *are* extremely common …

These should be worries, as should the fact that we have no photographs of aliens or landed spaceships that remotely pass muster. Indeed, there are no more than a handful of secondary witnesses to abduction cases (and never witnesses to a stranger being taken on board a UFO). Despite all of these grounds for caution, Dr Jacobs told me, 'You cannot investigate abductions without the ET context as a premise.' I must beg to disagree.

I am not disputing the way in which the ETH would solve many problems. It is an economical theory, because science knows it to be possible. We can envisage travelling to another world and perhaps conducting medical examinations on its inhabitants, collecting samples of plants and so on. That very fact seems to make it easier to accept that others might make such journeys in reverse. But why should we expect aliens to behave exactly as we would? Aliens, presumably, would be different in many ways, and there is something vaguely dissatisfying about their being a carbon copy of NASA astronauts.

However, the ETH has to be regarded as a front-running theory, if only because this is the guise in which the abductors appear. They say, almost without exception, that they come from space. We do not have to believe them, of course. And there is plenty of evidence that shows how the phenomenon lies. The range of planets from whence they arrive is vast and often nonsensical. It has more in keeping with a Buck Rogers comic book than with astronomical reality.

We may choose to think that this is because the aliens do not want us to know their true home and are playing games, and there are a number of cases where the answer 'You would not understand' is given to an abductee. On the other hand, we may consider this confusion to be related to most people's poor understanding of the universe. But then, why do very educated people, even those scientifically trained, come out with equally absurd planets of origin for their abductors? They sometimes even know the origin is nonsense but still have to report what they were told.

Astronomers and cosmologists cannot help us very much because they have no uniform attitude towards the existence of intelligent life in the universe. About the closest they come to a consensus is that the majority do believe that it probably does exist. Here is a selection of views.

Jerome Pearson, a USAF space scientist at Wright Patterson Research Center told an international space conference in Brighton in October 1987: 'The earth and moon are a double planet system. Because of the expected rarity of double planets, we may well be alone in our galaxy.'

Dr David Whitehouse a British astronomer, is less sure. In an article published on 24 December 1985 by *The Times*, (London). 'These close encounters of the absurd kind', he says: 'I shall feel more confident that aliens have landed when I see David Frost interview one ... as a subject for study UFOs are massively disappointing .... It is time we started pouring tough criticism on these shoddy ill-thought-out doctrines and let real science, infinitely more interesting, shine through. We are searching for life in outer space and could find it any time.'

Leading Soviet cosmologist Dr Vladimir Rubtsov, from Kharkov, kindly sent me his quite different views: 'The problem of visiting our planet by extra-terrestrials has not been practically considered within the framework of science .... The question whether there are among thousands of UFO-reports any observations of extra-terrestrial probes cannot have been solved just by slighting the problem as "unscientific". It needs and deserves a serious scientific study.'

Professor Allen Tough, a futurist from the University of Toronto, Canada, is doing his bit to analyse the problem. He did me the honour of asking for my comments on his paper 'What do extra-terrestrials plan for our future?' before it was published in the astronomical literature (reprinted by BUFORA's *JTAP*, September 1987). He says: 'Advanced extra-terrestrial beings from some part of our galaxy will probably play a major role in [Earth's] future .... It is quite possible that some UFO reports are triggered by an encounter with an extra-terrestrial being or spacecraft.'

As you can see, there is no real agreement, but encouraging signs that some space scientists are not throwing out all consideration of the abduction phenomenon, although they often regard it as synonymous with the UFO phenomenon. That could be a big mistake. Most UFOs are provably not alien in any way. Abductions are an entirely different matter and perhaps ought to be treated as such.

On the other hand, I recall the words of Professor Zdnek Kopal, with whom I took some astronomy lectures when I was at Manchester University. He was researching planets around other stars and, after showing that it was very probable that Barnards Star did have some, he advised that any aliens there might see our primitive war-like nature and think they would be doing the universe a big favour by wiping us out! 'My advice is this – if you hear that space phone ringing – don't answer!' he told us.

Budd Hopkins has a very specific theory about why the aliens are coming. He alleges that so many of his reports involve reproductive elements, to both male and female witnesses, that the only solution is to accept what these people are told by the entities. The aliens need our genes to develop their own stock and are endeavouring to create hybrid human/aliens which could live here *and* on their planet. This requires abducting young men to impregnate their females and also making human females of child-bearing age pregnant during an abduction, before returning some weeks later to extract the young foetus and bring this to term in their laboratories or an alien womb!

Of course, this idea is astonishing even amid the incredible abduction phenomenon. Inter-species fertilization is also something that seems very improbable in a biological sense, especially given the way the aliens are only partially human in appearance. But he claims that many cases support him, and we must note how almost every witness in our study (male or female) is indeed young. Also, sometimes they report experiences which confirm Hopkins' theory (for example, Mrs Verona's 'rape'). Those that do not tend to be rejected, as 'too old or infirm for our purposes' (as Alfred Burtoo claims he was told in Hampshire). The Church Stowe case might be very important in that regard, because you could interpret it as Elsie Oakensen being 'rejected' (as she feels she was) because she was past child-bearing age. Within minutes a group of younger, totally independent women seem to have become the focus for a second abduction attempt in the same area. It is not difficult to regard this as more than coincidence. But is it making too much out of too few examples?'

The idea of the ETH will remain prominent, because this is how the media will present the abduction phenomenon. It seems to be the answer most people want, and most media sources prefer to give the public what it wants to hear. It may prove to be the answer, but at this stage it is impossible to be confident, and I think we should bear in mind the sceptical words of space-writer Ron Miller, debating the ETH with Professor Michael Swords in the July/August 1987 issue of *IUR*: 'As I see it there is just too much attention being paid to the earth .... Too much if civilization and life are common; there would be too many other worlds at least as interesting as our own ... too much if life is rare; as some planet must be literally bankrupting itself to observe us.'

We have reached a difficult point in our search for an answer. Psychology alone does not fit. Nor does the theory of extra-terrestrial spaceships. I believe that an intermediary solution is necessary: either the third option that Mark Moravec proposed or my fourth one.

Moravec's option concerns a physically real phenomenon triggering a more subjective experience, thus providing a blend of the two. On a simple level, this might mean misidentification of, for instance, the full moon, an induced state where the mind believes it is experiencing a close encounter, and a resultant hallucination. In my estimation, that idea falls apart with many cases. What about the physical evidence of microwave or ultra-violet radiation?

This is why some researchers have begun to explore the idea of a new type of atmospheric energy that might have this associated radiation and then be able to create some kind of brain stimulation that induces hallucinations. This immediately removes the hurdle of the physical effects and, perhaps more importantly, the question of why witnesses are not psychologically unstable. They are, as we saw, visually imaginative. Perhaps the relevance of that is the impact of the created hallucination. If a person's visual skills mean that the result is a powerful illusion which might seem real, that could explain a great deal.

The Canadian brain specialist Dr Michael Persinger of Laurentian University has been in search of such a new energy source. In his paper 'Expected clinical consequences of close proximity to UFO-related luminosities' (*Perceptual and Motor Skills*, Volume 56, 1983), he developed his theory that there are what he calls 'transients' – floating columns of natural radiation that briefly appear and disappear in the atmosphere.

There is no doubt that he makes out an impressive case for how these radiation fields might scramble the electrical neuro-circuits of the brain. He shows how the intensity of effect would vary according to distance from the transient. At many yards only a ball of light would be seen. At closer proximity there would be 'sensations of tingling' and other electrostatic effects. Much nearer, an aura similar to that of an epileptic attack would occur, because current induction into the temporal lobe would alter the state of consciousness. This is remarkably like the 'Oz Factor' state posed in abduction cases.

If a witness came very close to one of these transients, he might well lose consciousness and suffer amnesia (a time lapse) and in rare cases severe burns or radiation poisoning. Mild after-effects of this sort (for example, nausea, headaches and diarrhoea) would not be uncommon, Persinger claims.

The abduction is explained in these very close encounters, he feels. The temporal-lobe distortion would create sensations of disassociation, out-of-body states, floating, misty visions, bright lights etc. The exact context in which these would be interpreted by the witness would depend on how he or she viewed the initial glowing radiation. In modern times this would often be as a UFO, or spaceship, with inevitable consequences during the subsequent 'vision'.

We can add to Persinger's theory. I have researched other so-called psychic phenomena (*Sixth Sense*), and there is no question that these often begin with a luminous phenomenon which might be interpreted as a ghost or vision, and which is followed by what appears to be the Oz Factor turning up in many diverse situations. What that certainly seems to prove is that the described symptoms are not specific to abductions but are indicative only of the altered state of consciousness the witness enters. The floating, time suspension and dreamlike status of the abduction is therefore not directly a part of the abduction itself, as it is often said to be. Here are some examples which help explain my point.

Mrs Dallas Williams wrote to me from Coventry to describe her 1982 experience. UFOs never entered into the reckoning, but it would be interesting to view this story as an abduction.

She was having some family tension at the time and was sleeping downstairs on the settee but missing her husband. Suddenly, as she puts it, 'I found myself awake, and I could see an oval-shaped light above me, about twenty-four inches in length and very white. It seemed to be oscillating .... All of a sudden I seemed to be pulled towards the light and merged with it ... the whole of me started to stretch horizontally and then I became aware that I was light as a feather. I started to glide towards the stairs ... into the bedroom where my husband lay .... The next moment I found myself lying on the settee. It was *so* vivid.'

Neuro-physiology professor Dr John Lilly reports in his book

The Centre of the Cyclone how he experimented in a sensory deprivation chamber, floating immersed in water for hours on end. This produced almost identical symptoms of floating, time distortion and Oz Factor. Indeed, I think the Oz Factor is simply the mind's way of inducing an artificial form of sensory deprivation, so that we pay less attention to normal, everyday things 'out there' and 'tune inward' instead. The loss of outside input manifests as disappearing noises, people, traffic etc, as in the Shropshire case where the women suddenly felt themselves going inward before the abduction.

'[I was] out of the body, out of the universe as we know it,' Lilly said of his experiments. Here he met 'entities that we cannot normally detect, but are there and have realities way beyond ours'. These entities spoke of his future, offered him a task to perform and then, '... gave me a very large amount of additional information, but on this they placed a seal. They said that I would forget it when I came back into the body, until such time as this information was needed. Then I would use it, "remembering" what they had put into me.'

It is hard to appreciate that these experiments, described in his book, occurred under scientific conditions in 1964, before the Hill and Villas Boas abductions were published. They are so exactly like what is now being described by abductees that one wonders if Dr Lilly could have been abducted from his sensory deprivation tank. Or is it that abductees (who are cocooned in a warm bed or driving on a quiet road and otherwise have sensory deprivation induced by the Oz Factor) enter the same conditions as Lilly did before undergoing a bizarre form of mental experience?

What do we make of the amazing adventures of Robert Harland, a professional magician, and self-confessed 'phoney medium'? He told me his story in great detail in 1980. It has never been published outside *Northern UFO News*, because I wanted to see if it was ever duplicated and to observe whether Mr Harland made capital out of his tale. He did not. But now, in the light of what we know of abductions, the story should be summarized.

In 1964 he went to a dentist in Middlesbrough for major oral surgery. This entailed the use of a gas anaesthetic, but at the last moment he decided he did not want this and fought the mask. It was too late, and Robert found himself floating free of his body, seeing the dentist bang his knee (an event later verified). He next observed a tall being with long white hair drift through the ceiling and explain telepathically that they must go together. The couple floated through the roof, and Robert found himself inside a UFO. He was shown around and given a lot of detail about its operation. The being told him that he had a message to convey, and Robert must carry it back. It concerned a terrible holocaust that the Earth would suffer in the future, when the crust would split apart. This was a cycle which the planet continually went through, returning to the beginning after the destruction. They wanted to help us break that chain of events.

Robert agreed to try but was told he would have to fight his way back into his body, which proved the case. Small, ugly creatures were tugging at him trying to prevent his return. Fortunately he evaded them and with a 'snap' was back in the surgery, seeing the dentist thumping him and looking very worried. He had apparently nearly died in the chair.

There are obvious links with the abduction phenomenon, but what do these stories from outside the standard UFO framework suggest? I think we are dealing with a consciousness event.

However, this must be much more than a hallucination. We seem to have to consider a phenomenon that puts witnesses into a particular state so that they can undergo an 'out-of-body experience' (OOBE). This should not be taken to mean that their spirit, or some such mystical aspect, literally does leave the body. Bristol University parapsychologist Dr Susan Blackmore has spent years looking into OOBEs and regards them as a vivid and consistent phenomenon of imagery (*Beyond the Body*).

The phenomenon which causes this transition into what Ian Watson called 'UFO consciousness' (as good a name as any) could occasionally be just a serious misperception, such as a star. More often it must be something more – for example, one of Persinger's transients, which accommodates the physical effects.

But we still have no answer to the amazing consistency between abduction cases. Can this simply be the result of human imagination, or does imagination need a helping hand?

We are at the leading edge of abduction research now, and

few have even come to embrace this question. Most still seem stuck in the debate between 'It's all imagination' or 'The aliens are kidnapping people.' In my view, both these views provide part of the answer, but neither works as a total solution. The result has to be a hybrid of the two.

In a series of articles, British writer Ian Cresswell has looked at this theory. He says: 'The origin of these images *is* subjective, and so is the process by which they emerge into consciousness .... But is their origin a human one, or something much deeper ...?' ('What dreams might come', *Magonia*, July 1984). He seems to favour a human 'superconsciousness', which he calls 'the dark side of the moon' of man's psyche.

Parapsychologist Scott Rogo, agrees with Cresswell. Rogo is one of the few perceptive thinkers who has actually studied abduction cases in the field, as opposed to many who write about them without ever going near an abductee.

Whilst sensibly keeping his mind open to other options, Rogo says ('Secret language of UFO abduction', *IUR*, July/August 1985): 'We ourselves have somehow created the mystery and are unleashing it into the world in vivid reality.' After a very impressive 1987 investigation into a new Californian abduction, he clarified his views ('The abduction of Sammy Desmond', *IUR*, July/August 1987): 'The abduction *is* a real physical event, but it reflects concerns or traumas buried within the subject's unconscious. It might be called an "objectified" dream – ie a system of symbolic imagery which suddenly erupts into the three-dimensional world.'

I believe the answer has to be something like that. There is fascinating work afoot in natural science, notably from biologist Dr Rupert Sheldrake. His *A New Science of Life* produced a storm in scientific circles when first released in 1981. The journal *Nature* even proposed the book as a candidate for burning, because it challenges the Darwinian theory of evolution. Yet it does so in a way that is exciting scientists all over the world, and it has been vindicated by every experiment so far carried out to test Sheldrake's 'wild' idea.

What he proposes is that biological form and experience are created by continual emphasis. If something is successful in furthering survival, then biological entities are more likely to be born with that factor. Similarly, if something becomes accepted as real, then it gains more and more actual reality. It would not be stretching Sheldrake's hypothesis too far to regard abductions as becoming real, because of their repeated emphasis within society. Similarly, the form they take will be identical because this form has become the standard template.

This idea offers a way to explain the small regional differences in our cases. In time these will gradually become diluted, as the abduction settles into a global form that has real stability.

Hard as this may be to comprehend, we are suggesting a person tuning into a stereotype mental image which has become quasi-real because so many people have experienced it, but it still retains many of the features of its subjective origins, whilst gathering more 'solidity' as time goes by.

There is one other possibility. This retains the advantages of the objective/subjective hybrid but makes the origin of this consciousness event outside mankind. In this sense there really are aliens, but they are not literally coming here in spaceships. Instead they are using individuals in 'UFO consciousness' as instruments for the transmission of a message and to conduct an investigation or analysis.

This strange suggestion has some merit. For example, it helps account for the apparent selectivity and conditioning of witnesses, such as in the Church Stowe case. This is very hard to explain with any of the theories put forward so far. Equally, it would explain the consistency of aliens in these cases as well as the science-fiction trappings.

The basic contact would be by aliens who really exist but who are using the minds of visually creative people to induce an experience. This is then lived through as an abduction. Since that abduction must be forged out of images already in the mind, we would expect the result to be individual 'visions' that follow a general outline – rather like giving the plot of a novel to ten film producers and seeing what they come up with. Each would produce a recognizable version of the same story, because they have an identical stimulus, but each result would also depend on the visual imagination of the producer.

This is so close to what we see in the abduction evidence that I feel it represents the best guess we can make at the moment. We have something like the following scenario.

A creatively visual person who has a track record of strange experiences, (seeing 'ghosts' or other hallucinations) finds him/herself in a position to be contacted by an alien intelligence. This intelligence is surveying the Earth in a manner totally different to that predicted by either science or science fiction. It is not crossing the immense void of space in machines; it is not beaming painfully slow radio signals across the light years to be picked up by our grossly expensive radio telescopes. These things are physically impossible, tediously slow or simply too old-fashioned. They reflect what we in the twentieth century consider to be 'state of the art technology', but almost certainly not twenty-first- or twenty-second-century technology. These beings are far more advanced and have harnessed the power of consciousness to cross the gulfs of space and seek out new life forms.

In this way the aliens communicate with members of our species able to listen. These receivers are people who use visual imagery and so can pick up the signals the aliens transmit, boost them and turn them into vivid pictures. The pictures will be so vivid that they will seem to be real, so far as the witness is concerned. Only a few clues will show that they are not. These clues include the fact that only those contacted will experience the abduction, that if abducted from a bed or a car this is where the witness will end the experience (because, of course, they never actually left there) and the inability to bring back physical proof from the UFO, because it was visited only in a mental sense.

The contact is precipitated by the Oz Factor. It may be accidental if the witness dozes off, or by chance contact with one of Persinger's transients, or deliberately induced by an alien probe selecting the appropriate person. The purpose of the contact would be two-way, perhaps to pass messages to us (such as warnings) and to extract data from us (such as examination of our genetic make-up, possibly to see if they can 'create a human' back in their laboratories).

What we experience as an abduction is a vision. It is not really happening, yet it is far more than a mere hallucination.

I am well aware that this is a daring hypothesis that is bound to be highly controversial, but I feel it is the best way to overcome the very obvious problems every other theory seems to introduce.

I am not expecting it to be acceptable as it stands, but I do hope that far-seeing scientists and abduction researchers will recognize that it is worth testing. For it *is* testable. All that is required is to gather a group of visually creative people together, find a way of inducing 'UFO consciousness' (perhaps by subjecting them to an artificial Persinger transient) and then, under controlled laboratory conditions, monitor the consequences.

Of course, this would cost money. But no advanced equipment is required. Besides, astronomers are currently spending millions of pounds and dollars from tax budgets all over the world, using radio telescopes to listen out for signals from intelligent lifeforms. If I am right, this is a vast waste of money that could be spent on so many other projects to the benefit of society.

And yet, with a strange irony, those messages from another world may well be coming at us all the time, only to be foolishly discarded by scientists who allow themselves to be bullied out of studying the abduction phenomenon – *not* because it has no substance, *not* because there is no evidence to work with, *not* because those who claim it are disturbed, or because those who promote it are making wild and unsupported statements, but simply because too many people regard the question of alien abduction as explained away, tied in with 'non-existent' UFOs or just plain crazy. I may not have dispelled all those illusions but I hope that I have persuaded just a few readers to take a second look at this fascinating and under-rated mystery of the Space Age.

Appendix I: Have You Been Abducted?

Of course, I am making no assumptions about what it means to have been abducted, but if some researchers are correct, many of you reading this book might have undergone an abduction experience without consciously realizing it.

If you suspect that this might be the case, try answering the following questions. If you find yourself replying 'yes' to three or more of them, then it's possible. But before you start celebrating, or panicking, you would be well advised to discuss the matter (in full confidence) with an experienced investigator. I will gladly forward your letter to someone who can be trusted if you write (with an SAE) to 37 Heathbank Road, Stockport, Cheshire SK3 0UP.

Have you seen more than one thing you think might have been a UFO?

If and when you saw a UFO, did you experience anything like the Oz Factor (page 22)?

Have you ever suffered a time lapse, suddenly finding yourself in a place where you did not expect to be or much later than you estimated it ought to be?

Have you had recurrent dreams about UFOs, aliens, floating sensations or strange messages about other worlds?

Do you undergo experiences that some people might call 'psychic' (especially 'out-of-body' sensations) on a more than sporadic basis?

Have you suddenly found yourself becoming very interested in conservation, artistic pursuits, the 'new age', love, peace and harmony or ecology, without any obvious cause for this interest?

Appendix II: Chronology of Cases

It would not be possible to list in chronological order all the cases that have happened, or even just those referred to in this book, but interactions are shown in an outline of some of the major events and dates.

In considering the effect one story might have on another, it must be recalled that until the past few years even well-publicized cinema films on an alien theme have attracted limited audiences. Science-fiction books certainly appeal to only a small section of the community, and UFO journals such as *FSR* and *IUR* have circulations measured in hundreds, or at most a couple of thousand. They generally do not go on sale to the public.

Surprisingly few abduction cases have received widespread media attention, although since 1978 (the year of Spielberg's film) there have been many more than before. The bibliography shows the same factor in the growth of relevant books published in the past decade.

24 June 1947: A pilot over the Cascade Mountains, Washington State, USA, observes strange lights and the UFO mystery is born.

14 August 1947: The first significant case involving a witness and alien beings takes place at Villa Santina, Italy.

January 1948: The US Government launches their first official probe into UFO sightings.

January 1950: The first book about UFOs appears, *Flying Saucers Are Real* by retired Major Donald Keyhoe (serialized in

Life magazine to enormous public interest).

1951: The film *The Day the Earth Stood Still* released in the USA, featuring friendly aliens coming to warn Earth against war.

November 1952: George Adamski claims to meet friendly Venusians in Californian desert and later go for rides in their UFO.

December 1952: The CIA become involved in UFO research and set up a covert study team under top physicist Dr H.P. Robertson. They discuss ways to make the subject look crazy.

Early 1950s saw a growth of space-fiction comic strips which inspired children of the period to get into space for real.

1953: The film *Invaders from Mars* begins trend of films depicting hostile invaders who kidnap humans. Adamski publishes his first book, and the contactee craze begins. The CIA comment favourably on its impact on UFO credibility in now released documents.

February 1954: 'Cedric Allingham' brings the contactee movement to Britain and Europe with his claim of meeting a Martian in Scotland (a book on the case published the following year).

October 1954: The first wave of sightings of alien beings takes place, mostly in northern Europe.

Mid 1950s highly popular radio serial, 'Journey into Space' and 'The Red Planet'. The second told of abduction of people to Mars and reflects the view at this time that the planets of our solar system could be inhabited.

October 1957: The Earth enters the Space Age with the surprise Soviet launch of a satellite into orbit. Within days a Brazilian farmer, Antonio Villas Boas, claims he was kidnapped by aliens and raped by a female entity on board. Case reported and investigated in January 1958 but not published.

September 1961: A young married couple, Betty and Barney Hill, from New Hampshire, USA, suffer a time loss during a car journey and, to relieve persistent nightmares, spend three years under psychiatric evaluation in Boston. Memory of an abduction with gynaecological features comes out.

Spring 1964: The story of the 1947 Villa Santina case first published. Shortly afterwards the Antonio Villas Boas case, which had been in hands of investigators for six years, is made public.

Late 1965: The story of the Betty and Barney Hill case made public and, after the release of the book by John Fuller a few months later, is syndicated all over the world.

Summer 1966: US Government forced by Congress to set up a scientific research group into UFOs with high profile.

December 1967: First of wave of modern abductions occurs to police officer Herb Schirmer in Nebraska, USA.

Late 1968: The results of the US Government study released. Nothing of any consequence is the conclusion, although one third of the cases are not explained by the teams of experts (including the Schirmer abduction). As the Apollo project is in full swing and interest in space travel at its maximum, the US Government announces it is closing its twenty-one-year-old UFO project.

July 1969: Man lands on the moon; interest in space travel begins to fade.

October 1973: Major wave of abduction cases occurs, mostly in the USA (including, in particular, the abduction and medical examination at Pascagoula, Mississippi).

October 1974: First ‘true’ abduction (the Aveley, Essex, encounter) takes place in Britain, although not reported for four years.

October 1975: Television film *The UFO Incident*, based on the Betty and Barney Hill abduction, screened in the USA. Within two weeks the Travis Walton abduction is reported at Snowflake, Arizona. Major news stories on this spread around the world. Only the second abduction to do this (the first being the Hill case in 1966).

December 1976: The Winchester, Hampshire, case becomes the first British abduction to attract media publicity, although the abduction phases came later and were not reported so widely. 1976 had become 'the year of the abduction' in Britain, with several occurring. Almost none were publicized, and most were reported only two or three years later.

Spring 1977: The biggest wave of UFO events ever hits Britain. Major publicity. None of these is an abduction.

December 1977: The Spielberg film *Close Encounters of the Third Kind* released in the USA. In February/March 1978 it receives major publicity in Britain and is chosen as the Royal Première film. Its true-to-life look at UFOs includes an abduction scene, but there is no wave of abductions on either continent.

November 1980: The next abduction wave in Britain occurs, including the police officer Alan Godfrey case. UFO books now appearing in abundance.

Spring 1983: The Spielberg film *ET* is released and is an enormous success, but again there are no abduction waves. Cases continue, however, all over the world. Very few are publicized.

October 1983: The alleged UFO contact between entities and the US Air Force near RAF Woodbridge, Suffolk, achieves huge global publicity.

December 1985: Whitley Strieber claims first memory of his abduction experiences.

February 1987: Strieber goes on major US promotions tour for his book (visiting Britain in May, Australia in June). His book is released in the USA in April. Huge focus of attention on abductions but, although quite a number of old cases surface in the USA, hardly any new cases are reported.

January 1988: A possible close encounter of the fourth kind finally takes place in Australia (see p. 163). Interestingly, Whitley Strieber's *Communion* has been a bestseller in Australia only a few weeks before. A woman and her three sons are travelling by car across the Nullabor Plain, near to where a major sighting occurred in November 1957 above a British nuclear test site. Their truck is sucked into the air, the witnesses suffer physical effects and, rather aptly, these Australians then report the Oz Factor! Major headlines feature the case ('UFO Hijack Terror' as the headline story in the British *Daily Star* proclaims). Typically, sceptics write it off without studying the case. An Adelaide scientist, Professor Peter Schwerdtfergger, says it is a 'dry thunderstorm' and *Daily Telegraph* science correspondent, Adrian Berry, a vitriolic debunker of such matters, dismisses it as a good example of the little-understood natural phenomenon of ball lightning. Perhaps it is one of these things, but such instant rejection without proper study is exactly what this book has urged that we avoid.

Bibliography

All books listed below are in English and are published in Britain, unless other origins are specifically given. Often there are several editions. Updated editions are mentioned only if important new text is added. One of the best suppliers of rare titles is 'Specialist Knowledge', a shop at 20 Paul Street, Frome, Somerset BA11 1DX, which also supplies books and catalogues by post, one of which lists books on stock in this subject. Send an SAE.

Letters in bold type indicate the subject of the book: **C** contactee story or personal account of an abductee; **S** case study of abduction by an investigator: **T** theoretical work on the nature of abductions. Others are general works, containing some relevant material. An asterisk indicates that the book is recommended as a significant contribution – in my (purely subjective) judgement.

1953: Adamski, G., and Leslie, D., *Flying Saucers have landed* (Spearman; updated 1970) **C**

1955: Allingham, Cedric, *Flying Saucer from Mars* (Mueller) **C**

1959: Jung, Dr C., *Flying Saucers: A Modern Myth of Things Seen in the Skies* (Routledge & Kegan Paul) **T***

1966: Fuller, J.G., *The Interrupted Journey* (Putnam, USA; updated 1980 by Souvenir, Corgi, 1981) **S***

1967: Lorenzon, C. and J., *Flying Saucer Occupants* (Signet, USA)

1969: Bowen, C. (ed), *The Humanoids* (Spearman; Futura, 1974) **S***

1970: Vallee, Dr J., *Passport to Magonia* (Spearman) **T***

1970: Keel, J., *Operation Trojan Horse* (Putnam, USA: Abacus, UK, 1973) *

1973: Webb, D., *Year of the Humanoids* (CUFOS, USA) **S***

1975: Vallee, Dr J., *The Invisible College* (Dutton, USA; Grafton, UK 1977, retitled *UFOs: The Psychic Solution*)
1976: Persinger, M. and Lafrenière, G., *Space-Time Transients and Unusual Events* (Nelson, USA)
1978: Watson, I., *Miracle Visitors* (Gollancz; Grafton, 1980) **T***
1979: Fowler, R. *The Andreasson Affair* (Prentice-Hall, USA; Corgi, 1980; also Prentice-Hall edition, *The Andreasson Affair – Phase Two* 1982), **S***
1979: Holtzer, Dr H., *The Ufonauts* (Grafton)
1979: Watson, Dr L., *Lifetide* (Hodder & Stoughton) **T***
1980: Gansberg, J. and A., *Direct Encounters* (Walker, USA) **S**
1980: Story, R. (ed), *The UFO Encyclopedia* (NEL)
1980: Hendry, A., *The UFO Handbook* (Sphere) *
1980: Johnson, F., *The Janos People* (Spearman) **S**
1980: Druffel, A. and Rogo, Dr S., *The Tujunga Canyon Contacts* (Prentice-Hall, USA) **S***
1981: Hopkins, B., *Missing Time* (Marek, USA) **S** *
1981: Basterfield, K., *Close Encounters of an Australian Kind* (Reed, Australia) **T** *
1982: Randles, J., *Alien Contact* (Spearman; Coronet, 1983), a case study of the Sunderland family encounters)
1983: Klass, P., *UFOs: The Public Deceived* (Prometheus, USA)
1983: Randles, J., *The Pennine UFO Mystery* (Grafton), detailed transcripts on the Alan Godfrey abduction case
1984: Rimmer, J., *The Evidence for Alien Abductions* (Aquarian) **T**
1984: Evans, H. *Visions, Apparitions, Alien Visitors* (Aquarian) **T***
1985: Randles, J. and Warrington, P. *Science and the UFOs* (Blackwell; Blackwell Inc, USA, 1987) the book that triggered the Whitley Strieber story
1987: Strieber, W. *Communion* (Morrow, USA; Century-Hutchinson, UK, 1988) **C***
1987: Hopkins, B. *Intruders* (Random House, USA) **S***
1987: Ballester-Olmos, V.J., *Encyclopedia of Close Encounters with UFOs* (Plaza & Janes)
1987: Sheldrake, R. *A New Science of Life* (Paladin, 1987)
1987: Randles, J., *Sixth Sense* (Robert Hale; Salem House, USA) on the Oz Factor and states of consciousness relevant to abductions
1988: Evans, H. and Spencer, J. (eds), *Phenomenon* (McDonald/Futura) *

Addresses

As well as the author, whose address appears on p. 224, journals and organizations referred to in the text may be contacted as follows (SAE advised):

BUFORA (*Bulletin* and *JTAP*)
16 South Way, Burgess Hill, Sussex RH15 9ST, UK.
CUFOS (International UFO Reporter)
2457 W. Peterson, Chicago, Illinois 60659, USA.
FUFOR (Fund for UFO research)
PO Box 277, Mount Rainier, Maryland 20712, USA.
MUFON (*Journal*)
103 Oldtowne Road, Seguin, Texas 78155, USA.
NUFON (*Northern UFO News*)
37 Heathbank Road, Stockport, Cheshire, SK3 0UP, UK.
IUN (*UFO Brigantia*)
84 Elland Road, Brighouse, West Yorks, HD6 2QR, UK.
Earth, 61 Ranelagh Ave., Bradford, BD10 0HF, UK.
Fortean Times, 1 Shoebury Road, London E6 2AQ, UK.
FSR, Snodland, Kent, ME6 5HJ, UK.
Magonia, 5 James Terrace, London SW14 8HB, UK.
Ovni Présence, CP 342, CH-1800, Vevey 1, Switzerland.

Index